On Eagles' Wings

On Eagles' Wings

Paige + Ken,

Enjoy

Debi Bell

Here is
Joy in the Journey!

For information write:
The Salvation Army
USA Southern Territory
Literary Council
1424 Northeast Expressway
Atlanta, GA 30329

ISBN: N: 978-0-86544-067-8

Editors: Linda & Lynell Johnson, The WordWorking Shop

Printed in the United States of America

Dedication

Dedicated to the pure in heart, who are blessed
because they see the Lord, high and lifted up; and
for those who cry, "Holy, Holy is the Lord Almighty."
You all inspire me to rise up on eagles' wings.

Foreword

ONE OF THE BEAUTIFUL things about the Bible is that it is a library of books, written by different authors at different times. We see the wide array of humanity on the stage of human history. This means that a particular book of the Bible can become a fresh word to us in a particular context. I believe the time has come for us to take a fresh look at the prophet Isaiah.

He lived in a time of drastic change, fickle government, fearful kings, threatening enemies, and hollow faith. Sound familiar? Isaiah addresses the haunting issues of humans— fear, threat, making our own wooden gods, expecting political leaders to save us, shoddy obedience. Reading the daily newspaper alongside the book of Isaiah might be a good thing to do.

And thankfully, Debi Bell has done just that. From parental advice to political reflection, she walks alongside Isaiah, allowing his words into our time. Her recognition of the breadth of God is assuring. We meet God the judge, the glorious one, the Kinsman Redeemer, the suffering servant of the

Lord, the deliverer, our hiding place, the warrior king, the tender shepherd, and the coming victor. While Commissioner Bell enlarges our understanding of God, she also calls for our response to this God. Hear carefully her call to obedience, costly sacrifice, and true peace.

If you find yourself fearful and losing hope, her daily visits with Isaiah may be exactly what you need.

Dan Boone
President, Trevecca Nazarene University

About This Book

ON EAGLES' WINGS IS designed for your personal devotional time in the rich, deeply layered writings of the prophet Isaiah, who frequently points the way to our Savior, Jesus. My prayer for you is that, as a result of your time with Isaiah, you will develop deep hope in the Lord and renew your spiritual strength, that you will "soar on wings like eagles." (Isaiah 40:31)

This is definitely an open–Bible devotional! Sometimes, the entire portion of Isaiah appears with a devotion, but many times, only the reference is listed, so you will need to open your Bible to that passage. At the end of some devotions are *More Scripture* references that either underscore the point of the devotion or expand your understanding of it. I encourage you to turn to those passages as well.

The devotions are numbered, and if you used the book daily, you would finish in six months. But with some of the longer devotions (especially ones that call for more study), you may want to spend more than one day. Following every devotion is a suggested prayer (or, in one case, a thought).

Each comes from my own heart, from the way I was convicted, challenged, blessed, or inspired. The Lord may prompt you to pray a different prayer. That's perfectly fine! God's Word is always multi–faceted and speaks to each of us in unique ways.

Note

Most of the Scriptures quoted are from the *New International Version* (2011) or *NIV* for short. But when it seemed appropriate, I've used a number of other versions and occasionally, a paraphrase like *The Message.* Below, I've listed versions with their abbreviations.

Modern English Version (MEV)
New Century Version (NCV)
New King James Version (NKJV)
New Living Translation (NLT)
New Revised Standard Version (NRSV)
The Voice (VOICE)

Contents

1

Isaiah—The Lord Saves

The vision concerning Judah and Jerusalem
that Isaiah son of Amoz saw ... (1:1)

NAMES AND THEIR MEANINGS are very important in the Bible. The name Isaiah means *Jehovah is salvation.* Isaiah's parents gave him a name that reflected their desire that he would know Jehovah and that the Lord would save him. Isaiah's parents may also have given him that name because they recognized the need of their nation to turn to God alone for salvation. Only God could save them from the Assyrians, the Egyptians, the Babylonians, or any other peoples who posed a threat. God alone could save them from the enemies of their nation and their souls.

Names and their meaning are equally important today. Parents typically give a great deal of thought to choosing their children's names. Parents name their children in hopes that they will reflect certain character qualities implied by the name. Perhaps they give a name to honor another person.

Parents may even give their child a name to make a personal statement. Some names give a clue to the events of the time or the mood of a nation. Some names reflect the spiritual convictions of the parents. Some are chosen just because they are popular.

Many bookstores and libraries have books on names. If you don't know the meaning of your given name (or the names of members of your family), look it up in a book or on the internet. Find out the history of your given name by asking your parents or a family member who might remember the reason(s) your name was chosen.

How did your given name affect you as a child? How did your given name contribute to who you became?

Prayer: God, give me more insight into who I am
and who You want me to be.

2

Family Name

The vision concerning Judah and Jerusalem
that Isaiah son of Amoz saw ... (1:1)

IN JEWISH TRADITION, A person is a Jew if his or her mother is
Jewish. Yet, in the Bible, lists of family names typically include
only males. The word *ben* preceding a name means *son of*. So
Isaiah would be Isaiah ben Amoz. The family name would
identify a characteristic of the father or possibly what he did
for a living. The meaning of Amoz is *strong, carried*, or *brave*.

Today, the last names of some English–speakers are like
"ben Amoz." For example, the name "Jackson" means "Jack's
son." Some last names reflect the industry of our ancestors.
For example, the English last name "Smith" may mean one of
your ancestors was a metal worker or blacksmith. That's true
in other languages as well. Obviously, last names indicate
ethnic origin: Yee, González, Kim, and O'Brien.

When everyone knows a family, a last name can be either
a blessing or a curse. It can open or close doors, depending on

the family's reputation. And the action of one single family member can be very important to the continuing of a good name or the destruction of a name.

When you receive Jesus Christ as your Savior, you become a redeemed member of the family of God; you take on His name. Jesus is often called our "Kinsman Redeemer." This is the fulfillment of an Old Testament practice of a family member paying off the family debt or paying the price to buy back the freedom of a relative living as a slave. (See the book of Ruth or Hosea.)

Because of our Kinsman Redeemer, we belong to the family of God and we are called Christians. This family name can be a blessing. It can open doors. It carries a great and wonderful legacy. However, many people in the history of the Church have dishonored the name Christian and the name of Jesus.

People have committed horrible deeds in His name. Sincere people have fought unjust wars in the name of God. Power–mongers have hidden behind the name of Jesus. More than one holocaust has taken place in the last 2,000 years because Christians did not really live up to their name. To live up to the family name Christian, to honor the name of Jesus, we must be so careful to *know* Him, the Lord who saves. We must live to bring honor to His name.

Do your actions bring honor or dishonor to the name of God? Do you live like a member of the family of God, a child of the King? How can members of the family of God be both exclusive and inclusive?

Prayer: Thank you, God, for making it possible for me to belong to Your family. Help me to honor the name of Jesus, my Kinsman Redeemer.

3

The Vision

The vision concerning Judah and Jerusalem that Isaiah son of Amoz saw during the reigns of Uzziah, Jotham, Ahaz, and Hezekiah, kings of Judah. (1:1)

ISAIAH, SON OF AMOZ, served as God's prophet during the same time span as the prophets Amos, Hosea, and Micah. Isaiah spoke God's Word to Judah, the southern kingdom, when the Assyrian empire was expanding. He enjoyed direct access to the kings of Judah. We could infer that he served as the court prophet, just as Nathan had when David was king. He may have been considered a member of the royal family.

The ministry of prophets is very important because they speak the message of God. A prophet may be called upon by God to foretell the future as it relates to God's plan. More often, God calls on the prophet to tell forth, or to speak, God's message for the present, so that people will respond and obey.

There are occasions when a prophet would refer to the

vision, the revelation, or the message God had given as a burden. It's true, a vision can be a burden. Very few people would sign on to be the tool God uses to confront His people. However, "Where there is no revelation, people cast off restraint; but blessed is the one who heeds wisdom's instruction." (Proverbs 29:18)

Throughout the book of Isaiah, God tells His people that they are both blind and deaf. They are blind because they have closed their eyes. They are deaf because they have plugged their ears. They have no understanding because they have hardened their minds. The prophet is God's man or woman who has eyes to see, ears to hear, and a mind open to the blessed truth that God cares enough about His people to give them the guidance they need.

Prayer: Open my eyes and my ears, Lord, and help
me not to harden my mind to what you have
to say to me.

4

A Layered Message

Isaiah 1:1

ISAIAH, SON OF AMOZ, both wrote and spoke about the vision, the message, God gave him. That vision still speaks to us today. A true vision or prophecy often has a layered message. What does the term "a layered message" mean? Imagine a mountain range. You see the tops of the mountains that only hint at the valleys. You see layers of the full picture, not the whole picture. What you see from afar only hints at the discoveries you will make when you set out to explore. This is how the vision of Isaiah yields its layers:

a) The message to the people of Isaiah's day

b) The message to the people of Judah who would one day be taken into exile in Babylon

c) The message to King Cyrus, whom Isaiah mentioned by name long before he was born as the one who would allow the Jews to return to Jerusalem from their Babylonian exile

d) The message to the nation of Israel about the Messiah who would one day come to redeem His people

e) The message meant for our day

f) The message to future generations who will live on after us

If you want to gain insight from the book of Isaiah, keep your eyes and ears open. Keep an open mind. God has a message for you. Are you ready to receive it? It will change your life.

Remember: The job of a prophet is to obey and please God, to deliver God's message without concern for his or her own popularity. When we are right with God, we will rarely be popular with the world.

Can there be lessons from this prophet that will help us today? Are you able to bear the burden of the prophet's message?

Prayer: Lord, help me to understand the layers of Isaiah's message and discern God's truth for me.

5

Notes on the Kings of Isaiah

Isaiah 1:1; 2 Chronicles 26–29

GREED FOR POWER AND riches, idolatry, and lack of respect for human life were hallmarks of the ruling families of Israel and Judah. Righteousness was not always taught to, or caught by, the children of the rulers. A righteous ruler often took the place of an evil one. The next generation's ruler was often compromised or the polar opposite of his parent.

Several kings of Judah fell under Isaiah's influence. Uzziah was a good king and God blessed him. But Uzziah became proud of his accomplishments. His pride moved him to enter the Temple to burn incense on the altar—something only the priests were supposed to do. Uzziah contracted leprosy, which made him unable to continue as king.

Jotham, Uzziah's son, reigned in his father's place until his father died. Then Jotham became king in his own right. He was a good king who rebuilt part of the Temple and strengthened Jerusalem's defenses. However, he tolerated idolatry.

Ahaz became king after Jotham died. He looked to other nations and other gods for help. He destroyed many of the rich furnishings of the Temple and shut the Temple doors. He set up altars to pagan gods throughout Jerusalem and the nation of Judah.

Hezekiah became king after Ahaz. He purged the land of idolatry, purified and restored the Temple, and sought God. He listened to Isaiah. He is remembered as a man of righteousness, faith, and prayer.

Obviously, dedication to God was not effectively passed on from generation to generation by the kings of Judah. The lesson to us? It is very important for us to train our children in the Word and way of God. Deuteronomy 4 indicates that God expects us to live and teach His Word. We can also have influence on the world around us. Living a righteous life is very important, but we must also share our faith with others if we expect to make a lasting difference for the Kingdom of God.

How can we inform our world right now about pleasing God? How can we inform and transform the next generations so they can please God?

Prayer: Help us, Lord, to walk in the paths of righteousness as examples to our children and to the world.

6

Addressing the Jury

Hear me, you heavens! Listen, earth! For the
Lord has spoken ... (1:2)

IMAGINE THAT GOD IS in a great courtroom and He is addressing the jury. He is calling on the heavens and the Earth to listen to His case and render their verdict.

In Genesis 1:1, we read, "In the beginning God created the heavens and the earth." The heavens and the earth were there from the beginning. They witnessed all that occurred before and after God created humans.

Perhaps God chose the heavens and the earth to be on the jury because they had borne faithful witness to Him. "The heavens declare the glory of God; the skies proclaim the work of His hands. ... their voice goes out into all the earth, their words to the end of the world." (Psalm 19:1,4)

Can the heavens and the earth hear? Let's go back to Genesis, Chapter 1. Repeatedly we read: "And God said, 'Let there be ... ' " and it happened. God separated light from

11

darkness. The sun, moon, and stars went to their right places in the heavens. The sky separated from the sea. The land rose from the waters. The vegetation sprang from the land. Creatures of the sea swam into being. Creatures of the sky flew into life. God spoke, and the animals knew where they belonged. Yes, the heavens and the earth can hear the voice of God, and they obey.

On the sixth day, God said: " 'Let us make mankind in our image' ... So God created mankind in his own image, in the image of God he created them; male and female he created them." (Genesis 1:26, 27) God blessed them and gave them authority to rule over the living creatures. The heavens and the earth stood as witnesses to what God said about humanity. They cooperated with God to provide light, air, nutrition, water, building materials, and all that humanity would need to live. God took care of humanity's spiritual needs Himself.

All was well until Adam and Eve rebelled. Sin entered the picture. Then God's plan of redemption went into effect—the plan He had in mind even before He laid the foundations of heaven and earth.

In this Scripture verse, God addresses the jury in His great court, where He serves as prosecutor and judge. The good news is that God also served as the Defender, the One who paid the penalty for the sin and rebellion of humankind.

Are you faithful to God? How can you faithfully declare His glory?

Prayer: Help me become as faithful to God as the
heavens and the earth are faithful to Him.

7

Presenting the Case

Hear me, you heavens! Listen, earth! For the Lord has spoken: 'I reared children and brought them up, but they have rebelled against me. The ox knows its master, the donkey its owner's manger, but Israel does not know, my people do not understand.' Woe to the sinful nation, a people whose guilt is great, a brood of evildoers, children given to corruption! They have forsaken the Lord; they have spurned the Holy One of Israel and turned their backs on him. (1:2–4)

GOD ADDRESSES HIS JURY and begins to present His case. "I reared children and brought them up, but they have rebelled against me."

Is there any challenge greater than that of raising children? "The ox knows its master and the donkey its owner's manger," but my children do not know or understand. Both the ox and the donkey have a reputation for stubbornness. Can either compare to a strong–willed 2–year–old or a rebellious teenager? If children would only cooperate, life could be so pleasant.

Many parents experience days when they wonder why they ever chose to have children. The dream family they hoped for looks more like a nightmare. This feeling of exasperation should give us some inkling of how God must feel at times about the humans He created. The amazing thing is that He knew what He was getting into. God was not blinded by some romantic image. He knew there would be days, weeks, months, years, and even eons when His heart would break over His children. But because God also knew of the rewards and joys we would bring, He created us anyway.

Your heart may be breaking or broken over the rebellious behavior of your children. Know this: God understands. Because He does, He stands with you through the trials ahead. James 1:5 tells us that if we need wisdom, we should ask for it. Don't give up on your children. Ask God to give you the measure of wisdom you need to deal with them one day at a time. Remember: God understands.

Prayer:　Lord, touch the children of our world and protect them. Keep their feet on the right path. Give us the wisdom and love we need each day to deal with them.

8

Hut in the Field *vs.* Strong Tower

Daughter Zion is left like a shelter in a vineyard, like a hut in cucumber field, like a city under siege. (1:8)

"DAUGHTER ZION" REFERS TO the nation of Judah, and more to the point, its capital, Jerusalem.

Before the building of the Temple on Mount Moriah, most of Jerusalem was on Mount Zion. *Zion* means "monument" or "raised up." At first, Zion referred only to the city of David, the area around the palace of David. Later it included all of Jerusalem and came to represent the southern kingdom of Judah.

To the nations of Israel and Judah, God was the Almighty. He was their Defender and Protector. Throughout their history, God proved His power. He warned them not to trust in military might and strategy. "Some trust in chariots and some in horses, but we trust in the name of the Lord our God."

(Psalm 20:7) In Proverbs and Psalms, God is named a Strong Tower of Defense.

Now God's beloved children, the nation of Judah, had turned their backs on Him. When they rebelled and abandoned God to make alliances with other nations, they abandoned their trust in their Tower of Defense. Unprotected, the people became "like a shelter in a vineyard, like a hut in a cucumber field, like a city under siege."

During the growing period and harvest time, watchmen stayed in the fields to guard against animals and enemies who would try to destroy the crops. The shelters and huts offered some protection against the elements. However, they were easy to assemble and just as easy to tear down. They could not serve as a protection against an army. Isaiah uses this illustration to warn God's people. If they put their trust in alliances with other nations, their defenses will be weak. The implied contrast is that if they put their trust in God and return to Him, He will again be their Strong Tower.

"The name of the Lord is a fortified tower; the righteous run to it and are safe." (Proverbs 18:10) Why do we ever run to anyone or anything else?

What are some of the things that you have relied on instead of God? The security of wealth? The stability of your reputation? The support of family and friends? The comfort and peace of your home? Faith that your body and mind will remain healthy?

All of these are blessings from God; however, they are not strong towers. They are like huts in a cucumber field, like shelters in a vineyard. If we turn from our Strong Tower and rely on them, God will allow us to be like a city under siege.

The comforts will slowly dwindle and we will find ourselves in desperate situations.

Prayer: Help us to be wise enough to recognize the difference between the Strong Tower of Your Name and the huts in the field of life. Help us run to You and put our faith in You, O Lord.

9

Obedience Is Better

Isaiah 1:10–14

GOD SPEAKS HARSH WORDS through the prophet Isaiah. He actually calls His people by the names of two cities remembered only for their depravity and destruction! (Genesis 13:10–13; 18:1–19:29) When we want to talk about a city that is particularly wicked today, we still call it Sodom.

In Isaiah's day, God spared a remnant of the nation of Judah, just as he had spared Lot's family from destruction. Not all were righteous and few deserved to be spared. But God's ultimate plan for the redemption of the world called for the preservation of the house of David and the remnant of Judah. In God's mercy, He did not cause the Daughter of Zion to become like Sodom and Gomorrah.

But God's people were rebellious. They were guilty of going through the motions of religion. They observed the monthly rituals, the weekly meetings, and even the special gatherings. They brought the finest sacrifices. They kept the letter of the Law and the traditions. Yet all this was meaningless because they did not have a relationship with the Lord God Almighty.

"Stop bringing me meaningless offerings!" God says.

Hear the prophet Samuel telling King Saul that obedience is better than sacrifice. (1 Samuel 15:22) Hear King David cry: "You do not delight in sacrifice, or I would bring it; you do not take pleasure in burnt offerings. My sacrifice, O God, is a broken spirit; a broken and contrite heart you, God, will not despise." (Psalm 51:16–17) Hear Jesus speaking to a Samaritan woman: "God is spirit, and his worshipers must worship in the Spirit and in truth." (John 4:24)

It's easy to become so involved in church services and serving in the church that we forget who church is about and who is the One we serve. It's easy to become so involved in the behavior, the traditions, and the activity of the church that we forget God. It is not the activity, the tradition, or the imitation of holy behavior that God wants most from us. God requires our hearts. He wants our obedience. Obedience that comes from a clean heart is what God will accept.

Jesus told the woman at the well that God looks for people who will worship Him in the Spirit and in truth. When God's Holy Spirit is working in our hearts and we respond, that is true worship. God requires hearts that embrace the Truth. The Truth is the Word of God.

Is your worship pleasing to God? Is your heart in it, or are you just going through the motions? Why is sacrifice often easier to give than obedience? Is God asking you to surrender an area of your life in obedience?

Prayer: Help us to worship in the Spirit and in truth.
Cleanse our hearts so that we truly obey.

10

God Refuses to Hear

*'When you spread out your hands in prayer,
I hide my eyes from you; even when you
offer many prayers, I am not listening. Your
hands are full of blood!'* (1:15)

IN 2 CHRONICLES 6:12–42, we find a record of Solomon's
prayer dedicating the Temple. In verses 20, 21, and 40 we
read that Solomon specifically asks God to have His eyes on
the Temple "day and night." Solomon asks God to hear the
prayers of the people, to keep His "eyes ... open" and His "ears
attentive to the prayers offered in this place."

In 2 Chronicles 7 we read God's response to Solomon, the
covenant He made with the people concerning the Temple. "I
have heard your prayer and have chosen this place for myself
as a temple for sacrifices. ... I have chosen and consecrated this
temple so that my Name may be there forever. My eyes and
heart will always be there. ... But if you turn away ... then I
will uproot Israel ... and will reject this temple ... " (vv. 12–20)

Such a time has come in Isaiah's day. Do you see the severity of the prophet's words to the people? How many years had the Temple that Solomon built stood on Mount Moriah? It had been there longer than most of Isaiah's hearers could remember. The very idea that God would abandon His Temple and His people was unthinkable. Some of the people would believe Isaiah, but most would simply see his words—even though they came from God—as an empty threat.

This particular message from Isaiah could be likened to Billy Graham's telling the American people that an alien nation was going to take over the government, export our leaders to another world, and tear down the White House. Some of us would give the message credence because of our respect for the messenger, but most of us would wonder if Billy had gone over the edge.

How could God refuse to hear our prayers? We believe God always hears prayer (especially when we push the right buttons). Would God really hide His eyes and close His ears from our prayers?

Yes, if our "hands are full of blood"! There are very few, if any, chemicals that will take out a bloodstain once it is set into the cloth. One small spot makes a garment useless and repulsive to us. How much more repulsive to God are the sin stains that cover the disobedient!

The blood of insincere sacrifice, ritualistic religion, and deliberate disobedience had stained the hands of the people. They were spiritually repulsive to God because of the filthy stains and grime of ritual, "religion," and rebellion.

Is it possible that insincere religion or deliberate disobedience stains your life? Are you burdening God with your rituals and sacrifices?

Prayer: Lord, help me to see any offense in me. Help me to see the sin stains on my life.

11

Let Us Settle the Matter

'Wash and make yourselves clean. Take your evil deeds out of my sight; stop doing wrong. Learn to do right; seek justice. Defend the oppressed. Take up the cause of the fatherless; plead the case of the widow. Come now, let us settle the matter,' says the Lord. 'Though your sins are like scarlet, they shall be as white as snow; though they are red as crimson, they shall be like wool.'
(1:16–18)

DESPITE HIS ANGER, GOD says that if His people will wash, they will be made clean. He calls us to spiritual regeneration and to social action.

When people truly know and love God, their actions reflect that relationship. They behave in a way that affords dignity to all living creatures. They develop a strong sense of caring about others. As an extension of the love they receive from

God, they feel compelled to help needy and weak people of their community.

Spiritual regeneration always results in social action. However, social action does not always result in spiritual regeneration. We must remember to keep first things first. Without the power of the Spirit, we may plunge into justice ministries, but our efforts will not likely succeed and may even cause us to burn out.

"Come now, let us settle the matter," says the Lord. "Though your sins are like scarlet, they shall be as white as snow; though they are red as crimson, they shall be like wool."

Remember the reason you serve God. Remember the God you serve. Most of all, remember that only the blood of the Lamb of God can take away the stain of sin—from us as individuals and from our churches.

" 'If my people, who are called by my name, will humble themselves and pray and seek my face and turn from their wicked ways, then I will hear from heaven, and I will forgive their sin and will heal their land.' " (2 Chronicles 7:14)

Prayer: Lord, make us clean. Wash us in the blood
of the Lamb and take away the stain of sin.
Then teach us to do right and seek justice.

12

You Choose: Blessing or Curse

'If you are willing and obedient, you will eat the good things of the land; but if you resist and rebel, you will be devoured by the sword.' For the mouth of the Lord has spoken. (1:19–20)

"IF YOU ARE WILLING and obedient ..." God always offers us a choice. He created humans with free will and allows us to exercise it. The choice here is painted as black and white: obey and be blessed with all good things or rebel and be cursed with destruction. However, the choice often feels more complicated.

We have already seen in Isaiah that God recognizes our blindness and deafness when it comes to His will. Circumstances blind us. The noise of the world deafens us. Personal desire hardens our hearts and clouds our understanding.

Many leaders fall by the wayside because they choose a moment of pleasure or satisfaction over a lifetime of blessing. How does this happen? Perhaps they are temporarily blinded by circumstances. Discouraged and tired, a young officer gives himself to lust and destroys his marriage, his family, and his ministry. A more seasoned officer feels used and useless and begins to take what does not belong to her. Her actions become easier and easier to rationalize, and soon she doesn't even realize that sin has taken her in.

Because of the clamor of fame or of urgent things, we allow our hearing to become dulled. The black–and–white choices of obedience and rebellion become greys. We allow the circumstances of living to blind us, to keep us from hearing. We choose not to ask God to keep our vision clear. We choose not to listen for the still small voice. We choose to make our hearts hard, and our reason becomes cloudy.

These are the choices of rebellion, which lead to the curse of destruction. But we can choose obedience, which leads to blessing.

The Lord God calls us to "settle the matter," to choose obedience. Dearly beloved, if you have made wrong, rebellious choices, know that there is a loving God waiting for you to return, to "eat the good things of the land" once again. Even if your life has become stained scarlet with sin, God can once again make you clean.

Prayer: God, help us to hear Your Word and see the way You make for us to escape temptation. Help us to recognize and choose obedience over rebellion. Forgive us when we fail You. Set our feet on the right path again.

More Scripture: Deuteronomy 11

13

Purging and Purifying

Isaiah 1:21–31

"SEE HOW THE FAITHFUL city has become a prostitute!" (1:21)
Once, Israel had one King, one Master, and one Husband—
God. The nation that had been like a faithful spouse is now
like a prostitute.

In 1 Samuel 8 we read how the elders of Israel met with
Samuel and demanded a king like the other nations had. This
grieved Samuel, their prophet and judge. Until this time, the
chosen nation had been a theocracy, a nation ruled by God
alone. God told Samuel that in asking for a king, the people
were not rejecting him, but God Himself. God granted the
people's request, but He instructed Samuel to line out the
dire consequences that would befall them under a king.

The people's habits of falling into idolatry and rebellion
began long before the time of Isaiah or even of Samuel. Look
at the early patriarchs and matriarchs. Jacob stole his brother's birthright rather than trusting God to fulfill His prom-

ises. Rachel stole her father's household gods as Jacob and his family ran away from Laban. Aaron made a golden calf for the people even as Moses was receiving the Law from God. Even after entering the Promised Land, everyone "did what was right in their own eyes" until God raised up a judge to lead them.

By the time of Isaiah, hundreds of years later, things had changed very little. The people kept promising to worship and obey God, but they didn't keep their promises. So once more God spelled out through His prophets the consequences of their rebellion. This time it would be exile. In Isaiah's day, the Assyrians took the northern kingdom of Israel into exile. The people of Judah, the southern kingdom, didn't believe it could happen to them because of the presence of God in the Temple. They believed that God would always defeat their enemies. But they also worshiped at "just–in–case" altars to other gods, and they made alliances with other nations.

God's holy nation was polluted, like tarnished silver. Isaiah compared their commitment to weak, watered–down wine. Their "trusted" leaders were rebels, partners with thieves. Isaiah said God would use the Assyrians and Babylonians as fire to burn off the people's impurities. Then God would bring back a remnant of the people and re–establish a righteous nation. "Zion will be delivered with justice, her penitent ones with righteousness." (1:27)

First comes purging and purifying; then comes redemption and restoration. As it was then, so it is now. We are in a constant state of purging and purification as God works in us to redeem and remake us into the image of Christ.

Verse 31 reminds us that all of our works will be tested

by fire. See 1 Corinthians 3:10–15. What will be left of your personal life after the fire of refinement? What will be left of our church? Our nations?

Prayer: Lord, refine us with the fire of Your Spirit. Help us to serve You as clean vessels fit for Your Kingdom.

14

The Mountain of the Lord

Isaiah 2:1–5

MORIAH MEANS "SEEN BY Yahweh." For Israel, the importance of Mount Moriah goes back to the day Abraham placed his son Isaac on the altar, which many people believe he did on that mountain. Centuries later, David would encounter the angel of death at the threshing floor of Araunah, located on Mount Moriah. David purchased this threshing floor, and Solomon built the Temple on the site. God filled the Temple with His glory, and His presence rested over the ark of the covenant.*

It is this mountain, the mountain of the Lord's Temple, that Isaiah prophesies "will be exalted above the hills." Later, Jesus says that when He, the Son of Man, is lifted up, He will draw all people to Himself. Mount Moriah, then, is symbolic of Jesus, the Messiah.

For Christians, all of the Old Testament points to Jesus. We believe that He is the true Son of promise whom Isaac foreshadowed—the Son, the Lamb, that God would offer as the ultimate sacrifice to take away the sin of the world. We believe that Jesus became flesh and dwelled (or "tabernacled") among us as the true Temple of God's presence and glory.

Jesus said that the Holy Spirit would teach us and guide us to the truth. (See John 16:13–15.) This is the very fulfillment of Isaiah 2:3: "He will teach us His ways so that we may walk in His paths."

Jesus told His disciples that they would be His witnesses in Jerusalem, Judea, Samaria, and to the ends of the earth. (Acts 1:8) I think of Acts 2 when I read the words of Isaiah 2:3: "The law will go out from Zion, the word of the Lord from Jerusalem."

In that city on the day of Pentecost, 120 followers of Jesus gathered in a meeting room to pray. By the end of that day, thousands had given their lives to God, and His Word began to go out to every part of the world.

We wait for the fulfillment of the rest of this portion of Scripture. On that day, a reverse of what happened in Genesis 11 will take place. There, we saw that pride and rebellion led the people, who all spoke one language, to unite and raise up a tower to the heavens. God was not pleased; He confused their language and divided the people. Isaiah 2:4 says that God will once again unite the nations, and they will live in peace. Together, the nations will "walk in the light of the Lord." (2:5)

Prayer: May Your Kingdom come and Your will be done. Bring peace to the nations.

*Mount Moriah is also a sacred place for Muslims because it was from here, 500 years after the Romans destroyed the Temple in 70 A.D., that they believe Mohammed ascended to heaven.

15

A Description of Decay

Isaiah 2:6–11

ISAIAH SAYS, "YOU, LORD, have abandoned your people." But then he goes on to describe a people who have abandoned Him. In this portion of Scripture, we see a description of spiritual decay.

The people are full of superstitions and are embracing the pagan ways of other nations. They have much silver and gold, many horses and chariots. And their land is full of idols: "… they bow down to the work of their hands, to what their fingers have made." The people of God have abandoned their true relationship with Him and turned to the idolatry and mysticism that other nations practice.

Isaiah prophesies to the people: "Go into the rocks, hide in the ground from the fearful presence of the Lord and the splendor of his majesty!" For the Day of the Lord is coming when He alone will be exalted and "the eyes of the arrogant will be humbled and human pride brought low." The people are clearly in trouble.

Are we like them? They didn't reach this state of decay overnight. They once worshiped God, and He rewarded them with every blessing. They had a God hunger that only He could satisfy. But over time, that "God hunger" became perverted; it drove them to other things. That can happen to us too. We can turn to psychics, to material things, to power, to prestige, to physical gratification—all to sate our "God hunger."

Once decay begins, it tends to continue. We become captive to our desires, and we refuse to bow before the only One who can truly satisfy our God hunger. We are anything but satisfied, but we will not admit it. Why not? Because of our pride.

Jesus reminds us, in a parable found in Luke 18:9–14, that God hears the prayer of the humble and refuses to hear the prayer of the proud. A religious man and a sinner go to the temple to pray. The religious man is so full of himself that he doesn't take time to recognize or confess his sin. The sinner acknowledges his sin and his need for God's forgiveness. Which prayer does God hear? This one: "God have mercy on me, a sinner."

Have you been trying to satisfy your hunger for God with other things? Maybe it's time to admit that.

Prayer: God be merciful to me, a sinner.

16

Pride and the Fall

Isaiah 2:12–22

"THE LORD ALMIGHTY HAS a day in store for all the proud and lofty, for all that is exalted, (and they will be humbled) ... The arrogance of man will be brought low and human pride humbled ... " (2:12, 17)

What is it that causes us to seek our own pleasure above all else? What drives us to feed our appetites even when we know it will ruin our life and the lives of others? The answer, in one word, is pride. It is the excessive arrogance that causes us to say: "I did it my way." It's not the same as self–esteem. It is a self–centered, self–destructive drive to put ourselves first, no matter the consequences. It demands its way and its rights. It doesn't care about the needs of others.

Pride is a thing God hates above all else. It can push even angels to do evil. Lucifer was one of God's grandest and most beautiful creations. But his pride caused him to rebel against God in an attempt to be greater than God.

In Genesis 3 we read that Lucifer, in the form of the serpent, appealed first to Eve's curiosity, then to her pride. He drew her attention to the Tree of Knowledge by asking a question: "Did God really say, 'You must not eat from any tree in the garden'?" Then he appealed to her pride by telling her that if she ate the fruit, she would be "like God."

Pride drove Cain to kill Abel. It built the tower of Babel. It led the way for King Saul as he departed the good path on which God had set his feet.

We can all fall prey to an excess of pride. Pride can cause us to feel too good about ourselves—or to despise ourselves. Pride can push us to feel overlooked and angry when promotions go to others. Pride can lead a preacher to be "entertaining" so people will admire her, not the Lord. Pride can lead us to compromise the truth of the Word of God, bending it to fit what we would like it to say. Pride can urge us to "re–create" God to be the kind of being we would like Him to be.

In Proverbs 16:18 we read: "Pride goes before destruction, a haughty spirit before a fall." Peter was thinking of Proverbs 3:34 when he penned these words: " ... clothe yourselves with humility toward one another, because 'God opposes the proud but shows favor to the humble.' Humble yourselves, therefore, under the mighty hand of God, so that he may exalt you at the proper time." (1 Peter 5:5–7)

Prayer: Lord, I repent of my pride. Grant me the gift
of humility.

17

Supply and Support

Isaiah 3:1–7

THE SECURITY AND PROSPERITY of a nation rely on many things, but those things can be summarized in this phrase: "supply and support." Support, in this passage, refers to leadership. Supply refers to the material things that are needed to sustain life. When Moses led the Jews to the Promised Land, they made a covenant with God to be His people. He would meet their material needs, and He would be their king and appoint men and women to assist Him in meeting their need for leadership. As long as the people kept their part of the covenant, God promised to meet their needs for supply and support.

Over the centuries, the nation of Israel repeatedly rejected God. By the time of Isaiah, He finally had had enough. The nation would go into exile. To make this happen, God would withdraw all supply and support.

Supplies of food and water would vanish. So would the

leaders: the hero, the warrior, the judge, the prophet, the soothsayer, the elder, the captain of 50, the man of rank, the counselor, the skilled craftsman, and even the con–artist enchanter. The result of this leadership gap, this lack of support, would be oppression. Inexperienced youth and children would take control, and people would "oppress each other—man against man, neighbor against neighbor."

This sounds like a history lesson we have never learned.

As long as good leaders lead, the nation or organization is preserved. When there is a leadership gap, fools come to power. People turn on each other rather than working together. They turn to their natural inclination for self–preservation rather than working for the good of the community. Self rules. Self demands. Self destroys.

There may be times when you are tempted to leave your church or leave your appointed place of service because you don't agree with or respect your leaders. Remember that God put you where you are for a reason. You cannot change things from the outside. Change occurs when good people remain faithful to God's call for their lives.

Jesus said that His followers should be like salt and light. Salt gives flavor, but it also heals and preserves. If we give up on our nation, our church, or our community, who will be the salt? If the light does not shine, how can those around us see the way? You are salt and light for your nation. You are salt and light for your church. You are salt and light for your community. Do not give up, or corruption and darkness will win.

You are salt and light when you remain faithful to God and live out His grace. Grace with a capital G is allowing the

Holy Spirit to lead you. Living God's Grace will result in loving, holy, righteous lives. You are salt and light when you are faithful where God has placed you.

Prayer: Supply and support, salt and light. Oh Lord, meet our needs today.

18

The Defiant Look

Jerusalem staggers, Judah is falling; their words and deeds are against the Lord, defying his glorious presence. The look on their faces testifies against them; they parade their sin like Sodom; they do not hide it. Woe to them! They have brought disaster upon themselves. Tell the righteous it will be well with them, for they will enjoy the fruit of their deeds. Woe to the wicked! Disaster is upon them! They will be paid back for what their hands have done. (3:8–11)

FOR A MOMENT THINK back to the last time you saw a defiant look on someone's face. Was it on the face of your 3–year–old? Your teenager? A person in the news? An employee? Or was it in the mirror? You know the look. It starts in the eyes. It is accompanied by a set of the jaw and a smirk that says: "I know what I'm doing, and you can't stop me."

The defiant look is one of pure rebellion. Occasionally it is amusing, but it is usually frustrating. When the look is aimed at me, I feel angry and want to retaliate. The defiant look tells me that the person cares more about the act of rebellion than about me. The defiant look disappoints me. I become a bundle of emotions.

I wonder how God feels when He sees the defiant look on our faces.

I woke up one morning and knew it was going to be one of those days. I told God He might as well mark me down for blowing it because I was not even going to try. I almost eagerly awaited temptation and allowed it to take me by the horns. I chose to sin. God intervened before I blew it in a big way, and He gave me a chance to reconcile my choices. But the defiance in my heart must have broken His.

Sometimes a defiant look is really a mask covering fear. Look in the faces of people caught up in a lifestyle that they know in their heart of hearts is wrong. You may see the defiant look. But don't let the mask keep you from loving and praying for them. Next time you see the defiant look, respond to it with a look that reflects God's love.

How can we help those who defy God by claiming their lifestyle is right because it feels so normal to them? How can we know whether something is really breaking God's law or is breaking a cultural interpretation of God's law?

Prayer: God, forgive us when we rebel against Your law and break Your heart. Touch those who are caught up in lives of rebellion and free them from the chains of sin.

19

Prosperity and Pride

Isaiah 3:16–4:1

THE NATION OF JUDAH had enjoyed years of prosperity and
the blessing of God. But when life became easier, the people's
priorities shifted. The pursuit of wealth instead of blessings
from God became the reason for living. Isaiah observed this
problem and addressed the women with a warning.

Why the women? I believe Isaiah spoke to them because
God has high expectations for women. When He created the
first woman, Eve, God called her a "helper," one who would
come alongside Adam just as God would come alongside His
people in battle. I believe God equipped women by giving them
a special sensitivity to Him. I realize this is a sweeping gener-
alization, but the more I study Scripture and observe human
nature, I believe it is a unique gift God gave to womankind.
The women of Isaiah's day neglected their gift and duty of
godliness to compete with each other in fashionable adornments and in attracting men with flirting eyes and swaying

hips. God would strip them of their adornments, dressing them in sackcloth; he would make them bald and unattractive and allow their men to fall by the sword. They would be reduced to pleading, "Take away our disgrace!" (4:1)

It's easy to become wrapped up in the indulgences of life and neglect the gift God has given us. I believe that the role of helper gives women both the privilege and the responsibility of coming alongside God to be His voice in the community and to intercede for our communities in prayer. When the pursuit of things like wealth and lust becomes our first priority, we become competitive instead of compassionate. We begin to treasure things and use people.

As God's ambassadors, we need to be careful about our appearance. It must not detract from our work for God. The focus is not so much on what we wear or whether we use make–up. The focus is on what we are like in our "inner selves." We must not become confused about the truly important things, or indulgence of self will become more important than concern for others.

The warning of this passage in Isaiah should speak to both women and men. We must all be careful about ordering our priorities. Anything that we put before God becomes an idol. And, ultimately, God will smash all idols. Enjoy the good things and the blessings God gives you. To do any less would be sin; however, to do any more is idolatry. How do we know what the right balance is? Jesus said: "Seek first his kingdom and his righteousness, and all these things will be given to you as well." (Matthew 6:33)

Note that after this passage, in Isaiah 4:2, true beauty is revealed. The true source of pride, for righteous women and men alike, is the "Branch of the Lord."

Prayer: Lord, help us to quit focusing on the wrapping and claim the gift.

More Scripture: 1 Peter 3:3–4

20

The Branch of the Lord

Isaiah 4:2–6

IN ISAIAH 2:2–5, WE read about the mountain of the Lord. Here, we read about the promises associated with the "Branch of the Lord." Both passages refer to the day of redemption. Each follows a long passage of warning and condemnation.

In this portion of Scripture, we can discover a promise of the redemption of all creation and the end of every curse. Before God expelled Adam, Eve, and the serpent from the Garden of Eden, He assigned a curse to each one that would pass from generation to generation until the day of redemption and healing.

He placed a curse on the land because of Adam. God told him that he would have to work very hard for food, something he had not had to do in the Garden. Isaiah now proclaims that the Branch of the Lord will heal the land and restore its original productivity.

God placed a curse on Eve that she would have pain in

childbirth and be subject to her husband. Isaiah proclaims that the Branch of the Lord will "wash away the filth of the women of Zion." He will cancel the curse leveled on Eve and her daughters. The Branch of the Lord will restore woman's position and equality.

God placed a curse on the serpent, that it would crawl on its belly and that there would be enmity between the serpent and the woman—and her offspring. This is the first prophecy about Jesus (the Branch of the Lord), that the serpent would strike His heel but that He would crush the serpent's head, winning victory over evil and even death.

Isaiah also prophesies (2:5–6) that in the day of the Branch of the Lord, God will return His presence to Mount Zion. When Moses led the Jews in the wilderness, God supplied a cloud by day and a pillar of fire by night to remind them of His presence, power, provision, and protection. God's Word through Isaiah promises that this manifestation will return.

Both Jeremiah and Zechariah foretold the coming of the Branch of the Lord, the Messiah. For those of us who know Him, the curses of the Garden have been canceled. But the day of the Branch of the Lord is also a day still to come in all its fullness because Jesus has not yet come again. When that day arrives, there will be a new heaven and a new earth.

In the meantime, the world around us is still fallen, dark, and corrupt. We who know Him are living in freedom, and we are about the business of reaching those who are still living under the curse. While we wait for the day of the Branch of the Lord, let us live holy (consecrated) and wholly (completely) in God's presence and promises.

Prayer: Let Your Kingdom come and Your will be done.

More Scripture: Genesis 3:6–9; Exodus 40:34–38; Jeremiah 23:5–6; Zechariah 3:8–10, 6:12–13

21

Shelter, Refuge, Hiding Place

Then the Lord will create over all of Mount Zion and over those who assemble there a cloud of smoke by day and a glow of flaming fire by night; over everything the glory will be a canopy. It will be a shelter and shade from the heat of the day, and a refuge and hiding place from the storm and rain. (4:5–6)

IF YOU WANT A great experience, go through the Psalms and mark all the verses that refer to God as shelter, shield, refuge, safety, and hiding place. Here's a start.

"Blessed are all who take refuge in him." (2:12)

"... you, Lord, are a shield around me ... " (3:3)

"In peace I will lie down and sleep, for you alone, Lord, make me dwell in safety." (4:8)

" ... let all who take refuge in you be glad; let them ever sing for joy. Spread your protection over them, that those who love your name may rejoice in you." (5:11)

"Surely, Lord, you bless the righteous; you surround them with your favor as with a shield." (5:12)

"My shield is God Most High, who saves the upright in heart." (7:10)

"The Lord is a refuge for the oppressed, a stronghold in times of trouble." (9:9)

"I love you, Lord, my strength. The Lord is my rock, my fortress and my deliverer; my God is my rock, in whom I take refuge, my shield and the horn of my salvation, my stronghold. I called to the Lord, who is worthy of praise, and I have been saved from my enemies." (18:1–3)

"The Lord is my light and my salvation—whom shall I fear? The Lord is the stronghold of my life—of whom shall I be afraid?" (27:1)

"The Lord is my strength and my shield; my heart trusts in him, and he helps me." (28:7)

"You are my hiding place; you will protect me from trouble and surround me with songs of deliverance." (32:7)

What a wonderful thing it is to be a child of God! When you do not know who to trust, trust the Lord.

Prayer: Oh God, be my hiding place.

22

God With Us

Isaiah 4:5–6

FOR THE PEOPLE OF Israel fleeing from Egyptian slavery, the presence of the Lord was visible as a cloud of smoke by day and a pillar of fire by night. (Exodus 13:21–22) When the cloud stopped, the people stopped to rest. When the cloud moved, they moved. The pillar of fire gave them the ability to travel at night by its light.

Have you ever wondered why God took the people through the wilderness rather than by the more direct and easily traveled coastal route? Exodus 13:17–18 informs us of one of the reasons. When the Israelites left Egypt, they considered themselves ready for war. But if they had actually faced the Philistines in battle early in their journey, they might have changed their minds and gone back to Egypt and slavery. If the people had traveled by the more direct route, they also would have missed the miracles of God's provision: the parted Red Sea, manna delivered from the sky, and water springing from a rock. If the people of God had not experienced the wilderness journey, their whole story would have been different. Our story would have been different too.

Isaiah's short reference to the cloud of smoke and pillar of fire would have evoked in the minds of his hearers many significant symbols of their religious and covenant history, of the lessons in trust and obedience they learned in the wilderness. To us, the description is also a reminder that God is our guide, the One who " ... will be a shelter and shade from the heat of the day, and a refuge and hiding place from the storm and rain." (4:6)

When we find ourselves in the wilderness on our journey, we may ask why God has allowed us to travel this difficult path. There's no real answer for that. But we have to understand that in the wilderness, if we trust God for everything, we will grow stronger, deeper, and richer in our spiritual lives and character. Then, just when we need it most, God will give us shelter, a hiding place where we can rest, reflect, and be restored.

Prayer: Lord, help me to trust and follow You in my journey, even when it feels like I'm in the wilderness.

23

The Lord's Vineyard

Isaiah 5:1–7

IN THIS CHAPTER, THE vineyard is used as a metaphor for the nation of Israel and the people of Judah, "vines" the Lord had once delighted in but now finds producing bad fruit.

God uses familiar objects and word pictures throughout Scripture to teach spiritual truths. Someone who is unfamiliar with vineyards may not understand the planting process, the cultivation methods, or the growth cycle. But we all can understand the difference between good fruit and bad fruit. The Lord had looked for good fruit—justice and righteousness—among His people. Instead, He found bloodshed and cries of distress. So He promised to destroy the vineyard and make it a wasteland.

Jesus told a parable about a landowner (the Lord) who rented His vineyard to some farmers (God's people). When it came time to collect its fruit, the landowner sent his servants (the prophets), and the tenants beat and killed them. Finally, he sent his son (Jesus), thinking he would be respected, but the tenants killed him too. Jesus asked what the owner of the vineyard would do to those tenants. His hearers said that those "wretches" would be brought to a bad end, and the landowners would rent the vineyard to other tenants. Jesus responded by saying, "I tell you that the kingdom of God will be taken away from you and given to a people who will produce its fruit." (Matthew 21:33–41, 43) He spoke prophetically of all those who would accept Him as King and become part of the new people of God.

Read a prayer for the restoration of the vine in Psalm 80.

Prayer: Help me to remain connected to Jesus, the true vine (John 15), so that I will bear good fruit.

24

A Personal Relationship

I will sing for the one I love a song about his vineyard ... (5:1)

THIS VERSE HELPS US to discover the kind of relationship Isaiah the prophet had with God. "The one" to whom Isaiah sings is God. In Deuteronomy 5:7 we read: "You shall have no other gods before me." To Isaiah, there is no god but the One God. And God is the first priority in Isaiah's life.

Isaiah says, "I will sing for the one I love." He loved the Lord his God with all his heart, soul, mind, and strength, just as the Law commanded. And remember, Jesus Himself says that this commandment is the most important of all. (Mark 12:28–30)

Those two truths are important for us to ponder today. All around us, many things and people clamor for our attention and first place in our priorities. It's all too easy to succumb and to forget that when we place anyone or anything before God, that person or thing becomes our god. We can no longer sing that the Lord is the "One I love."

Staying close to the Lord is often an issue of trust. If we don't really believe that He will take care of us, we begin to take matters into our own hands, and our devotion wavers. Can you trust God so completely as to know that if you obey that most important commandment and put Him before everything else, He will order your life the right way? Jesus tells us we must do exactly that. He says we shouldn't worry about our next meal or what we will wear because the Lord will provide for us, just as he does for the birds of the air and the flowers of the field. Jesus also teaches that we are to " ... seek first his kingdom and his righteousness ... " If we do that, He promises, all things will fall into place. (Matthew 6:25–34)

Prayer: Oh God, help me to truly recognize You as
the One I love. If I have allowed anything to
come before You, it is a false god. Remove all
idols and false gods from my life. Help me to
seek you first. Order my days.

More Scripture: Deuteronomy 4:29, 39; Deuteronomy 6:4–5

25

Carefully Prepared Soil

Isaiah 5:1–2

WHEN WE VISITED ISRAEL, I noted that the land grew a great crop of rocks. Our guide told us that in ancient times, after a person purchased a piece of land, the first order of business would be to clear the away rocks and stones. The guide also said that a landowner's enemies would often throw rocks into a field to slow down that process.

The owner of the vineyard in this parable of Isaiah is God. He too prepared the soil for choice vines by removing the stones.

Think of the parable of the soils that Jesus told. (Matthew 13) A farmer goes to plant his crop. The seed that falls on rocky soil springs up very quickly. However, the seeds don't have deep roots. Without a good root system, the plants could not survive the harshness of everyday reality. I wondered when I read this story, *Why were there still rocks in the soil if the farmer had prepared it for planting?* Maybe one of his enemies had come behind him and dumped a new crop of rocks on his land.

God scatters seeds of righteousness in our lives every day. Our enemy, the devil, is busy lobbing stones into the soil. We must work with God to keep the soil of our hearts and minds clear of stumbling stones and rocks, or the seeds of righteousness will sprout, but then wither and die without producing fruit.

What are some of the stones and rocks we might need to remove from our hearts and minds? Unforgiveness, disobedience, apathy, and lack of self–control are just a few examples. God looks for a good crop, for good fruit, which can grow only in good soil. For a check on whether you are producing good fruit, examine the list of the fruits of the Holy Spirit in Galatians 5:22–23. Then look at Philippians 4:8 for a clue about what we should put into our minds in place of any "rocks" that could stunt our growth in the Lord.

Can you set your heart and mind on "things above, not on earthly things"? (Colossians 3:1–2)

Prayer: God help me keep the soil of my heart free
from the stumbling stones and rocks of sin.

26

Tough Love

Isaiah 5:3–6

"YOU JUDGE," GOD CHALLENGED His people. "What more could I have done?" Now He was about to leave His vineyard, the nation of Israel and the people of Judah, to reap the consequences of their choices and actions. He would put the principle of tough love into action.

First God would remove the hedge. In Scripture and in life, a hedge offers protection. Two significant leaders and intercessors, Moses and David, asked God to protect the nation. The constant and consistent rebellion of the people finally caused the removal of that hedge of protection.

Second, God would break down the stone wall. The stones cleared out of a field made natural building material. Stone walls provided security, and God said he would break them down so that the people would be defenseless. They would lose not just their physical security but their psychological security as well. Feeling secure is important to individual as well as corporate well–being. If we don't feel secure, we can lose our personal sense of contentment and our sense of community. The fabric of society wears thin.

If the Lord brought the stone walls down, strangers would trample through the vineyard. Weeds and thorns would creep in where rich vines once had grown.

Finally, the Lord said that He would withhold the rain. One of God's agreements with His people, if they kept their promises, was to provide the rains in their season as a sign of His blessing. Taking away the rain, such a basic need, would be the final blow to the nation.

Did God abandon His people completely? No. A remnant would be spared. The Lord always provides a way of redemption. Before that, however, would come the time for tough love.

Is it possible that we sometimes need to provide this kind of tough love to people in our lives? Perhaps you are connected to someone who, through neglect and bad actions, is on the road to destroying herself. If she continues in destructive behavior, there could be severe consequences. It's very hard, but you may need to allow her to face those consequences. If you don't, she will likely never take responsibility for her actions. But that doesn't mean you abandon her completely. You must trust her to the Lord, who will provide a way for her to be delivered. He delivered you, didn't He?

Prayer: Lord, give me the wisdom I need about when
I need to use tough love. You set the example.
Help me follow it.

*Side note: Intercessors need to understand the hedge principle. When you pray for loved ones, ask God to put a hedge of spiritual protection around them. When you pray for the nation, pray for a hedge of spiritual protection around it.

27

The Myth of Success

*How terrible it will be for you who add more
houses to your houses and more fields to your
fields until there is no room left for other people.
Then you are left alone in the land. The Lord
All–Powerful said this to me: 'The fine houses
will be destroyed; the large and beautiful
houses will be left empty. At that time a ten–
acre vineyard will make only six gallons of
wine, and ten bushels of seed will grow only a
half bushel of grain.' (5:8–10 NCV)*

WHAT REALLY COUNTS IN life? Property? Prosperity?
Reputation? Family? Friends? If pieces of your life were taken
away one by one, how would you react? Think about Job. He
was a righteous man with a great reputation. He had it all: a
great family, land, possessions, and good health. But those were
not the most important things to him: God was. When Satan
was allowed to strip away everything from him but his life, Job

fell down in worship, saying, "The Lord gave and the Lord has taken away; may the name of the Lord be praised." (Job 1:21)

Hundreds of years later, God had also blessed the Israelites with many material blessings. But they had forgotten the source of their blessings. They always wanted more. Their hunger for riches was never sated. The rich got richer. They climbed the ladder of success only to look for another ladder. They added "more houses to ... houses" and "more fields to ... fields" until they were left alone. They neglected the important things. So the Lord was about to break down the prideful excess of the people until their "large and beautiful houses" were empty and their vineyards and fields completely unproductive.

Thousands of years later, we can easily fall prey to the error of the Israelites. Forgetting that our blessings come from the Lord, we begin to want more. Hunger for riches, achievement, fame, and success taunts us. We climb ladders and look for more ladders. Often the price of building empires is neglecting to build relationships, neglecting the spiritual and eternal. So many men and women reach their goals for power, property, prestige, and possessions to find that they are alone when they "arrive." They have no one to share in the glory of their victory.

What if your possessions, power, and reputation were taken away? Add your health to that list—and your family. What would be your reason for continuing? If you were in a truly strong relationship with God, you just might be able to say what Job said: "Though He slay me, yet will I hope in him ... " (Job 13:15)

Prayer: Lord, help me to get my priorities in order. Help me to enjoy the blessings of family, friends, success, and material wealth that You choose to give without grasping for more. Keep reminding me that these are only temporary. My real treasure is in you. Help me to live my life to make a difference for Your eternal Kingdom.

28

The Woe of Overindulgence

Isaiah 5:11–17

HERE IS A PICTURE of people consumed by the appetites of their flesh. They get up early in the morning and stay up late at night for the sole purpose of "partying." They give great banquets but have no regard for the Lord.

Now examine the lifestyle of a king who ruled Babylon during the time of the prophet Daniel (about 200 years after the time of Isaiah). The story is told in Daniel 5. King Belshazzar gave a great banquet to show off his wealth and power. All who attended were expected to indulge in food, wine, and everything else the king had to offer. It was in this setting that a very intoxicated King Belshazzar got an idea to bring out the sacred treasures that his father had looted from the Temple in Jerusalem. By choosing to use these vessels as part of the drunken revelry, Belshazzar was challenging God to show Himself.

As Belshazzar drank the wine, God did just that. His

hand appeared and wrote on the wall. (It's the first example of "holy graffiti.") As the king watched, "His face turned pale and he was so frightened that his legs became weak and his knees were knocking." (Daniel 5:6) Ultimately, Daniel offered the king a stark interpretation of the message on the wall: " ... you, Belshazzar ... have not humbled yourself ... Instead, you have set yourself up against the Lord of heaven." (5:22–23) Daniel told the king the consequences: his kingdom would be conquered, Belshazzar would die, and a new king would take his place.

What led Belshazzar to challenge God by using the sacred vessels? What led the people in Isaiah's day to run after drunken pleasure instead of their God? Pride. Every soul is hungry for the love of God. God gives that love freely to all who ask for it. Yet somehow, we humans refuse to accept that we have only to turn to God because turning to God would mean humbling ourselves. So we continue in our own way, indulging the appetites of the flesh to try to appease the soul. Pride turns to anger. Anger turns to rebellion. Rebellion turns to arrogance. Arrogance challenges God. And God will respond.

"So people will be brought low and everyone humbled, the eyes of the arrogant humbled." (Isaiah 5:15)

The handwriting is on the wall. Yet many refuse to see it or cannot bring themselves to understand it. Jesus says, "Let anyone who is thirsty come to me and drink." (John 7:37). "Let the one who is thirsty come; and let the one who wishes take the free gift of the water of life." (Revelation 22:17) Turn to God and feed your soul.

Prayer: Help me to see if I have been indulging in appetites of the flesh and refusing to humble myself before You. I want to walk in the path of right living.

29

Yoked to Sin

Woe to those who draw sin along with cords of deceit, and wickedness as with cart ropes, to those who say, 'Let God hurry, let him hasten his work so we may see it. The plan of the Holy One of Israel—let it come into view, so we may know it.' (5:18–19)

WHAT AN AMAZING PICTURE Isaiah paints for us here! People are dragging their great burden of sin along with cords of deceit and cart ropes of wickedness! Why would anyone want to live this way? The answer is found in verse 19, which hints of the people's arrogance, disbelief, and rebellion. Look at the attitude displayed in the words:

"Let God hurry ... The plan of the Holy One of Israel—let it come into view so we may know it." In effect, they are saying, with considerable arrogance, "If there really is a God, let Him show Himself." They are scoffing at God, not believing that the day of judgment will ever come.

The people of the early Church believed that Jesus would come back for them at any moment. For some, that meant being always ready, living holy and godly lives. For others, it meant living in fear because of the load of sin they were carrying. That fear produced an arrogance and rebellion that took advantage of God's grace and patience—to the point where some were saying, "Is He really coming back?" They were just like the scoffers of Isaiah's day.

Has anything changed today? The same responses to the day of Christ's return exist within and outside the Church. Some, eagerly anticipating it, commit themselves to living holy lives. Others, knowing their own sin, live in fear of ultimate judgment. That fear doesn't lead to repentance, however; they respond to God's grace with arrogance and rebellion. Each day, they grow more fearful, more angry, more rebellious, and more exhausted. They say to themselves: *He isn't really coming back.* They need to be reminded of the words of Peter: "The Lord is not slow in keeping his promise … Instead he is patient with you, not wanting anyone to perish, but everyone to come to repentance." (2 Peter 3:9)

Are you ready for the Lord to return? Or are you living in fear, exhausted by carrying a load of sin? Jesus says: "Come to me, all you who are weary and burdened, and I will give you rest. Take my yoke upon you and learn from me, for I am gentle and humble in heart, and you will find rest for your souls. For my yoke is easy and my burden is light." (Matthew 11:28–30)

Prayer: Lord, help me to come to You daily so that You can check my yoke and my burden to make sure they are the ones You gave me to carry.

30

Rationalization of Sin

Woe to those who call evil good and good evil, who put darkness for light and light for darkness, who put bitter for sweet and sweet for bitter. Woe to those who are wise in their own eyes and clever in their own sight. (5:20–21)

I WAS ON A diet, but that big hunk of chocolate cake looked so good. I knew it was not good for me and would inhibit my weight–loss plan. Yet my mouth watered. My resolve wavered. I thought, *One bite wouldn't hurt; I could exercise five extra minutes.* That one bite of cake was even better than I thought it would be. So I thought, *Maybe I can eat the whole piece. After all, I've been very good about sticking to my diet.* Soon that was gone, and I felt lousy. I berated myself, *How could I have been so stupid and weak?* I did not like how that felt, so I rationalized: *Oh well, one good piece of cake deserves another. I think chocolate actually will help me lose weight. Chocolate raises my blood sugar and gives me more energy to exercise. If my body didn't really need it, it would not crave it. Bring on the whole cake!*

When we rationalize wrong to make it seem right, one little "bite" leads to another. King David discovered this when he got involved with Bathsheba. First he spotted her and felt attracted. He found out that she was married. But because he was the king, he could do whatever he wanted, so he sent for her, they slept together, and she became pregnant. David tried to cover up that sin by sending for Uriah, her husband, so that he would go home, sleep with her, and think the child was his. But Uriah, a battle leader, would not take a privilege denied his men. So David arranged for Uriah's death in battle. When he married Bathsheba, David thought he had gotten away with his sin. But God knew what David had done, and the child of his sin died. He had to reap the consequences of adultery, deceit, and murder. (2 Samuel 11–12)

When we deceive ourselves that a sinful choice is right, we begin to move away from the Lord. At what point do past rationalizations dictate or limit our future choices? When do we become blind to the light of the truth so that wrong seems right?

Sin is sin. Sin leads to sin. Sin leads to destruction. Can anything break the cycle? Paul wrestled with this very problem in Romans 7:14–25. Here's what he says, paraphrased in a nutshell: "I want to do good, but I do wrong. Who will rescue me from this body of death? Thanks be to God, Jesus will."

Prayer: "You have delivered me from death and my feet from stumbling, that I may walk before God in the light of life." (Psalm 56:13) Lord, help me make right choices each day.

31

Woe to Corrupted Officials

Woe to those who are heroes at drinking wine and champions of mixing drinks, who acquit the guilty for a bribe, but deny justice to the innocent. (5:22–23)

AT FIRST THIS SOUNDS like another condemnation of those who run after wine. It is actually a condemnation of those who are trusted with governing the people but decide to seek their own pleasure. Instead of having a reputation for true heroics—being honest and upright and upholding justice for the innocent—their claim to fame is that they make a good drink.

It wasn't always so among the leaders of the Israelites. When Moses needed help in judging disputes among his people, his father–in–law, Jethro, gave him some sound advice. He said that Moses should " ... select capable men from all the people—men who fear God, trustworthy men who hate dishonest gain—and appoint them as officials over thousands, hundreds, fifties and tens. Have them serve as judges for the people ..." (Exodus 18:19–22)

The judges had to meet three criteria: they had to be people who feared God, who could be trusted by others, and who were absolutely honest. The officials mentioned in this passage of Isaiah didn't meet any of those criteria. They took advantage of their positions and used them for personal gain rather than for the good of the people. Power can corrupt people, but what occurs when corrupted people obtain power? It's the same today as in Isaiah's day. They seek their own personal gain and neglect the needs of the people they serve, and everyone suffers—individuals, families, the church, companies, and the nation. Often, corrupt leaders even end up destroying themselves.

Ideally, leadership should be sought by and entrusted to those who fear God, who know and love the Word of God, who pattern their actions and attitudes after the Word of God, and who seek the well–being of those for whom they have responsibility, not their own gain. Unfortunately, many people who seek leadership do not meet these qualifications.

Scripture teaches us that we are to pray for "all those in authority" (1 Timothy 2:2). That includes all leaders: those in government, the church, in business, and in schools. All leaders, even corrupt ones, must be covered in prayer. Pray that their weaknesses will not be exploited and exaggerated. Pray that they will have their eyes opened so that they can repent before their families and their own lives are destroyed.

If you are a leader, surrender yourself every day to God. Ask Him to help you live and lead in such a way that His Kingdom will grow. Ask God to help you have victory over your weaknesses. Ask for a heart for God's Word and for the people. Loving God and loving your people is the first step toward great leadership.

Prayer: Help our leaders to be people who fear God, who are trustworthy, and who hate dishonest gain. Help our leaders seek the needs of the people and honor God with their lives.

More Scripture: Titus 1:7–9

32

Therefore You Will Be Destroyed

Isaiah 5

THIS CHAPTER COULD READ as a heavenly proclamation of judgment. In most proclamations, a list of "whereas" clauses leads to "therefore" clauses. Look at the list of "whereas" clauses Isaiah supplies. Then look at the "therefore" and "so" clauses found in this chapter.

שׁ

Whereas you have neglected the laws of God;
Whereas you have indulged the flesh;
Whereas you have refused to humble yourselves;
Whereas you have yoked yourselves to sin;
Whereas you have mocked God;
Whereas you have rationalized evil as good;
Whereas you have trusted your own judgment;
Whereas you have turned away from God's direction;
Whereas you have denied justice to the innocent;
Whereas you love dishonest gain more than justice;

Therefore, you will go into exile;

Therefore, Death will expand its jaws;

Therefore, the arrogant will be humbled;

Therefore, destruction will come upon you;

Therefore, the wrath of God will consume you like flames lick
up straw;

Therefore, the Lord will strike you down.

ש

This summary of Isaiah 5 is clear and direct. Our actions
and choices can result in severe consequences. "Do not be
deceived: God cannot be mocked. A man reaps what he sows.
Whoever sows to please their flesh, from the flesh will reap
destruction; whoever sows to please the Spirit, from the Spirit
will reap eternal life. Let us not become weary in doing good,
for at the proper time we will reap a harvest if we do not give
up." (Galatians 6:7–9)

Prayer: Lord, give me wisdom each day to know Your
Will. Give me courage each day to follow it.

33

I Saw the Lord

Isaiah 6:1–4

WHAT AN AMAZING CLAIM Isaiah made: "I saw the Lord"!

Isaiah served as a prophet to the royal court, and the death of King Uzziah was a moment of crisis. It was then that Isaiah encountered the Lord as King of kings, exalted and sitting on a throne. The train of His robe filled the Temple. A king's garment or robe was an extension of his person. So God's personality filled the Temple.

Celestial beings called seraphs, or "burning ones," attended God. In Revelation 4, these seraphs lead worship. They cry out: " 'Holy, holy, holy is the Lord Almighty,' who was, and is, and is to come." The seraphs give triple emphasis to God's holy personality, a burning presence that purifies everything it touches. The seraphs call God "Lord Almighty," indicating the power of His presence. They also proclaim that God's glory—his honor, praise, renown, and eminence—fills the earth.

In Isaiah's vision, the sound of the seraphs' voices shook the doorposts and the thresholds, and the Temple filled with smoke. In the Old Testament, cloud and smoke were manifestations of the glory of God filling a place. They testified to something—or maybe, in this case, someone—being sanctified or set apart for God's use.

Isaiah saw the glory of the Lord in the midst of that smoke, felt His presence, understood His personality, and experienced His power. It is wonderful to know that in Jesus, we can "see" the Lord for ourselves. John 1:14 tells us, "The Word became flesh and made his dwelling among us. We have seen his glory ... " How can that be? John 1:18 says, "No one has ever seen God, but the one and only Son, who is himself God and is in closest relationship with the Father, has made him known." When the Apostle Philip asked to see the Father, Jesus explained that if His disciples had seen Him, they had seen the Father. (John 14:8–11)

This is the miracle of the incarnation: God chose to reveal Himself to the "whosoever" through Jesus Christ. To love and know Jesus is to know God's presence.

To ponder:

Exodus 16:10 The glory of the Lord appears in a cloud

Exodus 40:34–38 The glory of the Lord fills the Tabernacle

2 Chronicles 7:1–3 The glory of the Lord fills the Temple

Ezekiel 10, 11:22–23 The glory of the Lord departs from the Temple

Prayer: Help me to appreciate the glory of Your presence.

More Scripture about people who encountered God in remarkable ways: Genesis 16:7–14 (Hagar in the desert); Genesis 32:22–32 (Jacob wrestles with God); Exodus 3:1–4:17 (Moses at the burning bush); 1 Samuel 3 (calling of the boy Samuel); Daniel 3 (Shadrach, Meshach, and Abednego in the fiery furnace)

34

I Have Seen

'Woe to me!' I cried. 'I am ruined! For I am a man of unclean lips, and I live among a people of unclean lips, and my eyes have seen the King, the Lord Almighty.' Then one of the seraphim flew to me with a live coal in his hand, which he had taken with tongs from the altar. With it he touched my mouth and said, 'See, this has touched your lips; your guilt is taken away and your sin atoned for.' (6:5–7)

WHEN ISAIAH EXPERIENCED THE wonderful holiness of God, he was in awe. But instantly, he was also in despair. He recognized that he was utterly sinful and worthy only of death. Isaiah knew that something as ugly as sin cannot survive in the presence of God's holiness.

In Exodus 33:18–23 we read of Moses requesting that the Lord allow him to see His face. The Lord told Moses that no one could see His face and live, so He made provision for Moses to experience a part of the glory of His presence and survive.

The Lord also made provision for Isaiah. One of the holy beings that attended God flew to the altar and, with a pair of tongs, picked up a burning coal. The holy being touched the coal to Isaiah's mouth and told him that his guilt and sin were taken away. Atonement was made for Isaiah.

When we finally surrender to the Lord, our most precious dream and worst nightmare are realized. The precious dream is that He is real and He loves us. The worst nightmare is that we cannot survive in His presence; His purity, holiness, and beauty are too much for us. When we stand in the presence of God, all lies are stripped away. When we truly see God, we truly see ourselves. The comparison is not pretty. Yet just as the Lord made provision for Moses and Isaiah, He has made provision for our guilt and sin to be taken away.

To ponder:

What is the significance of the seraph taking the coal from the altar with tongs? (The seraph was a holy being of fire and the burning coal would not burn him.) Notice that the seraph holds the burning coal in his hand as he touches it to Isaiah's lips.

Why did Isaiah call himself a man of unclean lips instead of a man with an unclean heart or mind? How does the consecration of his lips prepare him for his role?

Prayer: Lord, like Isaiah, I know I am a person of unclean lips. Touch me with a coal from your altar today.

35

A Layered Vision

Then one of the seraphim flew to me with a
live coal in his hand, which he had taken
with tongs from the altar. (6:6)

I ALWAYS FIND IT interesting to note the details of dreams
and visions recorded in Scripture. There are often layers of
meaning to uncover.

When we are trying to interpret a dream or vision in
Scripture, other passages of Scripture can give us keys. For
example, a study of the setup of the wilderness Tabernacle
as described in Exodus can help us to understand Isaiah's
vision. A comparative study in Hebrews can help us to understand the spiritual significance of the Tabernacle, the Temple,
and the role of Jesus as both sacrifice and Great High Priest.

By God's instruction, the wilderness Tabernacle of the Old
Testament was patterned after the "heavenly Tabernacle."
Later, by God's instruction, the Temple was patterned after
the wilderness Tabernacle. Jews of the day would have under-

stood the altar in Isaiah's vision to be the altar of burning incense that stood in the Holy Place. That altar symbolized the continual prayers, the intercession, offered to the Lord by the priests on behalf of the people.

Once a year the high priest anointed the altar of incense with blood from an animal that was sacrificed to the Lord as the atonement offering. The high priest also carried the blood of this sacrifice into the innermost room of the Tabernacle, the Most Holy Place. Only he could go behind the curtain that shielded that sacred chamber, and only once a year, to atone for the people's sins.

The writer to the Hebrews calls Jesus the Great High Priest (4:14). When Jesus died on the Cross as the Lamb of God, " ... he entered the Most Holy Place once for all by his own blood, thus obtaining eternal redemption." (9:12) Jesus " ... offered for all time one sacrifice for sins ... " (10:12) No longer would an earthly high priest be needed to atone for the people's sins. "He is able to save completely those who come to God through him, because He always lives to intercede for them." (7:25)

At the moment of Jesus' death, the curtain separating the Holy Place from the Most Holy Place was torn in two from top to bottom. (Matthew 27:51) No longer would an earthly obstacle shut people off from the dwelling place of God. "Therefore, brothers and sisters, since we have confidence to enter the Most Holy Place by the blood of Jesus, by a new and living way opened for us through the curtain, that is, his body, and since we have a great priest over the house of God, let us draw near to God with a sincere heart and with the full assurance that faith brings, having our hearts sprinkled to cleanse us from a guilty conscience ... " (Hebrews 10:19–22)

What can take away our guilt and sin? The blood of Jesus and the faithful prayers of intercession that He offers for us. Jesus said of Himself, "I am the way and the truth and the life. No one comes to the Father except through me." (John 14:6)

Prayer: Help me to recognize that the way of salvation is through Jesus alone.

36

The View Is Great

Isaiah 6:1–7

Isaiah saw the Lord. His view of God caused him to worship the beauty of God's holiness and to repent of his own sinfulness.

When we stand in the presence of God, we recognize His personality, His purity. God is holy.

> *Our response to God's holiness is worship. We bow down before God and adore Him. He is Creator, the First and Last, Eternal One.*

When we stand in the presence of God, we realize His power. God is almighty.

> *Our response to God's power is holy fear. God holds in His hands the power of life and death. He is the Almighty King, Master of everything.*

When we stand in the presence of God, we reach for His provision. God is merciful.

Our response to God's mercy is awareness of our own unworthiness and acceptance of the redemption He offers. God is Redeemer, Savior, and King of kings.

Have you encountered the real presence of God? Seek God in the pages of Scripture. Seek God in honest and earnest prayer. Jesus promised that God hears and will answer true seekers. (Matthew 7:7–8) God promises, "Call to me and I will answer you … " and "You will seek me and find me when you seek me with all your heart." (Jeremiah 33:3; 29:13)

God desires to meet with you. He has made a Way. (John 14:6) The view is great from there.

Prayer: Lord, help me to seek You with my whole heart. Prepare me to meet with You.

37

I Heard the Lord

Isaiah 6:8–13

"THEN I HEARD THE voice of the Lord saying: 'Whom shall I send? And who will go for us?' And I said: 'Here am I. Send me!' "

God communicated with Isaiah through sight and sound. Isaiah saw the Lord, heard the song of the seraphim, and worshiped. He saw himself and repented. He heard the Lord and volunteered.

Who would go and proclaim God's message? Who would tell the people about God's plan? Isaiah wasted no time in answering: "I have seen and heard these wonderful things for a reason. I will go."

He volunteered before he knew the message he would be delivering. He volunteered before he knew how the message would be received. Isaiah had learned to trust the Almighty King and respond in quick and complete obedience.

It's not always like that with us. It is often through the

breaking of our own will and the denial of our own desires that we learn to obey.

A child who has disobeyed is told to sit in a chair for a "time out." His body sits, but his mind is at play. The motorcyclist wears a helmet because it is safe and it is the law, but she imagines riding free to feel the wind. The young man wears a suit and tie but dreams of sandy beaches where he can run with abandon. Complete compliance and obedience—of body and mind—is rare. When it happens, it is most often the result of complete trust.

Isaiah was given a clear vision of God. That vision, combined with God's provision of atonement, worked together to form in him a bond of complete and utter trust and the desire to respond to God with quick and complete obedience. His questions were gone. His rebellious human nature was submitted. Isaiah responded: "I am here. I am available. Send me."

Another giant of Scripture, Moses, had a meeting with God (Exodus 3). What was his reaction to God's request: "So now, go"? Moses didn't respond right away with complete obedience. He first had excuses and questions.

Look at God's call of some others and their responses: Joshua 1; Jeremiah 1; Ezekiel 1–3; Amos 7:14–17; Luke 1:26–38; Matthew 4:18–22; Matthew 28:19–20; Acts 26:12–19.

How have you responded and how will you respond to the call of God on your life?

Prayer: Help me to go where and when You send me.
               Help me to trust and obey.

38

Go and Tell

Isaiah 6:9–10

THE ETERNAL INVITATION TO "come and see" is followed by
the command to "go and tell."

What was Isaiah to tell the people? The message came
in riddle form: "Be ever hearing, but never understanding;
be ever seeing, but never perceiving. Make the heart of this
people calloused; make their ears dull and close their eyes.
Otherwise they might see with their eyes and hear with their
ears, understand with their hearts, and turn and be healed."

Isaiah's mission was to bring truth to the people. However,
the people would not understand and respond. God sent
Isaiah to deliver a message to a people who would refuse to
accept it. Do you ever feel as though the Lord has sent you
on a mission to people like that? Isaiah would never know all
the results of his faithful obedience to God's command to "go
and tell." In the same way, we may never know the results of
our faithful obedience, but we still must obey God's command.

Why would anyone want to preach the truth to a group of people who are either unwilling or unable to hear and respond to it? Good question.

Look at Matthew 13. Here we see Jesus speaking to the masses. They came to hear His stories and see the miracles He would perform. They came hoping that Jesus would endorse their version of the truth. They came looking for Him to meet their perceived needs. They saw what they wanted to see and they liked some of what Jesus said, but then they got too near the Truth. Threatened by it, they tried to ignore, to discredit, and eventually to kill it. But Truth always wins. It may take time. It may even seem as though Truth is defeated, but it will prevail.

Isaiah had great influence over many individuals during his ministry, yet the people, the nation, did not respond and turn to God so that He could heal them. When David's son Solomon became king, God had promised His people that if they would humble themselves, turn from their wicked ways, and seek His face in prayer, He would hear and heal their land. (2 Chronicles 7:14) Some 250 years later, during the reign of Hezekiah—and the time of Isaiah—the nation of Judah experienced a small revival. They took down the visual symbols of rebellion and participated in ritual and religious observances. However, they did not really return to God in their hearts. Repentance begins and revival continues when the heart recognizes Truth and chooses obedience.

In the same chapter of Matthew where the crowd took offense at what Jesus said, He had these encouraging words for His disciples: "Blessed are your eyes because they see, and your ears because they hear." (Matthew 13:16) " ... the knowledge of the secrets of the kingdom of heaven has been given to you ... " (Matthew 13:11)

Prayer: Holy Spirit, help us to see, hear, and understand the Truth. Help us to faithfully go and
tell what we have seen. Anoint our lips to
speak Your Word. Open hearts to understand
so that they may turn and be healed.

More Scripture: 2 Chronicles 33:10–17; Luke 2:8–20; Mark 16:6–7; Romans 10:12–14

39

Divine Destruction

Then I said, 'For how long, Lord?' And he answered: 'Until the cities lie ruined and without inhabitant, until the houses are left deserted and the fields ruined and ravaged, until the Lord has sent everyone far away and the land is utterly forsaken. And though a tenth remains in the land, it will again be laid waste. But as the terebinth and oak leave stumps when they are cut down, so the holy seed will be the stump in the land.' (6:11–13)

"FOR HOW LONG, LORD?" was Isaiah's question. How long will this people refuse to hear? The answer was not a happy one. God knew that the people would not respond until He allowed the destruction of Judah and the exile of the survivors.

It is not God's will for His children to suffer loss of any kind. But some of us are so stubborn that destruction of the things we hold dearer than God is the only way for Him to save us. Parents (and even people who don't have the responsibility for raising children) learn very quickly that all children are not the same. Something that works for one child may have the opposite effect on another. Punishment for a compliant child may consist of "the look," while a strong–willed child needs a firmer response.

It is the same with God and His children. How long will it take you to hear and obey? What things will God have to pry from your hands before He can get your attention?

God wants to bless you. You must have your hands free to receive these blessings. Let go of the things you treasure. If they are good for you, God will give them back. Trust God and receive His blessings with open arms. Clenched fists only guarantee bruised knuckles.

Prayer: Help us to listen and obey so that we may be blessed as we walk Your way.

40

Stand Firm

Isaiah 7:1–9

AHAZ, KING OF JUDAH, was nervous. Pekah, the son of
Remaliah, the king of Israel,* had formed an alliance with
Rezin, the king of Aram. Their joint forces attempted to invade
Jerusalem, the capital of Judah, but they could not overpower
it. Still, " ... the hearts of Ahaz and his people were shaken, as
the trees of the forest are shaken by the wind." (7:2)

The Lord assured Ahaz, through Isaiah, that He knew all
about his enemies' threats to destroy the land of Judah. "Yet
this is what the Sovereign Lord says: 'It will not take place, it
will not happen ... If you do not stand firm in your faith, you
will not stand at all.' " (7:7, 9)

Isaiah reminded Ahaz that if he would trust God for the
security of the nation, God would take care of His people.
That was part of the Lord's covenant with David and those
who followed him on his throne. If the king sought the Lord
with his whole heart and led His people to obey His Law, the
Lord would bless that king's rule.

Sadly, Ahaz decided not to trust God. Instead, he gave the king of Assyria silver and gold from the Temple in Jerusalem and from the royal palace and offered to be his slave if the mighty Assyrian army would attack Aram and Israel. The Assyrian army did just that, capturing Damascus, the capital of Aram, and putting King Rezin to death. Ahaz traveled to Damascus to swear allegiance to the king of Assyria. While there, he saw an altar to a pagan god and ordered that a copy of it be placed in the Jerusalem Temple. He stripped the Temple of many of its sacred furnishings to please the Assyrian king. With Ahaz at the helm, the nation was driven onto the reefs of compromise with worldly power and of spiritual corruption. (2 Kings 16)

Ahaz knew about God, so he gave Isaiah an audience, but he wouldn't entertain the prophet's message. That's because he had no personal faith in which to stand firm.

How can you stand firm in a faith you do not have? You can't! That's why it's so important for Christian parents, pastors, and teachers to teach the basics of the Bible and of faith so that when children and new believers need to stand firm, they have a faith on which to stand. Read the Bible together and encourage Scripture memorization. Pass on a love for God's Word. If we know what God's Word says, we can know what we believe. If we know what we believe, we can stand firm.

Prayer: Lord God, help us to love Your Word. Help us to grow in our faith. Help us to stand firm.

More Scripture: Ephesians 6:10–18

*The story of the division of the nation of Israel into two kingdoms—Judah in the south and Israel in the north—is told in 1 Kings, beginning in chapter 11.

41

Twisting Scripture

Isaiah 7:10–25

"AGAIN THE LORD SPOKE to Ahaz ..." through the prophet Isaiah. He told Ahaz to ask for a sign, but Ahaz refused to do that. We should find this interesting, because Ahaz alludes to Deuteronomy 6:16 when he says, "I will not ask; I will not put the Lord to the test." Ahaz knew Scripture and used it when he thought it was to his advantage. He wanted to rationalize his reason for not following Isaiah's instruction. But Isaiah wasn't fooled. He became full of righteous anger and prophesied the conquest of Judah by Assyria.

Scripture has been twisted, used as rationalization, since the serpent used God's own words to trick Eve in the Garden of Eden. When Jesus was in the wilderness, the devil tried to get Jesus to use Scripture as a kind of "magic." Quoting Psalm 91:11–12, Satan challenged Jesus to throw himself off the highest point of the temple to show that the angels would not allow Him to fall. Jesus answered, "Do not put the Lord your

God to the test." It was the same Scripture from Deuteronomy that Ahaz had used, but Jesus used it as the Lord intended. By doing that, He defeated Satan. (Luke 4:9–13)

Scripture quoted correctly and from a right motive defeats evil. However, remember that the evil one also knows how to quote Scripture. People who quote it incorrectly or from an evil motivation are trying to use the Holy Word as a mask for their true intentions. Be careful whom you trust. The best way to separate what is true from what is false is to know the Word of God, not just as words you memorize but as the Truth that God intended. Then you can defeat Satan.

Prayer: Lord, help us to be as "wise as serpents, and innocent as doves." (Matthew 10:16 *NRSV*) Help us to recognize Truth.

42

Assyria: The Lord's Tool

Isaiah 8:1–10

MOST PEOPLE OF OUR day would not choose to stick a child with the name Maher–Shalal–Hash–Baz. But even before Isaiah's son was conceived, the Lord told him to write that name on a scroll. It means: "quick to the plunder, quick to the spoil." Isaiah and his wife, who was also a prophet, then had their son and, following God's instructions, named him Maher–Shalal–Hash–Baz. The Lord told Isaiah that Samaria (the capital of the northern kingdom of Israel) and Damascus (the capital of the kingdom of Aram) would be plundered by Assyria before the child learned to say "my father" or "my mother." That would happen in just a little over two years.

This prophecy was both good news and bad news for King Ahaz and Judah. It was good news because Assyria would take care of their problem with the kingdoms of Israel and Aram. It was bad news because Assyria would also humble Judah. The prophecy that spells out trouble for Judah sounds poetic: "Because this people have rejected the gently flowing waters of Shiloah and rejoices over Rezin [king of Aram] and the son of Remaliah [Pekah, king of Israel], therefore the Lord is about to bring against them the mighty floodwaters of the Euphrates ..." (8:6–8)

The gently flowing waters of Shiloah refer to the provision of God. Psalm 23 portrays the Shepherd causing His sheep to rest beside still waters. Those still waters represent safety for the sheep—for the people of God. The mighty floodwaters of the Euphrates are anything but safe. They represent the Assyrian army that would sweep into Judah. Anyone bright enough to put two and two together would have understood the warning.

But even in the warning there was hope. The "river" that would pass through Judah would come up to its neck but not destroy it. Judah would survive as a nation, while Israel* and Aram would not. Though the king, the nation, and the people of Judah would be humbled, God—Immanuel!—would rescue them. God planned to use Assyria to get the people's attention before it was too late.

God's judgment is always on time. God's judgment is always just. God does not abandon us as long as there is hope for reconciliation. Immanuel, "God is with us," even when the floodwaters reach to our necks. What does God have to do to get our attention?

Prayer: Lord, God, help our nation return to You and trust Your Word.

---

*For a complete account of the end of the kingdom of Israel, read 2 Kings 17. The "remnant" of the people not taken into exile mixed with people the king of Assyria sent to settle the "empty" land. Those people became the Samaritans.

43

In God We Trust

Isaiah 8:11–17

WHAT MAKES YOU REALLY afraid? As a child, I was afraid of the dark. When it was time to turn off the lights at night, I would flip the switch and run for the bed. I would try to make it under the covers before the light actually went out. But I was never fast enough. My heart would pound until I got completely under the covers, which I trusted to protect me. I know that sounds silly now. If there really were something to be afraid of in the dark, how would a blanket and sheet guard me? As I matured, I realized there were more substantial things to fear. But I also learned to commit both my real and irrational fears to God. When I learned about God's promises for protection and provision, I realized He was using fear to teach me about trusting Him.

Many of life's experiences seem to teach us not to trust people, much less an unseen God. We learn to trust what we ourselves can see, feel, and know. It takes a great leap of faith to trust God.

King Ahaz and the nation of Judah were not willing to take a leap in faith and trust in God alone for their protection. Instead, the king made an alliance with Assyria that compromised the political and spiritual life of the nation. (See 2 Kings 16 for the details.)

God instructed Isaiah not to go along with the people who were trusting Assyria to deliver them from Israel and Aram. Instead of fearing those nations, Isaiah said, "The Lord Almighty is the one you are to regard as holy, he is the one you are to fear, he is the one you are to dread." (8:13)

But the alliance with Assyria turned the nation of Judah away from being a God–fearing people. They not only had to comply with the laws of Assyria, but they also had to accept its gods.

Isaiah took his stand against such idolatry: "I will wait for the Lord, who is hiding his face from the descendants of Jacob. I will put my trust in him." (8:17)

When you are afraid, will you trust in God's provision and protection, or will you turn elsewhere for help? If you fear the Lord, you need not be afraid of anything else. Psalm 23:4 says, "I will fear no evil, for you are with me; your rod and your staff, they comfort me."

Prayer: Oh Lord, help us to trust in You with all our hearts. Help us overcome our fears by trusting in You.

More Scripture: Psalm 23, Psalm 34, Psalm 56, Proverbs 3:5–6, Luke 12:1–12

44

Sanctuary or Stumbling Stone

'He will be a holy place; for both Israel and Judah he will be a stone that causes people to stumble and a rock that makes them fall. And for the people of Jerusalem He will be a trap and a snare. Many of them will stumble; and they will fall and be broken, they will be snared and captured.' (8:14–15)

PARADOX AND PROPHECY GO hand in hand. Speaking to Isaiah, the Lord says of Himself that He will be a "holy place," a sanctuary, and then, in the same breath, that He will be a "stone that causes people to stumble and a rock that makes them fall ... a trap and a snare." During His ministry, Jesus referred to Himself as the cornerstone of the true sanctuary of God, yet also a stone that would cause many to fall and be crushed. (Luke 20:17–18)

How can this be? The Apostle Paul explains, "For the message of the cross is foolishness to those who are perishing, but to us who are being saved it is the power of God. ... Jews demand signs and Greeks look for wisdom, but we preach Christ crucified: a stumbling block to Jews and foolishness to Gentiles, but to those whom God has called, both Jews and Greeks, Christ the power of God and the wisdom of God." (1 Corinthians 1:18, 22–23). If we choose to trust and obey God, He will be a "holy place," a sanctuary for us. If we reject God's way and turn to our own wisdom, He will be a stone that causes us to stumble and fall, a snare that will trap us.

Have you ever lost your balance and fallen in public? I have, and I found it quite humiliating. No one likes to be on the floor, where we feel at our most vulnerable. We can choose to stay there, covering our eyes and hoping to dissolve into the floorboards. If you're like me, your reaction might be to attempt to spring back up before the situation becomes even more embarrassing. But when you do that, you may not notice that you are hurt, and you can easily injure yourself even more. So is there another alternative?

Spiritually speaking, after you "fall," you have three clear choices:

1) Lie there, completely humiliated. (" ... worldly sorrow brings death." 2 Corinthians 7:10)

2) Continue to struggle (sin) and risk more injury.

3) Humbly turn to the One who can help. ("Godly sorrow brings repentance that leads to salvation ... " 2 Corinthians 7:10)

Which will it be for you? Cornerstone or stumbling stone? Sanctuary or snare? Choose today.

Prayer: Almighty God, help us remember that You
alone are the solid cornerstone for the building of our lives.

More Scripture: Isaiah 28:16, Romans 9:30–33, 1 Peter 2:6–8,
James 4:5–10

45

No to the Psychic Network

Here am I, and the children the Lord has given me. We are signs and symbols in Israel from the Lord Almighty, who dwells on Mount Zion. When someone tells you to consult mediums and spiritists, who whisper and mutter, should not a people inquire of their God? Why consult the dead on behalf of the living? Consult God's instruction and the testimony of warning. If anyone does not speak according to this word, they have no light of dawn. (8:18–20)

ISAIAH AND HIS CHILDREN were signs and symbols from God for the people, but the people insisted on looking elsewhere for help. Instead of looking to God, the people consulted mediums and spiritualists. Sound familiar?

Because God created us to hunger for His presence, all humans have the desire to connect with God. When circumstances and choices turn people away from making that connection, they go after counterfeits and diversions, and Satan gladly points the way. You might think that falling prey to superstition and dabbling in the occult is a problem only for non–Christians. But how many Christians read their horoscopes every day and only bother to read the Bible occasionally? How many church attendees can tell you all about palm reading and ESP but cannot tell you what the Ten Commandments are and where in the Bible to find them? How many can list the signs of the zodiac but can't list the Beatitudes or the fruits of the Spirit?

God specifically forbade His people to be involved in occult activities. (See Leviticus 19:26,31 and Deuteronomy 18:10–13.) But how can you tell whether something that is spiritual is of God? "This is how you can recognize the Spirit of God: Every spirit that acknowledges that Jesus Christ has come in the flesh is from God, but every spirit that does not acknowledge Jesus is not from God. This is the spirit of the antichrist, which you have heard is coming and even now is already in the world." (1 John 4:2–4)

In a search for spiritual connection, have you turned to counterfeits and diversions from the truth? Ask God to help you clear them out of your mind and heart. Only He can set you free from these things, through the blood of Jesus Christ. Call upon the name of the Lord today.

Prayer: Lord, shine the light of Your truth and love
into every corner of our hearts.

46

Deep Darkness

Distressed and hungry, they will roam through the land; when they are famished, they will become enraged and, looking upward, will curse their king and their God. Then they will look toward the earth and see only distress and darkness and fearful gloom, and they will be thrust into utter darkness. (8:21–22)

WHEN PEOPLE CHOOSE DARKNESS over light, their stress levels escalate. Why not just turn back to the light? Wouldn't that be the normal, intelligent thing to do? But many people don't. "Distressed and hungry, they will roam through the land ... " They continue scrabbling around in the dark, looking to themselves and their own appetites for hope. Finding none, they look upward and curse God. Then they look around them and see only " ... distress and darkness and fearful gloom ... " (8:21, 22)

The Apostle Paul describes the descent into "utter darkness" that happens when people turn away from Truth. The further they move away from God, the emptier and more hopeless they become, and the more they turn to depravity of mind, body, and spirit. (Romans 1:18–32)

Unless we are on our guard, it is all too easy to spiral into darkness. That's why it is so necessary to stay grounded in God's Word. "Consult God's instruction and the testimony of warning. If anyone does not speak according to this word, they have no light of dawn." (8:20)

If you've been wandering in the dark for a while, you may fear coming back into the light. When your eyes become adjusted to a darkened room, bright light can cause discomfort. The choice is to turn away to the comfort of the dimness or to become adjusted to the light, which will make everything clear. God's Word is Light; its Truth will illuminate everything.

Prayer: God, poke holes in the darkness that surrounds us and expose us to the light of your Truth. Save us from the dark desires that would shadow Your light.

More Scripture: Psalm 19, Psalm 119

47

Great Light

Isaiah 8:20–9:2

ISAIAH PROPHESIES THAT HOPE is on the horizon for the people "thrust into utter darkness." (8:22) He says there will be "no more gloom for those who were in distress," and then he specifies who those people are: the lands of Zebulun and Naphtali. (9:1) You can find these on a Bible map showing the allocation of lands to the 12 tribes of Israel. Zebulun and Naphtali are in the northern part of Israel, around the Sea of Galilee. This is where Jesus would grow up and also where much of His teaching and healing ministry would take place.

Isaiah points to that day: "The people walking in darkness have seen a great light; on those living in the land of deep darkness a light has dawned." (9:2)

I am definitely not a morning person. If I want to see the sun rise, it is easier for me to stay up and wait for it. On those rare occasions when I have been conscious at sunrise, I have really enjoyed the experience. One of those times was when we were in Israel. We had arrived on a night flight. On a bus on the way to breakfast, there were signs that dawn was coming. The desert gave off a wonderful aroma. The sky began to change colors ever so subtly. Steam rose from the water in irrigation ditches. The birds and beasts of the day began to stir. Then, suddenly, the sun made its full appearance. This is how the light of dawn arrives. This is how Jesus came.

At first, few noticed the coming of the Son of God. He was an ordinary human baby, who grew unassumingly into a man. Then, when He began His public ministry at the age of 30, He began to attract attention as He taught about the Kingdom of God. People came from miles around to witness the signs as He healed the bodies, minds, and souls of men, women, and children. On the Cross, He defeated the darkness, and He rose again like the dawn. The Great Light made His appearance. One day soon, He will come again, not like a gradual dawn but in full splendor like the noonday sun.

Prayer: God, help us to see the light of hope even when it shines dimly in our overwhelming darkness.

48

Express Your Joy

You have enlarged the nation and increased their joy; they rejoice before you as people rejoice at the harvest, as warriors rejoice when dividing the plunder. For as in the day of Midian's defeat, you have shattered the yoke that burdens them, the bar across their shoulders, the rod of their oppressor. Every warrior's boot used in battle and every garment rolled in blood will be destined for burning, will be fuel for the fire. (9:3–5)

"GOD, YOU HAVE CAUSED the nation to grow and made the people happy. And they have shown their happiness to you, like the joy during harvest time, like joy of people taking what they have won in war." (9:3, *NCV*)

Are you truly happy about what God has done in your life? Has the Lord "shattered the yoke" that burdened you? Has the "rod" of oppressive sin been broken and the victory been won? Then express your joy. Live a joy–filled life and glorify God. God has given us many blessings, and we take them for granted too often. We don't notice them until they are gone.

Make a list of your most valued blessings. Perhaps they are home, family, friends, church. Make a list of the little joys that you look forward to each day. Perhaps that first cup of coffee, a quiet time with the Lord, the laughter of a child. Now think about those things that sustain you and help you to flourish, like breathing, the beating of your heart, your body's ability to mend, sunshine, rain, fresh air, and food. Don't you think it's about time to say thank you to God for the joy of living? Celebrate your joy!

Prayer: Wow! Lord, when I stop to count my blessings, I realize how amazing my life is. Help me celebrate each day by taking the time to thank You!

49

A Child Is Born

For to us a child is born, to us a son is given,
and the government will be on his shoulders.
And he will be called Wonderful Counselor,
Mighty God, Everlasting Father, Prince of
Peace. (9:6)

CAN YOU READ THIS verse without hearing the majestic notes
of George Frideric Handel's "Messiah"?

"For to us a child is born, to us a son is given ... " I see
this prophetic Word of Isaiah as the ultimate birth announcement. And God sent that announcement way in advance.
Hundreds of years before the baby Messiah was conceived
in His mother's womb, the Lord told the universe about His
plan. Two thousand years after the birth of the Messiah, we
still stand in awe of these words: To us a child is born, to us
a son is given!

There is usually a sense of hope surrounding the birth
of a baby, a wonder at the potential for good this new life

will bring. What did the birth of the Messiah into our reality mean for this world? What difference does the birth of this boy child make for you?

Prayer: Thank You for Your Son, who became flesh
and moved into the neighborhood so that we
could know You!

50

His Name

He will be called Wonderful Counselor, Mighty God, Everlasting Father, Prince of Peace. (9:6)

WONDERFUL COUNSELOR. CONSIDER THE meanings of the word *wonderful:* amazing, extraordinary, awesome, marvelous, beyond comprehension. Consider the meanings of the word *counselor:* advisor, guide, mentor, instructor, teacher.

Mighty God. Consider the meanings of the word *mighty:* strong, powerful, great, vast. Consider the meanings of the word *God:* omnipotent one, omniscient one, holy one, supreme being, divine creator, sovereign.

Everlasting Father. Consider the meanings of the word *everlasting:* eternal, unending, perpetual, immortal. Consider the meanings of the word *Father:* originator, author, abba (daddy), loving parent, provider.

Prince of Peace. Consider the meanings of the word *prince:* royalty, monarch, ruler, rider on a white horse. Consider the meanings of the word *peace:* reconciliation, accord, order, serenity, rest.

Isaiah was prophesying the coming of the Lord Jesus. He is the Prince of Peace, the King of kings who invites the weary and burdened to come to Him and find rest. He is the Wonderful Counselor who reveals wisdom and promises His followers that when He departs, He will send another Counselor to guide them. He is the Alpha and Omega, the First and the Last, the Beginning and the End—the Everlasting Father who calls His disciples His children and demands that we all become like children if we are to be part of His Kingdom. He is, finally, the Mighty God, the rider on the white horse who is called Faithful and True, who has eyes like blazing fire and wears a robe dipped in blood, going out to wage war and to destroy the forces of evil.

Prayer: Remind me, Lord, of all your magnificent
names. Thank You for coming to Earth to
bring my salvation.

51

The Government Is
His Responsibility

... and the government will be on his
shoulders ... of the greatness of his
government and peace there will be no end.
He will reign on David's throne and over
his kingdom, establishing it and upholding
it with justice and righteousness from that
time on and forever. The zeal of the Lord
Almighty will accomplish this. (9:6–7)

WHAT ARE THE OUTSTANDING features of the Messiah's
reign? Peace, justice, and righteousness are its hallmarks. It
is also a reign without end, one that is guaranteed: "The zeal
of the Lord Almighty will accomplish it."

For hundreds of years, people looked for the Messiah's government to come as an earthly one. Some people are still looking for that. Because we are so wrapped up in our physical life,
it is sometimes hard for us to comprehend spiritual reality.

Scripture is the account of God translating spiritual truth to us so that we can comprehend it. God gave Moses and His people a tent, a Tabernacle, at the center of the community to physically represent the Spirit dwelling among them. When the people ceased wandering and settled in the Promised Land, God gave permission for them to build a Temple, where His "Glory," His presence, would dwell. Many centuries later, Jesus came as a human being to show what God is like: "The Word became flesh and made his dwelling among us. We have seen his glory, the glory of the one and only Son, who came from the Father, full of grace and truth." (John 1:14)

Isaiah foretold His coming: "A child has been born to us; God has given a son to us. He will be responsible for leading the people. ... Power and peace will be in his kingdom and will continue to grow forever. ... He will make it strong by ruling with justice and goodness from now on and forever. The Lord All–Powerful will do this because of His strong love for His people." (Isaiah 9:6–7, *NCV*)

The Messiah's reign of "justice and goodness" will last forever. Through Him, the Kingdom of Heaven is here. Yet Jesus taught His followers to pray: " ... your kingdom come, your will be done ... " (Matthew 6:10) There are two reasons He instructs us to pray this way. First, this prayer gives God permission to do the necessary work in our own lives so that His Kingdom will grow and His will be done through us. Second, it prepares the way for God to expand His kingdom into the lives of others. When we claim His promises, God is faithful to bring them about. He will do what we ask because of His great love for us, His people.

Prayer: May Your Kingdom come, Lord, and let it begin with me.

52

But First

Isaiah 9:8–21

NOTE THE CHORUS IN this passage: "Yet for all this, his anger is not turned away, his hand is still upraised." (9:12, 17, 21)

No one would be spared: not the elders or the lying prophets, not the young men or the fatherless or the widows, "for everyone is ungodly and wicked, every mouth speaks folly." (9:15–17)

Before the promise of the Messiah would see light, a great darkness of judgment would overshadow the chosen people of God. They were not ready to receive the promise. Their hearts were full of pride and disobedience. God's anger would have to be spent before redemption could occur.

The nation would experience destruction of homes and security and removal of rulers and leaders. The people would see their nation destroyed and be exiled to a foreign land. What would it take for the God's chosen ones to truly love and obey God as they had once promised?

What does it take today for God to get people's attention? How long will it be before they turn to God?

Prayer: God, give people eyes to see and hearts that will repent before it is too late.

53

And Justice for All

How terrible it will be for those who make unfair laws, and for those who write laws that make life hard for people. They are not fair to the poor, and they rob my people of their rights. They allow people to steal from widows and to take from orphans what really belongs to them. How will you explain the things you have done? What will you do when your destruction comes from far away? Where will you run for help? Where will you hide your riches then? You will have to bow down among the captives or fall down among the dead bodies. But the Lord is still angry; his hand is still raised to strike down the people. (10:1–4, NCV)

WHEN A NATION TURNS away from God, it does not continue to care for the needs of its people. The first to feel the effects of such neglect are the weaker members of the community: the poor, the widows, the orphans, the elderly, and the children.

In a nation truly united under God, there would be justice for all. Remember Superman's motto: "truth, justice, and the American way"? Those words sound old–fashioned and dated today. Many Americans have a tough time remembering the words to the Pledge of Allegiance, much less remembering to practice the ideals it contains. How then do we expect to hold our lawmakers responsible for the laws they make? After all, our elected officials represent the collective body of the nation. If we as individuals cease to care about God and our community, the laws made by the representatives of our nation will reflect that apathy.

We can agree that good laws protect all the people. Poor laws exploit the weaker members of the community and rob people of their rights. God is not pleased with poor laws. There is no excuse for people who make and apathetically accept poor laws. Eventually the whole community pays.

Get involved with the government of your country and your local community. Take time to educate yourself by exploring the resources available to you. We all are important to the process. If you just stand by because of apathy or fear, you will have to live or die with the government you contributed to. Most important of all: Pray for those who are in positions of political leadership, that they will make sound decisions based on what is good for their people. (1 Timothy 2:1–2)

Prayer: Lord, You know the condition of the heart of every leader. Convict and convince them to seek Your heart and obey Your Word.

54

God Is in Control

Isaiah 10:5–16

MANY PEOPLE WONDER IF God is really in control. They point
to world leaders who are responsible for atrocities and crimes
against humanity and ask: "If God is in control, why would
He allow these things to happen?" The people of Isaiah's day
asked the same question. The prophet Habakkuk asked the
same question. God gave the same answers to Habakkuk and
Isaiah that He gives to us. Yes, God is sovereign and He is
in control, whether we understand or not. We don't have to
understand. We just have to trust.

God promised His people that He would protect and bless
their nation as long as they obeyed and trusted Him. He also
promised that if His people turned from Him, He would give
them up to other nations until they trusted Him again. God
gave many warnings and intervened many times on the people's behalf, but they did not return to Him as a nation.

Does this make God some kind of supernatural egomaniac

who punishes people for not adoring Him? No, it does not. God, our Creator, gave us free will to choose good or evil. He knows what will happen when we choose evil. The problem is, we don't always believe His warnings. So when the consequences of our actions come back on our heads, we demand to know why God is punishing us.

A dad warns his daughter to get out of the way after she's pushed a swing, or else she will be hurt. But the child soon forgets that warning, pushes the swing, and turns her back on it. Then she cries, "Why did the swing hit me?" If she had listened and trusted that her dad knew what he was talking about, she could have avoided being hurt.

We need to trust and obey, even if we can't understand why. The Lord knows best, and His warnings can keep us away from dire consequences. "Trust and obey, for there's no other way/ To be happy in Jesus,/But to trust and obey." God is the same yesterday, today, and forever, and He is always in control.

Prayer: Lord, there are many things in life that seem unfair to me. I get upset when evil people seem to win the day. Help me to keep my eyes on You.

More Scripture: Habakkuk 1–3

55

The Tools in God's Hands

Isaiah 10:5–16

THE KING OF ASSYRIA became a tool in God's hands to punish His chosen people. Why would God then turn and punish him for what he had done? Because God knew the king's wicked nature. The Lord said, "I will punish the king of Assyria for the willful pride of his heart and the haughty look in his eyes." (10:12) The king boasted that he had plundered and subdued God's people by the "strength of my hand." (10:13) He didn't realize that he would have been able to do nothing unless the Lord had allowed it.

When Jesus was put on trial, the Jewish leaders demanded his crucifixion. Pilate, the Roman governor, gave in to the demands of the mob and handed Jesus over to the soldiers to be killed. Yet Jesus told Pilate that he would have no power unless God had given it to him. (John 19:1–11) Both the leaders and Pilate were tools in God's hands. They didn't know it, but they were serving a greater purpose than they could possibly realize.

One important thing to understand is that God didn't cause the king of Assyria or the Jewish leaders or Pilate to sin. They all had free will, and they chose to do evil. The other important thing to understand is that we won't always be able to understand what God is up to. Most of the time, we can only see what is in front of us, and we may think that God is being unnecessarily harsh—or not harsh enough.

When God's people were being defeated by the king of Assyria, they no doubt asked why God would turn such a wicked man against them and allow him to win. After Good Friday, Jesus' disciples were crushed. They no doubt were asking why, if He was the Messiah, the Lord would allow wicked men to defeat Him.

In the 37th Psalm, David tells us, " ... do not fret when people succeed in their ways, when they carry out their wicked schemes," for eventually, " ... the power of the wicked will be broken ... " He encourages us, "Hope in the Lord and keep his way. He will exalt you to inherit the land; when the wicked are destroyed, you will see it." (vv. 7, 17, 34)

When things seem unfair, when the wicked seem to be prospering, remember that we can't see the big picture God sees. But we need to trust that He is in control.

Prayer: Lord, I can't see Your plan, but I know that
You have one. Help me to hope in You.

More Scripture: Read all of Psalm 37, plus Psalm 73.

56

Holy Flame

The Light of Israel will become a fire, their Holy One a flame; in a single day it will burn and consume his thorns and his briers. The splendor of his forests and fertile fields it will completely destroy, as when a sick person wastes away. And the remaining trees of his forests will be so few that a child could write them down. In that day the remnant of Israel, the survivors of Jacob, will no longer rely on him who struck them down but will rely on the Lord, the Holy One of Israel. A remnant will return, a remnant of Jacob will return to the Mighty God. (10:17–21)

READ THIS PORTION OF Scripture, then turn back to Isaiah 9:18. There, evil is compared to a small fire that grows to consume everything in its path. Having lived in Southern

California, I am well acquainted with what can happen when a careless person tosses out a cigarette or a faulty machine spews out an unchecked spark. At first there is a small fire. Soon the flames send out embers, which duplicate themselves. If the land is dry, precious fields, forestland, and homes are consumed by the exploding flames. There is mass destruction. But when all is burned away, the land is fertilized from the ashes and seeds sprout new growth. Often, forest managers practice controlled burning so that the forest remains healthy.

That is what Isaiah prophesies for the people of Israel. God, the Light of Israel, their Holy One, will be like a fire and a flame that will first consume thorns and briers, then forests and fertile fields. When the fire is spent, very few trees will be left standing. This is the devastating destruction that God, in his anger, will allow to come from Assyria. When that controlled burning is spent, only a small number of trees—the remnant of the people—will be left.

Are there some things in your life that you need to allow the Lord to burn away so that you can be purified? Surrender those things to God and allow Him to sanctify you with His holy fire.

Prayer: Holy Spirit, burn bright in my life so that I can be a light for You.

57

I Will Restore

Isaiah 10:20–27

DESTRUCTION HAS COME AND only a small number of people are left. Isaiah prophesies that those few will turn from their allegiance to the king of Assyria and "will truly rely on the Lord, the Holy One of Israel." No longer will the people need to fear the Assyrians, the Lord says, because " ... my anger against you will end and my wrath will be directed to their destruction." (10:20, 25)

The Apostle Paul writes: "Do not take revenge, my dear friends, but leave room for God's wrath, for it is written: 'It is mine to avenge; I will repay,' says the Lord." (Romans 12:19)

That's what Isaiah is prophesying here. He says that the enemy will be vanquished, and the Lord " ... will raise his staff over the waters, as he did in Egypt." The yoke that has held Israel captive will be lifted from their shoulders and broken. (10:26, 27)

We often sing, "God will make a way where there seems

to be no way." Sometimes, when it seems like we are beset on all sides by people who are bent on our destruction, we want to lash out against them, to take matters into our own hands. That way lies our own destruction. Instead, we should be turning to the Lord and trusting Him to set us free.

A word here for those whose "enemy" is a spouse or significant other who is abusive. Be assured that the Lord did not bring this wrath upon you; His anger burns at anyone who would harm one of His own. For you, the first step in trusting the Lord to set you free may be leaving that relationship, for your own safety. But the same advice that Paul gave the Romans applies here as well. It's not up to you to take revenge. That is the Lord's business. It may not seem like it right now, but the Lord is in control. His promise to you is found in the prophet Joel: "I will repay you for the years the locusts have eaten ... " (2:25) Morris Chapman's song echoes that promise: "What was lost in battle,/What was taken unlawful/Where the enemy has planted his seed ... I will restore to you all of this and more."

Prayer: Lord, help me to trust You completely, knowing that You will make a way.

58

It Looks Hopeless

*See, the Lord, the Lord Almighty, will lop off
the boughs with great power. The lofty trees
will be felled, the tall ones will be brought
low. He will cut down the forest thickets with
an ax; Lebanon will fall before the Mighty
One. A shoot will come up from the stump
of Jesse; from his roots a Branch will bear
fruit.* (10:33–11:1)

WHAT LOOKS MORE HOPELESS than a "forest" of tree stumps?
The lushness and life of the woods are gone, and in their place
is a haunting, barren landscape. But if you were to return to
the same spot six months later, hope would rise in your heart
as you saw new life springing from the stumps.

This was the picture of hope that Isaiah wanted to plant
in the imaginations and memories of his readers. Because of
the sin and rebellion of the people, God would destroy Israel
like a lumberjack cuts down a mighty forest. The promise of

new growth in a devastated forest became a symbol of hope for the re–establishment of the nation of Israel. Specifically listed as future ruler of this kingdom was the One who would come through the family of Jesse, the father of David.

The Branch would spring from the root of Jesse. Look at Jeremiah 23:5–6 for more prophecy concerning the Branch. "The branch" symbolized a ruler, a king whom God would provide. The Spirit of God would be the source of the king's power, wisdom, and judgment. The Spirit of God would "rest upon" the king and teach him.

We understand this to be a prophecy about the Messiah and His rule. Jesus went one step further with this promise, saying that the Spirit would come to us to be our teacher (John 14:26, 16:13) and come upon us to give us power (Acts 1:8).

Everything looked hopeless at the end of Chapter 10, but God would restore hope, and He promised even richer things for His people.

Are there areas of your life that resemble a ruined forest? If you turn that barren area over to Him, life will return to the forest in God's time. He never leaves us without hope. Remember the hope of the Branch.

Prayer: Lord, there are areas in our lives, in our communities, that resemble a ruined forest, a desert land. Help us to claim the promise of hope found in the Branch growing from the stump. Let Your Spirit rest upon us and teach us the right way to go.

59

Like a Belt—Clothes of the Kingdom

Goodness and fairness will give him strength,
like a belt around his waist. (11:5, NCV)

CLOTHING DESIGNERS TRY TO dictate the fashions and clothes we wear. The teens of the 60s revolted by choosing to wear old jeans and T–shirts. Soon that became the uniform of the baby boomer. Designers caught on to the fad and began to capitalize on denim. People began to pay designer prices for what had once been considered cheap clothes. Are designer labels really worth the price we pay for them?

Most of us would answer no. Still, we do invest time and money in our wardrobe because we want to look good. But how much thought do we give to our spiritual wardrobe? Do we know what the best–dressed citizens of the Kingdom of Heaven wear? There are references to Kingdom clothes throughout Scripture. How many can you list? Here are a few to get you started:

A garment of praise (Isaiah 61:3)

Garments of salvation and a robe of His
   righteousness (Isaiah 61:10)

The full armor of God (Ephesians 6:11–18)

After Adam and Eve sinned by eating the fruit of the Tree
of the Knowledge of Good and Evil, they became concerned
that they were not clothed. They sewed fig leaves together to
make coverings for themselves, then tried to hide from God.
Later, God shed the blood of innocent animals and covered
Adam and Eve with their skins. This was a type or foreshadowing of the fact that we cannot hide our sins from God. Only
the shedding of blood can do that. Jesus, the Lamb of God,
allowed His blood to be shed to cover our sins. Only the robes
of righteousness designed by Jesus are acceptable in God's
sight.

Are you covered?

Prayer: Lord, in my sin, I am naked before You.
Through Your grace, please dress me in the
robes of righteousness that only Jesus can
provide.

60

The Lion and the Lamb—
Prayers of Reconciliation

The wolf will live with the lamb, the leopard
will lie down with the goat, the calf and the
lion and the yearling together; and a little
child will lead them. The cow will feed with
the bear, their young will lie down together,
and the lion will eat straw like the ox. The
infant will play near the cobra's den, and
the young child put its hand into the viper's
nest. They will neither harm nor destroy
on all my holy mountain, for the earth will
be full of the knowledge of the Lord as the
waters cover the sea. (11:6–9)

ISAIAH FORETELLS A DAY when natural and historical
enemies will reconcile and even become friends. The preda-
tor and prey are symbolic of nations, tribes, people groups,

neighbors, and individuals who will someday be reconciled with each other and with God.

In the list of predators and prey, note especially the cobra and the baby, for they represent the offspring of the serpent and of Eve. All creation was turned upside down because Adam and Eve rebelled against God. In Jesus, that curse is canceled for us "who are in Christ Jesus" (Romans 8:1), but not all has been restored. One day, " .... the creation itself will be liberated from its bondage to decay and brought into the freedom and glory of the children of God." (Romans 8:21) Isaiah describes the day when all will be right with His children: "They will not hurt or destroy each other on all my holy mountain, because the earth will be full of the knowledge of the Lord, as the sea is full of water." (11:9, *NCV*)

Should we just stand by and wait for that glorious day? That isn't what Scripture teaches.

Daniel knew God's promise through Jeremiah that after 70 years, the Jews would return from exile. But he didn't simply wait for that day. He was moved to plead with God to do what He had promised. (Daniel 9:1–19)

Jesus instructs us to pray: " ... your kingdom come, your will be done, on earth as it is in heaven." (Matthew 6:10) That's a prayer every Christian should be praying. God's Word promises a new world of peace. It's up to us to pray for that new world to come.

Prayer: Let Your Kingdom come and Your will be done.

61

Intercession Needed

Isaiah 11:6–9

ALL CHRISTIANS SHOULD BE praying for the day of reconciliation that Isaiah describes. But some are also called to
be intercessors, also known as gap–standers, prayer warriors,
and lookouts on the walls.

" ... I have put guards on the walls to watch. They must
not be silent day or night. You people who remind the Lord
of your needs in prayer should never be quiet. You should not
stop praying to Him ... The Lord has made a promise, and by
his power he will keep His promise." (Isaiah 62:6–8, *NCV*)

If God calls you to be an intercessor, allow Him to teach
you through His Word and lead you by His Spirit about how,
when, and where to pray. If this is your calling, it won't be
easy. When you begin to intercede for the reconciliation of lost
lambs, broken families, and warring nations, you are entering
a battleground.

Make and keep an appointment with God each day and

be sure you are open for quick prayers as nudges come. Start your prayer time with thanksgiving. Then pray for protection: for yourself, your loved ones, and your property, so that Satan cannot use these as distractions. Then pray Scripture. Know what God says so that you can claim God's promises.

Your call to intercession may be very specific. In Isaiah 32:9–14, women are specifically called on to intercede for their nation. Complacent, secure women—and men—wake up! Get serious about prayer. Repent, weep over sin, and seek God's face on behalf of our nation.

Read Isaiah 32:1–5 to see what kind of world we would have if every government authority, every person who exercises power over another, would give their hearts to God. If every leader of this world were reconciled with God, they would rule in godliness, wisdom, justice, and righteousness. God's Holy Spirit would lead them. The fruit of justice and righteousness is peace.

As intercessors, for whom should we pray?

- Pray for rulers and leaders to reconcile with God.

- Pray for tribes, nations, and neighbors to reconcile with each other.

- Pray for family members to reconcile.

- Pray for individuals to become reconciled with God. Pray for the lost lambs.

Prayer: Lord, if you want me to be an intercessor, give me Your Spirit to protect and guide me.

62

The Lost Lambs

Isaiah 11:6–9

GOD'S PLAN FOR WORLD reconciliation starts with individuals. We are all called to pray for the lost lambs.

Some time ago, God got my attention and gave me a lesson about loving and praying for the lost. I was watching a TV show called "Nash Bridges." The main character, Nash, thought that a man who was out of prison on a three–day pass to help find a murderer was not cooperating. He asked the man why he was so distracted. Did the man want a drink, drugs, a woman? The man, played by Willie Nelson, looked very rough and hard, and he didn't respond to Nash's sarcasm. He simply and quietly asked to see his son, who was in an AIDS hospice. In the next scene, the father enters the room, goes to his son's bed, and reaches out to touch his hand. The son is a long–haired, rough–looking young man most of us would be afraid to meet on the street. He wakes up, gives his father a weak smile, and says: "I knew you would come."

That moment of tender love reminded me that in the eyes of God, every sinner is the one lost sheep. When we reach out to a lost lamb, we are the hand of the Father reaching out in love.

Who stands in the gap for the lost lambs of God today? Who prays for them? Who is in those AIDS hospices praying with and loving people back to their heavenly Father? Who is on the street corners and in the poor neighborhoods loving God's lambs back to Him? Who is in the office buildings of top executives and on Rodeo Drive loving the rich and powerful back to God? Even if you cannot go to those places physically, you can pray. Your prayers, in the power of His might, will send the right people to the lost lambs of God.

Prayer: Lord, so fill me with Your love that I can see
and pray for one of Your lost lambs today.

63

Lift Him Up

Isaiah 11:10–16

"AT THAT TIME THE new king from the family of Jesse will stand as a banner for all peoples. ... God will raise a banner as a sign for all nations ... " (11:10, 12 *NCV)*

"Just as Moses lifted up the snake in the wilderness, so the Son of Man must be lifted up, that everyone who believes may have eternal life in him." (John 3:14–15)

"Jesus said, ... I, when I am lifted up from the earth, will draw all people to myself.' " (John 12:30, 32)

"Rouse, then, soldiers, rally round the banner," begins a familiar chorus. The "banner" that comes to mind for me is the Salvation Army flag. In the wilderness days of the Israelites, besides the pillar of cloud and pillar of fire they followed, each of the 12 tribes had a banner or standard, a pole with a symbol on top of it. When the leader of the tribe lifted the banner, the people of that tribe would gather around it to hear their instructions. When the cloud moved, the people organized themselves around their tribal banner and followed it.

Isaiah prophesied that a new king from the family of Jesse, the Messiah, would be a banner around which all nations could rally and unite. Jesus, the fulfillment of that prophecy, said that when He is lifted up, He will draw all people to Him. In Jesus we put aside the things that do not matter and we focus on the important things. When we focus on the presence of God among us, we unite. There is peace. Sin is conquered.

Yet the last portion of this chapter speaks of Israel and Judah being at war with the surrounding nations. Look back to the books of Exodus through Deuteronomy. God gave specific instructions to the Israelites for the annihilation of the peoples living in the Promised Land. Instead of obeying God, the Israelites mixed with those people and became polluted by their practices. The lesson is: Compromise with sin and sin will defeat you. Those nations were symbolic of the compromise with sin. When the earth is full of the knowledge of the Lord, all who practice sin will be annihilated. (Revelation 6:15–17)

In the promised land of holy living, there are many things to defeat, "peoples" to conquer. What sin habits in your life need to be annihilated? Are you making any compromises with them that are keeping you from living a truly holy life?

Jesus came to be lifted up on the Cross so that we could be free from sin. Rally around Him, our true banner. Be free from sin. Live your life for God.

Prayer: Jesus, set me free from the habits that would hold me back from You.

64

A Hymn of Praise

In that day you will say: 'I will praise you,
Lord. Although you were angry with me,
your anger has turned away and you have
comforted me. Surely God is my salvation; I
will trust and not be afraid. The Lord, the
Lord himself, is my strength and my defense;
he has become my salvation.' With joy you
will draw water from the wells of salvation.
In that day you will say: 'Give praise to
the Lord, proclaim his name; make known
among the nations what he has done, and
proclaim that his name is exalted. Sing to
the Lord, for he has done glorious things; let
this be known to all the world. Shout aloud
and sing for joy, people of Zion, for great is
the Holy One of Israel among you.' (12:1–6)

"AT THAT TIME YOU will say: 'I praise you, Lord! ... Praise the Lord and worship him. ... Shout and sing for joy ... because the Holy One of Israel does great things before your eyes.' " (12:1, 4, 6 *NCV*)

" 'God is the one who saves me; I will trust Him and not be afraid.' " (12:2 *NCV*)

"You will receive your salvation with joy as you would draw water from a well." (12:3 *NCV*)

" 'Praise the Lord and worship him. Tell everyone what he has done and how great he is. ... Let all the world know what He has done.' " (12:4, 5 *NCV*)

What has God done for you? Make a list of those things. Have you praised Him for His goodness to you? Take the time to experience the joy of truly praising God. God is the One who saves us. We can trust God. Isn't that enough to praise Him about?

After his great sin, David had lost the joy of his salvation, and he pleaded with God to give it back to him: "Create in me a pure heart, God, and make my spirit right again. Do not send me away from you or take your Holy Spirit away from me. Give me back the joy of your salvation. Keep me strong by giving me a willing spirit." (Psalm 51:10–12 *NCV*) David knew that sin had broken his connection to God. When we are mired in guilt because of our sin, we cannot praise God. Don't allow the devil to pound the wedge of guilt between you and God. Get right with Him. Confess your sin. He is faithful and just to forgive and to cleanse you from all unrighteousness. (1 John 1:9)

If you allow the Holy Spirit of God to work freely in your life, you will have joy. (See Galatians 5:22 and Romans 14:17.) Joy is not a fickle emotion that depends on circumstance. Joy is a benefit of a rock–solid trust in God that gives peace in the midst of all circumstances. Joy is a result of knowing God is in control.

Prayer: Fill me today with the joy of Your salvation.

65

Judgment Day

A prophecy concerning Babylon that Isaiah son of Amoz saw: Raise a banner on a bare hilltop, shout to them; beckon to them to enter the gates of the nobles. I have commanded those I prepared for battle; I have summoned my warriors to carry out my wrath—those who rejoice in my triumph. Listen, a noise on the mountains, like that of a great multitude! Listen, an uproar among the kingdoms, like nations massing together! The Lord Almighty is mustering an army for war. They come from faraway lands, from the ends of the heavens—the Lord and the weapons of his wrath—to destroy the whole country. Wail, for the day of the Lord is near; it will come like destruction from the Almighty. Because of this, all hands will go limp, every heart will melt with fear. Terror will seize them, pain and anguish will grip them; they will writhe like a woman in labor. They will look aghast at each other, their faces aflame. (13:1–8)

THE WARNING CAME EARLY in the people's covenant relationship with God. God told them that in years to come, when they fell away from Him, He would send destruction, famine, and plague. Ultimately, the army of a foreign nation would remove them from their land. (Deuteronomy 28:49–68) The first time that nation shows up in Scripture is 2 Kings 20:12–19 after the illness and healing of King Hezekiah. The king of Babylon sends envoys to congratulate Hezekiah on his recovery. Hezekiah, wanting the Babylonian king to know what a great nation Judah is, shows his visitors all the treasures in the royal palace and warehouses. When Isaiah hears of this, he prophesies that a day will come when those treasures and many of the people of Judah will be carried off to Babylon. In Isaiah 13:1–8 we see the further development of that prophecy.

It wasn't until a hundred or so years later that the Babylonian King Nebuchadnezzar actually captured Jerusalem and took all but the poorest people of the nation into exile. But the exile had a positive outcome. While in Babylon, the people of Judah concentrated on the Law and their relationship with God. Exile became like a furnace that purified and solidified the people.*

When the day comes that we have to face the consequences of our actions and choices, it may be too late to learn from them. It would be so much simpler if we could learn from history. That is why we have the written Word of God. God is not mocked; we will reap what we sow. While there is time, check your actions and choices to see that you are following the Lord, not other influences.

Prayer: Help us learn from history and remain faithful to You.

More Scripture: Galatians 6:1–10

* The story of the Babylonian invasion and the beginning of the exile is told in 2 Kings 24–25. The prophets Jeremiah, Ezekiel, and Daniel provide a great study for this time period.

66

The Lord's Mercy

The Lord will show mercy to the people of Jacob, and he will again choose the people of Israel. He will settle them in their own land. (14:1 NCV)

PSALM 102 IS A prayer of one person who represents the people of God and the city of Jerusalem. The psalmist expresses great love for the nation. The heart–breaking, emotional plea and the physical investment of an effective intercessor come through in his words. Intercessory prayer is not for wimps! Look at verses 3–11. This intercessor is really committed to the subject of his prayer.

The intercessor lays claim to God's mercy and promise in verses 12–22. Look especially at verse 13: "You will come and have mercy on Jerusalem, because the time has now come to be kind to her; the right time has come." *(NCV)*

The promise that the Lord will have mercy on His people and restore Jerusalem is recorded in many places in the words of the prophets. The intercessor is aware of God's promises and is led to plead for God's mercy and for the fulfillment of His promise. The prayer of the psalmist is that God's plan will come about in God's time. Isaiah 14:1 clearly points to that plan.

Has God made you aware of problems in your community or family? Look for Scripture promises that relate to those problems and lay claim to them. Before you "do battle" in prayer, ask God to show you how to pray righteously, fervently (with all your might), and effectively.

Prayer: Lord, we plead for Your mercy to us. Restore our nation. Bless our communities. Bless our families.

67

Join the Family

Then non-Israelite people will join the Israelites and will become a part of the family of Jacob. (14:1 NCV)

AS THE SONG GOES, "I'm so glad I'm a part of the family of God." Aren't you glad to be a part of this family? John 1:12 declares: " ... to all who did receive him, to those who believed in his name, he gave the right to become children of God ... " Romans 8:14 *(NCV)* says, "The true children of God are those who let God's Spirit lead them." Isn't that amazing?

That means the promises of the Old Testament given to the family of Jacob, the descendants of Abraham, belong to us! We are children of the King of kings!

How did this happen? Paul writes to the Colossians: "At one time you were separated from God. ... the evil things you did were against God. But now God has made you his friends again. He did this through Christ's death in the body so that he might bring you into God's presence as people who are holy ... " He says, "God has freed us from the power of darkness and brought us into the kingdom of his dear Son. The Son paid for our sins, and in him we have forgiveness." (Colossians 1:21–22, 13–14, *NCV*)

How do I take advantage of this offer? I acknowledge that I need God; confess that I have sinned, broken the laws of God; and recognize that my sin separates me from God. "Everyone has sinned ... all need to be made right with God by His grace, which is a free gift." (Romans 3:23, 24 *NCV*) "When people sin, they earn what sin pays—death. But God gives his people a free gift—eternal life in Christ Jesus our Lord." (Romans 6:23 *ERV*) Once I have acknowledged my need for God and confessed my sins, all I have to do is ask for forgiveness, and I receive a new life. Then God and His people join in saying, "Welcome to the family!"

Then, how do I live? I get to choose. If I choose to devote myself to God's Word and to prayer, I will learn about the rights, privileges, and responsibilities I have as a child of the King, and I will build a relationship with Him. Then I will be living like a member of the royal family. But if I choose to neglect the Word and time in prayer, I will live as a pauper— at best, a poor relation.

Are you a member of the family? If so, are you living as a pauper or as a child of the King?

Prayer: Lord, I'm so grateful that you have adopted me as Your child. Help me to live worthy of that honor.

68

Trusting in God's Plan

Isaiah 14

IN A VISION, GOD allowed Isaiah to see the future of the Babylonians, the Assyrians, and the Philistines. They would all be vanquished, and Israel would be restored: "They will make captive of their captors and rule over their oppressors." (14:2)

Most of those living in Isaiah's day, including the prophet himself, would not see his prophecies come to pass. Can we trust God's promises for tomorrow when we are living in the turmoil of today? When the people of Judah were exiled to Babylon, Jeremiah prophesied that they would be freed in 70 years. (Jeremiah 29:10) Seventy years? That's a long time to wait for the Lord's promise to come true! Could we wait that long? Wouldn't we be pleading with God to change his mind and end our bondage sooner?

The Apostle Paul gives us this promise: "We know that in everything God works for the good of those who love him. They are the people he called, because that was His plan." (Romans 8:28 *NCV*)

There may be times in your life when that promise doesn't ring true. You might be in the midst of a horribly oppressive situation at work. You might be dealing with the devastating illness or loss of a loved one. You might be experiencing blow after blow to your finances. In those circumstances, it can be hard to believe that God has a plan. We cry out for solutions, healing, restoration that doesn't seem to come.

Like the prophet Habakkuk, we plead, "How long, Lord, must I call for help but you do not listen?" (Habakkuk 1:2) He was complaining about the wickedness and injustice surrounding him in Jerusalem. God answered that He would use the Babylonians to bring judgment upon the people. Then Habakkuk complained about the people being swallowed up by such a wicked nation. The Lord answered that there would be a solution, but it would not come right away: "It is not yet time for the message to come through, but that time is coming soon … It may seem like a long time, but be patient and wait for it …" (Habakkuk 2:3 *NCV*) The prophet responded in trust: though he couldn't yet see the answer, " … yet I will rejoice in the Lord, I will be joyful in God my Savior. The sovereign Lord is my strength; he makes my feet like the feet of a deer, he enables me to tread on the heights." (Habakkuk 3:18–19)

While you wait for God's plan to unfold, bless His holy name. It may seem counterintuitive, but offer to Him the sacrifice of praise.

Prayer: "Blessed be Your name/On the road marked with suffering/Though there's pain in the offering,/Blessed be Your name." (Lyrics by Matt Redman)

69

A Distanced Cousin

Isaiah 15

Background reading: Genesis 18–19, Numbers 21–24, Judges
3:12–30, and Ruth.

"A PROPHECY AGAINST MOAB: Ar in Moab is ruined, destroyed
in a night! Kir in Moab is ruined, destroyed in a night! ... In
the streets they wear sackcloth; on the roofs and in the public
squares they all wail, prostrate with weeping. ... the armed
men of Moab cry out, and their hearts are faint. My heart
cries out over Moab ... " (15:1, 3, 4)

This is a harsh prophecy about Moab's coming destruction. The Moabites were "relatively" kin to the Israelites.
Here's a brief history. When God choose to destroy Sodom
and Gomorrah for its evil, He answered Abram's request and
spared his nephew Lot and his two daughters. (Genesis 18–19)
The daughters got Lot drunk so they could sleep with him
and become pregnant. The older daughter gave birth to a son
and named him Moab. His descendants were the Moabites.

The younger daughter gave birth to a son and named him Ben–Ammi. His descendants were the Ammonites.

Hundreds of years passed, and the Israelites and Moabites became more distant from one another both physically and spiritually. The Israelites spent 400 years in Egypt, and when they left, they were a mighty nation. But because of disbelief and disobedience, they spent a generation, 40 years, in the desert. When the time came for them to enter and claim the Promised Land, their journey took them through the land of Moab. The Moabites, who had given themselves over to worshiping other gods, were terrified. They knew they could not win against this mighty throng in battle, so Balak, their king, tried to defeat the Israelites by asking Balaam, a prophet, to curse them. But Balaam couldn't do that because the Israelites were blessed by God. Before King Balak, Balaam issued three messages blessing rather than cursing the Israelites. Then Balaam prophesied Moab's destruction.

Isaiah echoes that prophecy. Read the words of Balaam in Numbers 23:19. God's Word is sure and we can count on it. We can count on His promises of blessings and of curses.

The Moabites were of the family of Abraham, but poor choices distanced them from the blessings of the family of Abraham. Poor choices set the descendants of Lot on a path that led away from God. The choices we make in our lives today will also affect the lives of our descendants. Will our choices yield blessings or curses?

Prayer: Lord, help me to make wise choices in my life. Cause my life to bring blessing instead of trouble to others.

70

A Messiah for All

Then a new loyal king will come; this faithful king will be from the family of David. He will judge fairly and do what is right. (Isaiah 16:5 NCV)

IN THE MIDDLE OF a very harsh prophesy about the destruction of Moab and its people, we have this promise about the coming Messiah. Throughout the book of Isaiah, we receive hints—and sometimes fairly clear indications—that the Messiah the people of Israel looked for would not only save them, but would also provide salvation for the people of the enemy nations that surrounded them.

God called the people of Israel to be a holy nation, one separated out for God. The designation as "separate and special" people sometimes produced a prideful attitude in God's chosen people. But they also often turned to the gods and the armies of other nations for help instead of relying on God; in doing so, they became compromised. It was both pride and compromise that led to the exile in Babylon and the destruction of Jerusalem. In exile, the people again listened to the call of God to come out and be separate. When they were miraculously returned to their homeland, with great dedication and vigor, the people of Judah crafted codes and laws that would help keep them separate once more.

It would have been a great shock, then, for them to learn that the promised Messiah would not just save them, but also the whole world. God's chosen people wanted to hang on to their special calling. It's not surprising that in the early Church, Jews who accepted Jesus as their Messiah struggled with the idea that Gentiles could be saved without first converting to Judaism.

Today it may come as a surprise to some Christians that people do not have to "convert" to Christianity to be saved. When a jailer asked Paul and Silas what he must do to be saved, they replied, "Believe in the Lord Jesus and you will be saved … " (Acts 16:30–31, *NCV*) They did not say, "You have to join a church and adhere to its doctrine and rituals." The doctrines and disciplines of church membership are important parts of our faith, but they are not necessary to salvation. Paul and Silas told the jailer that being saved was as simple as believing in Jesus. We must be careful of what we tell those who want to know what they must do to be saved. Let's keep it simple.

Prayer: Lord, help me always to remember that the Gospel really is for "whosoever," to keep Your message of salvation simple, and to allow You to lead and save the lost. I will do my part and let You do Yours.

71

Compassion, Not Revenge

My heart cries for Moab ... I am very sad ...
(16:11 *NCV*)

WE WHO CLAIM JESUS Christ as our role model must extend
true compassion to all, even our enemies. Jesus said that the
true children of God love their enemies and return good for
evil. (See Matthew 5.) The Apostle Paul writes: "My friends,
do not try to punish others when they wrong you, but wait for
God to punish them with his anger. It is written: 'I will punish those who do wrong; I will repay them,' says the Lord. But
you should do this: 'If your enemy is hungry, feed him; if he is
thirsty, give him a drink. [Extending kindness to your enemy]
will be like pouring burning coals on his head.' Do not let evil
defeat you, but defeat evil by doing good." (Romans 12:19–21
NCV) As a follower of Christ, you are to melt the heart of your
enemy through kindness and let God deal with them.

It is very difficult for people to understand this principle
until they taste the bitter pill of revenge and unforgiveness.

If you have ever taken revenge, you realize how little it satisfies. Unforgiveness and smoldering anger cause more hurt to the one who harbors them than to the one(s) on the receiving end.

We all long for justice; that is, unless justice means that we or our loved ones suffer. Praise God that He is merciful, or we would receive the justice we deserve. Jesus is God's greatest expression of compassion for an enemy. "God shows His great love for us in this way: Christ died for us while we were still sinners." (Romans 5:8 *NCV)*

Prayer: Lord, help me take up the challenge of Matthew 5:43–48. Help me to love my enemies and to do good things for those who do not deserve it. Let my kindness melt the heart of my enemy.

72

You Forgot God

Isaiah 17

"YOU HAVE FORGOTTEN THE God who saves you; you have not remembered that God is your place of safety." (17:10 *NCV*)

"At that time people will look to God, their Maker; their eyes will see the Holy One of Israel. They will not trust the altars they have made, nor will they trust what their hands have made, not even the Asherah idols and altars." (17:7–8 *NCV*)

"Then God spoke all these words: 'I am the Lord your God ... You must not have any other gods except me. You must not make for yourselves an idol ... You must not worship or serve any idol, because I, the Lord your God, am a jealous God ... I show kindness to thousands who love me and obey my commands.'" (Exodus 20:1–6 *NCV*)

Chapter 17 of Isaiah continues to describe the destruction that will take place in the Middle East. The focus is on Aram (in particular its chief city, Damascus), and Israel. Look at the second half of verse 3. "Those left alive of Aram will be like the glory of Israel ... " *(NCV)* That sounds OK until you look at the description of Israel in verses 4–6. Its wealth will be gone. The land will be empty like a field after harvest, like an olive orchard that has been picked clean. The picture is bleak. Why this destruction? The salt of the earth, the chosen people, forgot God. When the chosen people of God remain true, the world around them is affected by the blessings they receive. When they forget God, the world around them is affected by the destruction they bring upon themselves. Jesus said that His followers are the salt of the earth. (Matthew 5:13) One of the properties of salt is that it works as a preservative or antiseptic. God's chosen people are the preservative of the morality and spirituality of the world. When God's people become corrupt, the world loses.

But after the destruction takes place, the remnant, the few survivors, will turn away from false gods and idols and look to God once again. In 2 Chronicles 7:14, God's Word tells us that when we sin, we don't have to wait for destruction to come: " ... my people, who are called by my name, will be sorry for what they have done. They will pray and obey me and stop their evil ways. If they do, I will hear them from heaven. I will forgive their sin, and I will heal their land." *(ICB)* It is not too late for us to be "salt" in our communities and our nation. God's people turn away from false gods and idols. God's people humble themselves to seek God's face and pray. God's people love and obey God.

It's time to check out your level of "saltiness." How effective are you for God's Kingdom? Do your friends and neighbors know by your words and actions that you belong to God? Is God number one in your life? Do you live each day for His sake? If anything or anyone comes before God, you are guilty of worshiping false gods or idols. You have forgotten God— or you have put Him aside for other things. Remember, God blesses obedience.

Prayer: Lord, examine all of me. If anything or anyone has risen above You in my priorities,
reveal it to me. Help me keep You first. Help
me to obey You and live my life for the sake
of Your Kingdom. I love You, Lord.

73

God Is Watching

The Lord said to me, 'I will quietly watch from where I live, like heat in the sunshine, like dew in the heat of harvest time.'
(18:4 *NCV*)

THERE ARE TIMES WHEN we feel as if God has abandoned us. We cry out, but He seems not to hear us. Yet God is with us, watching over us. We may not feel it, but we can know it.

I think of the story of a woman who had been taken from her home and sold as a slave. Her owner was a woman who had not been able to have a child. It was a time when a woman's value was determined by how many children she gave her husband. Guided by the law and culture of the day, the woman decided to use the slave's body to conceive a child. When the slave became pregnant by the woman's husband, she reacted with joy—and a little superiority. The woman became jealous and treated her slave harshly. The slave woman escaped into the desert.

That is where she met God. Alone, hungry, tired, and desperate, Hagar met God at a well. She had not known Him before, but He assured her that she was not forgotten or alone, that He would take care of her. Hagar gave God a new name: Lahai Roi, "the Living One who truly sees me." God told Hagar that she would have to return to Sarai, her owner, and she was ready to obey because she had met the living God who saw her in her desert place. (Genesis 16)

Is God your Lahai Roi? The Living One who is present like heat in the sunshine or the welcome dew at harvest time? When you are in the middle of the worst day of your life, remember Lahai Roi, the God who sees you. In fact, every day of your life, remember Lahai Roi, the living God. He knows all about you and wants what is best for you.

Prayer: Lord, help me to remember that You are the Living One who truly sees and knows me.

74

Exodus Revisited

Isaiah 19

"LOOK THE LORD IS coming on a fast cloud to enter Egypt. The idols of Egypt will tremble before Him, and Egypt's courage will melt away." (19:1 *NCV*)

Examine Exodus 3–14. These chapters tell of God's working to free the Israelites from slavery to Egypt. Through a series of plagues, God showed Himself more powerful than all the gods and idols of Egypt. The final plague attacked the Egyptians' families and national stability by killing the first-born of every household; that is, every household that did not have the blood of a lamb on its doorposts. Those households belonged to the Israelites, who were told by God how to protect their children.

The Egyptians were so glad to get rid of the Israelites that they paid them to leave. After a few days, however, reality set in. The Egyptian economy was built on slavery, and without the Israelites, that economy would collapse. Pharaoh sent his army after them. In Exodus 14:19, we read that the cloud and the angel of God came between the Israelites and the Egyptians. God parted the Red Sea, and the people passed through on dry ground.

The cloud became a symbol to the Egyptians of the great God, the One God Jehovah. It reminded them of the 10 plagues, the Exodus, and their final defeat at the Red Sea. No wonder that even hundreds of years later, the Egyptians would tremble and their courage melt away when they heard that the Lord was coming again in "a fast cloud."

This cloud of Isaiah 19:1 would bring disaster. Isaiah 19:2–15 prophesies internal wars, drought, famine, and government failure. Yet verses 16–25 declare that the ultimate outcome of this disaster will be different from the first time God visited His wrath on Egypt. This time, the people will turn to God and He will listen to their prayers and rescue them and heal them. Isaiah foretells a time when Egypt, Assyria, and Israel will be united: "The Lord All–Powerful will bless them, saying, 'Egypt you are my people. Assyria, I made you. Israel, I own you. You are all blessed!' " (v. 25 *NCV*)

What is our responsibility on hearing this promise? When God impresses the truth of an unfulfilled prophecy upon us, our responsibility is to pray for God's will to be done. If you understand the promise of Isaiah 19:20–25, begin to pray for the accomplishment of God's will in the Middle East. God is allowing you to be a part of His work through your prayers.

Prayer: Help the people turn to You in the day You reveal Yourself. Open their eyes to see You.

75

Virtual Reality and Visual Aids

In the year that the supreme commander, sent by Sargon king of Assyria, came to Ashdod and attacked and captured it—at that time the Lord spoke through Isaiah son of Amoz. He said to him, 'Take off the sackcloth from your body and the sandals from your feet.' And he did so, going around stripped and barefoot. Then the Lord said, 'Just as my servant Isaiah has gone stripped and barefoot for three years, as a sign and portent against Egypt and Cush, so the king of Assyria will lead away stripped and barefoot the Egyptian captives and Cushite exiles, young and old, with buttocks bared— to Egypt's shame. Those who trusted in Cush and boasted in Egypt will be dismayed and put to shame. In that day the people who live on this coast will say, "See what has happened to those we relied on, those we fled to for help and deliverance from the king of Assyria! How then can we escape?"' (20:1–6)

THIS IS A SHORT, unusual chapter. It covers a three–year period for the prophet. God instructed Isaiah to strip and behave as a war captive for three years. His strange behavior and nakedness symbolized the fact that Egypt and Cush would lose in war with the Assyrians. It warned the people of Israel to avoid putting trust in the military might of those nations as allies. It reminded them to trust in God alone.

Through Isaiah, God was making an extreme statement, which called for an extreme commitment on the part of the prophet. He might not have completely understood God's orders, but He trusted Him enough to obey.

Is there anyone or anything that you trust more than you trust God? Daily, we face problems that pull at us, that keep us from trusting God.

When our jobs and paychecks are secure, we trust God. But what happens when He allows our jobs and paychecks to end?

By God's design, we need others, and family and friends are essential to our emotional well–being. But our need to avoid loneliness, taken to an extreme, can draw us away from God. What happens when a believer marries a non–believer, even though God's Word tells him not to do it? What happens when we go along with friends and abuse alcohol or other drugs, even though we know it's wrong? Such believers end up leading a divided life.

What about your possessions? Do you possess them or do they possess you? What about habits and pleasures? Is anything or anyone more important to you than your relationship with God?

Jesus said that it is impossible to serve two masters. Every day we make choices that determine who or what is our master. When we choose God, it's an extreme commitment to trusting Him above all else.

Prayer: Lord, keep me from putting my trust in anyone or anything but You.

76

Prepare the Battle Shields

They set the table; they spread the rugs; they eat and drink. Leaders, stand up. Prepare the shields for battle! (Isaiah 21:5 *NCV*)

"GET UP YOU OFFICERS, oil the shields!" (21:5 *NIV*)

This 21st chapter of Isaiah warns of the war and destruction that will come to Babylon. The leaders are taking their ease. But they are warned to stand up and get ready for battle.

Can you imagine soldiers going into battle without preparing themselves or their equipment? That is unthinkable, yet we often go onto the spiritual battlefield with little or no preparation.

Prayer is one of those paradoxical concepts. On one level it's so simple. It is talking to God, and everyone can do it. We children of God have ready access to our Father's ear, and we know He hears our prayers. On another level, every time we pray, we enter into a spiritual battle that requires great faith and perseverance. Carefully read Ephesians 6:10–18, which speaks about the full armor of God and the battle waged in prayer. Look to verse 16: "And also use the shield of faith with which you can stop all the burning arrows of the Evil One." *(NCV)* Prepare and oil the battle shields.

You are involved in a spiritual battle. The war is not on its way; it is here. Isaiah 21:5 gives us a glimpse of leaders who talk of battle but don't prepare their most essential equipment. It is easier to talk about spiritual warfare than it is to engage the enemy. We don't have the luxury of ignoring the spiritual battle any longer. Too many of us have played at praying. Now God is calling us to get real. God is calling for His prayer warriors to prepare and join the battle. Before you begin to participate in God's directed intercession for revival in the Church and the evangelism of the lost, you need to put on the whole armor of God. We stand in His strength. " 'You will not succeed by your own strength or by your own power, but by my Spirit,' says the Lord All–Powerful." (Zechariah 4:6 *NCV)*

The battle belongs to the Lord. We must be prepared to follow His direction. Officers, leaders, soldiers, quit sitting around talking about it. Hear God's order to prepare the battle shields, for the enemy has arrived and battle is engaged.

Prayer: "Oh, thou by whom we come to God, the life, the truth, the way! The path of prayer Thyself hath trod: Lord, teach us how to pray!" (From the pen of James Montgomery in Song #784 of *The Song Book of The Salvation Army)*

77

Did You Forget Something?

Isaiah 22:1–14

HAVE YOU EVER BEEN haunted by the feeling that you have forgotten something very important? It may occur just as you shut the door of your house or close the garage door on your way to work. The feeling may come over you when you are 10 miles into a long journey. You can't put your finger on it; the feeling just teases you. You're tortured by trying to figure out what you may have forgotten. Did you leave the water running in the backyard? Did you unplug the iron? Did you feed the dog? What did you forget?

The people of Jerusalem prepared for war. They fixed the holes in the walls. They designed and built weapons. They stored up water and food. Everything was ready. Yet that nagging feeling haunted them. They were forgetting something very important. They were forgetting the Lord. Worse, they were ignoring the Lord.

God promised His people that He would fight for them if

they would obey His instructions. The Temple stood as proof of His presence among them. As long as the Temple stood, they were not really that worried. The Temple became like a good luck charm instead of a reminder of their covenant. They made all the preparations for winning a battle except turning to God.

God called them to fast, repent, and pray. Instead of obeying this call, the people partied. They took the fatalistic view that despite their preparations, they could very well die in battle. So they thought they might as well eat, drink, and be merry in the meantime.

When you make plans, don't forget to consult God first. As you proceed with your preparations, don't forget to obey Him. The success of our plans and preparations does not depend on our efforts, but on His Spirit and blessing.

Prayer: You alone are God. Our days and our problems are in Your hands. The battle belongs to You. Thank You for going ahead of us to prepare the way.

More Scripture: 2 Chronicles 20

78

Keys to the Kingdom

'In that day I will summon my servant,
Eliakim son of Hilkiah. I will clothe him
with your robe and fasten your sash around
him and hand your authority over to him.
He will be a father to those who live in
Jerusalem and to the people of Judah. I will
place on his shoulder the key to the house
of David; what he opens no one can shut,
and what he shuts no one can open. I will
drive him like a peg into a firm place; he
will become a seat of honor for the house of
his father. All the glory of his family will
hang on him: its offspring and offshoots—
all its lesser vessels, from the bowls to all
the jars.' (22:20–24)

THE KEEPER OF THE keys, the gatekeeper, is also called a steward. A *steward* is a caretaker, manager, or representative put in charge of an estate or another person. Stewards are trusted with and held responsible for taking care of the resources of their employer. In most cases they can make decisions that are just as legally binding as if the owner had made them. A good steward studies the master's character and practices and tries to do exactly as the master would do.

The Lord considered Eliakim so trustworthy as a steward that He gave Him, literally, the keys to the kingdom. Eliakim had such great authority that " ... what he opens no one can shut, and what he shuts no one can open." The Lord said he would become " ... a seat of honor for the house of his father," something that would carry through to later generations of the family. (20:22–23) What had Eliakim done that the Lord entrusted him with so much responsibility? We know only that the Lord calls him "my servant," just as he had called Moses His servant, saying "he is faithful in all my house." (Numbers 12:7) Coming from the Lord, that is high praise.

We are God's stewards, and as such, we have great responsibility for the people, the money, and the time He has entrusted to us. Once we recognize this truth, we will use God's resources as God would use them.

We don't have to guess what it means to be a good steward. The Lord set down principles for us to follow, and we find these principles in Scripture. As we learn and follow these principles, we can make right decisions about the resources with which He has entrusted us.

How do you spend your energies, your money, and your

time? Begin each day by giving that day back to God. Let Him know you are available. Pay your tithes and gladly give your offerings. Choose as God would choose. Then you will find that you are a good steward worthy to hold the keys of the Kingdom.

Real stewardship is recognizing that all we have, including our very lives, belongs to God. "For you know it was not with perishable things such as gold or silver that you were redeemed from the empty way of life handed down to you from your ancestors, but with the precious blood of Christ, a lamb without blemish or defect." (1 Peter 1:18–19)

Prayer: Help us to remember that we are Your stewards. This knowledge will be a great strength during our most trying days.

More Scripture: Compare this passage to 1 Chronicles 9:26–27, Matthew 16:19, and Revelation 3:7–8.

79

God's Plans Succeed

Isaiah 23

THIS CHAPTER OF ISAIAH speaks of destruction and restoration of the city of Tyre. Tyre was a rich seaport that seemed indestructible. The people were not conquerors but merchants. The prophecy begins, "Wail, you ships of Tarshish" because shipping was the city's lifeblood. Its wealth was unparalleled; its "merchants are princes, whose traders are renowned in the earth." (23:8) Because it was such a crossroads, perhaps like New York City today, Tyre was also a place of many cultures and diversions of all kinds. The citizens of Tyre were a proud people who had no reason to believe that anyone would have reason to destroy their city.

Isaiah also foretold that after 70 years, the "span of a king's life," Tyre would be restored to " ... return to her lucrative prostitution and ... ply her trade with all the kingdoms of the earth." The difference this time would be that the profit and earnings of the city would be set apart for the Lord, to be used by " ... those who live before the Lord, for abundant food and fine clothes." (23:15, 17, 18)

Tyre, that rich city, destroyed for 70 years, then restored? Many people hearing Isaiah's words might have considered their prophet to be one brick short of a load. It would be hard for them to believe that a city so rich and prosperous would fall, and if it did, that the Lord would see fit to bring it back to its former glory. Isaiah himself may have wondered at God's message. But he was faithful and obedient to deliver it because he knew and trusted God.

Like Isaiah, we must get to know God so well that we trust and obey, that we take Him at His word, even if what He says seems outlandish and even if others scoff at us when we proclaim it. If God's Word says it, it will come to pass. God's plans succeed.

Prayer: Lord, in the context of our world, Your way
and Your Word sometimes seem strange to us.
Help us to be willing to trust in Your Word.

80

The Lord Will Punish the World

Isaiah 24

THIS CHAPTER IS A real doomsday report! "The Lord will destroy the earth and leave it empty ... " (24:1 *NCV)* According to verse 2, no one, regardless of social standing, will be exempt from destruction.

Why will it occur? Verse 5 states it is because the people of the Earth have ruined it. They have not followed God's teachings nor kept their part of the covenant with God. In the beginning God created the Earth, and He gave humankind specific instructions to take care of it. After the Fall, humankind no longer enjoyed the paradise that was Eden. But humans still had a sacred responsibility to take care of the Earth. We have often neglected that responsibility. The rainforests are disappearing because of greed and ignorance. We are rapidly depleting our natural resources. We have become a "throwaway" society. Our landfills and junkyards testify against us. We have polluted the air, land, and water, including the farthest reaches of the oceans. Nature is out of balance, so much so that our very existence is threatened.

In Romans 8:19–23, the Apostle Paul says that the whole world awaits the day of redemption when " ... creation itself will be liberated from its bondage to decay ... " But before that day will come the Day of Judgment and Destruction.

What can we do? In a sense, nothing, for God's Word is true and His prophecies will come to pass. However, that is not a reason to take a fatalistic viewpoint like "eat, drink, and be merry, for tomorrow we die" or "pollute, indulge, and ignore, for the world will end anyway." Instead, God's Word should serve as a wake–up call to remind us that from the very beginning, God put us in charge of the Earth, and He meant that we should take care of it, not destroy it.

What can you do? You can avoid contributing to the wasting of our natural resources. You can be good stewards of all God gives you. Don't throw trash on the ground. Leave every place better than you found it. Be sensitive to the needs of others.

Admittedly, it is easy to go to extremes with conservation. Some people even go so far as to worship nature, the creation of God, rather than God the Creator. It must be kept in balance. But that absolves no one of the responsibility of stewardship of God's Earth.

Prayer: Help us to work to restore the natural balance of our Earth before it is too late. Nature tells of Your Glory and points to a concerned Creator. Help people to care.

81

Something to Sing About

Lord, you are my God; I will exalt you and praise your name, for in perfect faithfulness you have done wonderful things, things planned long ago. You have made the city a heap of rubble, the fortified town a ruin, the foreigners' stronghold a city no more; it will never be rebuilt. Therefore strong peoples will honor you; cities of ruthless nations will revere you. You have been a refuge for the poor, a refuge for the needy in their distress, a shelter from the storm and a shade from the heat. For the breath of the ruthless is like a storm driving against a wall and like the heat of the desert. You silence the uproar of foreigners; as heat is reduced by the shadow of a cloud, so the song of the ruthless is stilled. (25:1–5)

"LORD, YOU ARE MY God. I honor you and praise you, because you have done amazing things. You have always done what you said you would do ... You are like a shelter from storms, like shade that protects from the heat." (25:1, 4 *NCV)*

We serve a mighty God! Do you believe that God really cares about the details of your life? Do you believe that God can do something about your problems? These five verses talk about the fact that God keeps His word. He cares for people in need and will come to their assistance. He vanquishes the "ruthless," our enemies.

People often turn to God and give Him glory only when they are desperate. Too many times we humans have to get to the end of our "hoarded resources" before we plead with God for help. Do not wait until you have no other recourse before you turn to God. God wants to show mercy to you now. He wants to be kind to you.

Do not wait for trouble to sing the praises of God. He cares about every detail of your life. Let God be God in your life. Get to know Him "up close and personal." Then you can sing His praise not only after He rescues you but also in the good times of your life.

Prayer: You are my shelter. You are my Shepherd.
Lead me in the paths of righteousness for
Your name's sake.

82

God's Dinner Party

The Lord All–Powerful will prepare a feast on this mountain for all people. It will be a feast with all the best food and wine ... On this mountain God will destroy the veil that covers all nations ... he will destroy death forever. The Lord God will wipe away every tear from every face. He will take away the shame of His people from the earth. The Lord has spoken. At that time people will say, 'Our God is doing this! We have waited for him, and he has come to save us. This is the Lord. We waited for Him, so we will rejoice and be happy when He saves us.' (26:6–9, NCV)

WHEN JESUS TAUGHT HIS followers to pray, He instructed them to ask God to supply their daily bread. He chose His words carefully for His disciples, who certainly knew about

God's provision for the needs of the Israelites in the wilderness. God rained down bread (manna) for them each day, but He commanded them to gather only what they needed. In His physical provision for His people, God was teaching them a spiritual principle.

From the beginning, God provided for our physical needs by creating a world designed to sustain life. As far as we know, no other planet in our solar system can do that. God also provided for our spiritual needs. Jesus told the people that he came to be the spiritual Bread of Life. (John 6:25–71) God began preparations for this banquet of salvation at the very beginning of creation, and timed its fulfillment perfectly: " … at the right time, God sent His son. A woman gave birth to Him under the Law." (Galatians 4:4 *NLV)*

Jesus made a direct connection between feeding the 5,000 and offering Himself as the Bread of Life. After that great miracle, the crowd ran after Him. But He rebuked them for their eagerness to pursue "food that spoils" rather than "food that endures to eternal life." (John 6:26–27) They were physically hungry and didn't realize that they were spiritually starving. When Jesus declared that He was the Bread of Life sent down from Heaven by the Father, most of them rejected Him. Even many of His disciples abandoned Him.

Jesus makes the same offer to us today. He says, "I am the Bread of Life. Whoever comes to me will never go hungry, and whoever believes in me will never be thirsty." (John 6:35) He alone can give us true life, and He alone can sustain us. Every time we eat, we should keep this spiritual truth in mind. Remember Him at every meal and give thanks.

For the rest of the story, read Revelation 21 and 22. A great dinner party awaits us! Jesus is the host. We are the guests of honor. The Spirit and the Bride say: "Come!"

Prayer: Give us this day our daily bread.

More Scripture: Matthew 22:1–14. Many are invited, but few are chosen.

83

True Peace, Perfect Peace

Isaiah 26:1–4

"You, Lord, give true peace to those who depend on you, because they trust you. So, trust the Lord always, because he is our Rock forever." (26:3–4 *NCV*)

"You will keep in perfect peace those whose minds are steadfast, because they trust in you. Trust in the Lord forever, for the Lord, the Lord himself, is the Rock eternal." (26:3–4 *NIV*)

"Thou wilt keep him in perfect peace whose mind is stayed on thee … " (26:3 *KJV*)

"Jesus said, 'Don't let your hearts be troubled. Trust in God, and trust in me.' " John 14:1 *(NCV)*

"I leave you peace; my peace I give you. I do not give it to you as the world does. So don't let your hearts be troubled or afraid." John 14:27 *(NCV)*

The buzzword for the 60s, "peace," was accompanied by a flash of the two–fingered peace sign. The huge generation of Baby Boomers was coming into adolescence and young adulthood. Society was not wholly prepared. Schools were overcrowded.

Parents were overwhelmed. While the Vietnam War raged, society also raged as it underwent a reluctant metamorphosis. It seems ironic that one of the most unsettled eras of modern age chose the word *peace* as its buzzword. It sounds ironic until we realize that the buzzword reflected the deepest desire of that generation

Since the rebellion of Adam and Eve in the Garden of Eden, humans have hungered for peace. What we too often fail to recognize is that this hunger is really a desire for a right relationship with God. When we have a right relationship with God, we have peace, the kind of peace that cannot be attained by human effort.

Why is it so difficult for humans to recognize their need for a right relationship with God? Why do we tend to look for peace in all the wrong places? Could it be that we are like self–willed and stubborn children? Such children rarely admit they are wrong, which only gets them into deeper trouble. They are a lot like straying sheep that want to go their own way and put themselves into great danger.

Are you seeking peace? Claim the promise and challenge of Isaiah 26:3–4. God gives perfect and true peace to those who steadfastly trust Him. We can trust Him. We can trust Him for salvation. We can trust Him to meet our needs.

Jesus told His followers that the secret to peace, true and perfect peace, was to seek first the Kingdom of God and the righteousness of God. When you have a right relationship with God, God will take care of the rest. (Matthew 6:33)

Prayer: Peace, perfect and true peace, is a gift from
You, God. Give us peace.

More Scripture: Philippians 4:6–9

84

The Right Path

The way of the righteous is smooth; O Upright One, make the path of the righteous level. Indeed, while following the way of Your judgments, O Lord we have waited for You eagerly; Your name, even Your memory, is the desire of our souls. At night my soul longs for You, indeed, my spirit within me seeks You diligently; for when the earth experiences Your judgments the inhabitants of the world learn righteousness. (26:7–9 NASB)

WHEN ISAIAH SAYS THE path of the righteous is level and smooth, he is not indicating that that path is easy, only that God has cleared a path for the righteous to follow. The same truth is echoed in Psalm 23:3–4: "He guides me in the paths of righteousness for His name's sake. Even though I walk through the valley of the shadow of death, I fear no evil, for you are with me; your rod and your staff, they comfort me." *(NASB)* For the sake of God's name and reputation, He makes a way for the righteous to follow. Isaiah and the Psalmist David discovered the path by following God's Law. We discover it by God's grace. When we seek God with all our heart, He reveals Himself to us and sets our feet on the right path. "For You have delivered my soul from death, indeed my feet from stumbling, so that I may walk before God in the light of the living." (Psalm 56:13 *NASB)*

How do we choose the right path? Both David and Isaiah point us in the right direction. An intimate knowledge of God's Law sets us in the right direction. Jeremiah gives us the next clue: "You will seek me and find me when you seek me with all your heart." (Jeremiah 29:13) When we seek God, we will find Him.

Nature is known to take the path of least resistance. But in life, the easiest path is not always the best path. Following the right path requires self–denial, trust, and obedience. Jesus said: "Enter through the narrow gate. For wide is the gate and broad is the road that leads to destruction, and many enter through it. But small is the gate and narrow the road that leads to life, and only a few find it." (Matthew 7:13–14)

Here is an expanded version of Jesus' teaching from Matthew 7:13–14 *(VOICE)*: "Go through the narrow door. For the wide door leads to a wide path, and the wide path is broad; the wide, broad path is easy, and the wide, broad, easy path has many, many people on it; but the wide, broad, easy, crowded path leads to death. Now then that narrow door leads to a narrow road that in turn leads to life. It is hard to find that road. Not many people manage it."

Let us be like Isaiah, who prays, "My soul yearns for you in the night, in the morning my spirit longs for you." (26:9) If we seek God, we find the Shepherd, who leads us in the right path. His reputation is at stake, and we can count on Him.

Prayer: Lead me, O Lord, in the right way and help me walk in it each day.

85

Salvation for the World

As a pregnant woman about to give birth
writhes and cries out in her pain, so were we
in your presence, Lord. We were with child,
we writhed in labor, but we gave birth to
wind. We have not brought salvation to the
earth; and the people of the world have not
come to life. (26:17–18)

GOD CHOSE THE NATION of Israel to serve as a vessel of salvation to the world. They were set apart, separated for His purpose. The nation of Israel was a unique nation in that they had only one God. Other nations worshipped and recognized many gods.

God chose the nation of Israel to bring the Light of Truth into a dark world. It is the nature of humans to focus on the letter rather than the spirit of the law. Once our focus is off what is important, we either major in the minors or disregard the truth and go our own way. That is what occurred with the people of Israel. In Isaiah's day the people thought of their separateness as either a burden or a special blessing that put them above others. They missed the mark and misunderstood the call. They either ignored the Light of Truth or kept it to themselves. They turned their backs to the Light of Truth because being different required too much effort. Or they selfishly held it close, feeling that the Light of Truth was too good for anyone who was not one of God's chosen people.

Isaiah laments that the nation of Israel felt the labor pains of change. But they were not the earnest strivings of lasting, eternal change that would spread the Light of Truth, but the hard, pointless travail of temporary, cosmetic change that would simply lead further into darkness.

If you are a Christian, God has chosen you to serve as a vessel for the Light of Truth. Jesus lives in you and desires to shine through you. But it is our nature as humans to focus on the peripheral rather than the heart of anything. Does majoring on the minors of your faith distract you from your holy purpose? God made a way for the world to receive salvation. Now God calls you to take the Good News of His love to the lost and dying of that world. Do not "give birth to wind" and throw away the opportunities God gives you to share the good news. We can bring the Light of Truth to those who are still in darkness. Get focused on Truth, and make effective, lasting, eternal change.

Prayer: Your Word is Truth. Truth is light. Help us to live the Truth in such a way that our very lives bring the lost out of their darkness.

86

Promises and Prayers

HERE ARE SOME PROMISES and prayers from Isaiah (*NCV*).

26:12 "Lord all our success is because of what you have done, so give us peace."

28:12 "God said to them, 'Here is a place of rest; let the tired people come and rest. This is the place of peace.' "

30:15 "This is what the Lord God, the Holy One of Israel, says: 'If you come back to me and trust me, you will be saved. If you will be calm and trust me, you will be strong.' "

30:18 "The Lord wants to show His mercy to you. He wants to rise and comfort you. The Lord is a fair God, and everyone who waits for His help will be happy."

41:10 "So don't worry, because I am with you. Don't be afraid, because I am your God. I will make you strong and will help you; I will support you with my right hand that saves you."

41:13 "I am the Lord your God, who holds your right hand, and I tell you, 'Don't be afraid. I will help you.' "

43:1–3 "Now this is what the Lord says. ... 'Don't be afraid, because I have saved you. I have called you by name, and you are mine. When you pass through the waters, I will be with you. When you cross rivers, you will not drown. When you walk through fire, you will not be burned, nor will the flames hurt you. This is because I, the Lord, am your God, the Holy One of Israel, your Savior.' "

54:10 " 'The mountains may disappear, and the hills may come to an end, but my love will never disappear; my promise of peace will not come to an end,' says the Lord who shows mercy to you."

59:1 "Surely the Lord's power is enough to save you. He can hear when you ask him for help."

Prayer: Lord, lead me to the prayer or the promise I
             need today.

87

Trumpet of the Lord

In that day the Lord will thresh from the flowing Euphrates to the Wadi of Egypt, and you, Israel, will be gathered up one by one. And in that day a great trumpet will sound. Those who were perishing in Assyria and those who were exiled in Egypt will come and worship the Lord on the holy mountain in Jerusalem. (27:12–13)

"WHEN THE TRUMPET OF the Lord shall sound, and time shall be no more ... When the roll is called up yonder, I'll be there." Remember that old Gospel song? When I learned those words, I imagined the trumpet of a Salvation Army soldier playing them. Now, after growing in my understanding of Scripture, I realize the "great trumpet" in this passage of Scripture is a shofar, an instrument made from a ram's horn, used to call the people together for prayer, information, or war. In this case, the shofar would sound to bring the people who had been scattered by war and exile back to " … worship the Lord on the holy mountain in Jerusalem." (27:13)

We read in Exodus 19:13 that not until the shofar sounded one long blast would the people be allowed to approach Mount Sinai to be near the presence of God. But first the people were to consecrate themselves, wash their clothes, and "be ready" to meet with God. (Exodus 19:10)

Paul tells us that at the end of days another trumpet will sound. (1 Corinthians 15:52) Now is our time of consecration and preparation. Are you ready to meet God? It matters very little if God uses a brass instrument or a ram's horn. When I hear the trumpet's call, I want to be ready. When the roll is called up yonder, I want to be there.

Prayer: Lord, help us to be ready to hear the sound of
Your trumpet call.

88

A Cryptic Message

In that day, the Lord will punish with his sword—his fierce, great and powerful sword—Leviathan the gliding serpent, Leviathan the coiling serpent; he will slay the monster of the sea. (27:1)

BABYLONIAN MYTHOLOGY INCLUDED A story of creation by a god who had to first subdue the serpent Leviathan, also known as Chaos. One of Babylon's great gods was this serpent. Leviathan also figures in apocalyptic writings. Since Satan used the serpent in the Garden of Eden as his vessel for temptation, it could be that Leviathan represents any enemy of God or His people. Certainly in the context of Isaiah 27, Leviathan represents darkness and the enemy of light.

In Revelation 19:11–15, we read of the Lord's avenging sword. "I saw heaven standing open and there before me was a white horse, whose rider is called Faithful and True. With justice he judges and wages war. His eyes are like blazing fire, and on his head are many crowns. He has a name written on him that no one knows but he himself. He is dressed in a robe dipped in blood, and his name is the Word of God. The armies of heaven were following him, riding on white horses and dressed in fine linen, white and clean. Coming out of his mouth is a sharp sword with which to strike down the nations. ... "

Revelation 19 goes on to speak of a great battle that will take place on the final day of the Lord. Isaiah speaks of this battle and the day of reckoning for Babylon. Prophets reveal "mountain ranges" of truth, with the near future and the distant future bound together. When the message is cryptic, we must use clues from Scripture to begin to unravel the mystery of the prophecy. Isaiah speaks of the near future when God will deal with Babylon and of the distant future when God will deal with Satan.

God's ultimate weapon, His fierce, great, and powerful sword, is His Word. It is described in Hebrews 4:12: "For the word of God is alive and active. Sharper than any double–edged sword, it penetrates even to dividing soul and spirit, joints and marrow; it judges the thoughts and attitudes of the heart."

In John 1, Jesus is called the Word. It was this Word, Jesus, who spoke creation into being. Jesus is the King of kings in the Revelation account who defeats the beast with the sharp sword coming out of His mouth. He has already won the ultimate victory for us. We need to claim this victory over sin, darkness, and deceit. Choose for yourself this day to live as a victor and not as one defeated. Praise God for the victory found in Jesus Christ, the living Word of God.

Prayer: May Your Kingdom come and Your Will be done.

More Scripture: Romans 7–8

89

The Restored Vineyard

Isaiah 27:2–13

REREAD ISAIAH CHAPTER 5 and refresh your memory about
God's vineyard, which represented the nation of Israel and
the people of Judah. The Lord planted the best vines and did
everything possible to cultivate and protect His vineyard,
only to be disappointed: "Then he looked for a crop of good
grapes, but it yielded only bad fruit." (5:2) So God allowed His
vineyard to become a wasteland. However, He never ceased
to care for it and looked to the day He would restore it. But,
as Isaiah prophesies in this passage, Jacob's (Israel's) guilt
would require atonement before restoration could come.

The problem for the people was one of disconnection. By
worshiping at other altars and around Asherah poles, they
had separated themselves from the true God. Still, Isaiah
prophesies a flourishing future for Israel: "In days to come
Jacob will take root, Israel will bud and blossom and fill
all the world with fruit." The Lord promised that he would

sound a "great trumpet" to draw those who were perishing in Assyria and exiled in Egypt back to " ... worship the Lord on the holy mountain in Jerusalem." (27:6, 13)

The Lord dealt harshly with His people, but He never abandoned them; they were part of His grand plan. God chose Abraham, Isaac, Jacob, and their descendants to serve as a holy and separated people who would serve as a conduit for the Messiah. The Messiah, the true vine, would bring living fruit into the world: Light, Grace, Truth, and Salvation.

In John 15, Jesus declares that He is the true vine and that His followers are the branches. The branches must remain connected to the vine to live and to bear fruit. Jesus is the Vine, we are the branches, and God is the Gardener. Hallelujah, what a Savior!

Prayer: Lord, bless us and help us to bear good fruit
that is useful for Your Kingdom.

90

True Values

Isaiah 28:1–9

"THE LORD IS TRYING to teach the people a lesson; he is trying to make them understand his teachings." (28:9 *NCV*)

In Chapters 28 through 33, Isaiah prophesies six "woes" concerning various nations and God's own people. We will look at the woes in order, then come back to other verses of interest in these chapters.

The first woe is a message about the demise of Samaria. Isaiah calls it the "wreath" of Ephraim, alluding to the time in Israel's history when the country divided after Solomon's death. Jeroboam, of the tribe of Ephraim, led all the tribes except Judah, Benjamin, and the Levites in revolt against King Rehoboam, son of Solomon. Jeroboam established Samaria as his capital city. Jeroboam's kingdom became known as Israel, often referred to as the northern kingdom. He set up a new system of religion to prevent the people from going back to Rehoboam. In the day of Isaiah, Samaria was still a very prosperous city, even though the Assyrians were beginning to conquer the people of the northern kingdom.

Isaiah compared the city of Samaria, the nation's pride, to a withering wreath of flowers. It wore a "crown" of victory—note that drunken revelers often wore wreaths on their heads—that would be thrown to the ground and trampled underfoot. However, Isaiah prophesies that there will be some who would receive a crown of lasting value. "In that day the Lord Almighty will be a glorious crown, a beautiful wreath for the remnant of his people. He will be a spirit of justice to the one who sits in judgment, a source of strength to those who turn back the battle at the gate." (28:5–6) In Revelation, Jesus told the churches that He would give the crown of life to all those who overcome.

We face daily challenges to choose between the things of the world and the things of God. The things of the world may appear as the better value at times, but the things of God have lasting value. The Apostle Paul reminds us that the things we see are temporary, but the things of God are eternal. (2 Corinthians 4:18) How do the eternal things of God affect the values of your life? Are your real values, the "code" by which you live your life, based on the temporary or the eternal?

Prayer: God, we need Your help to recognize true value in the sea of falsehood that surrounds us.

91

Stuck in a Rut

Isaiah 29:1–14

THE SECOND OF THE six woes is against "Ariel," or Jerusalem. In verse 1, God charges "the city where David settled" with being stuck in a rut of ritual. The years pass and the cycle of festivals is repeated, but they don't really mean anything to the people.

Rites and rituals can be good object lessons. They are forms that should school our thoughts and actions to enable us to love and serve God. They should serve as a means to an end. But if they become the end in themselves, we are stuck in a rut that prevents us from recognizing what is true.

"The Lord says: 'These people come near to me with their mouth and honor me with their lips, but their hearts are far from me.' " (29:13) The people repeated the memorized words of their rites and rituals. They conformed to the expected behaviors. They acted like, looked like, and even sounded like they loved God, but their hearts did not respond or belong to Him.

There's nothing wrong with committing Scripture, doctrine, hymns, and church vocabulary to memory. In fact, it's really important to do. It's also important to conform to the behavior expected of us as Christians. But when it's conformity for conformity's sake, it's empty ritual.

Think about it. When you pray before a meal, do you repeat the same words every time? When was the last time you really returned thanks to God for the meal? Do you pay attention to the hymns you sing and the Scripture you read? Do you understand what the words really mean? What about your devotions? Have you fallen into a rut there?

The Lord goes on to say: "Their worship of me is made up only of rules taught by men." (29:13) God gave Moses the Ten Commandments, the blueprints of the Tabernacle, and the regulations for living everyday holy lives. As the years passed, the religious rulers added rule upon rule and regulation upon regulation.

We have a tendency to do the same thing. In Ephesians we read that we are saved by grace through faith. Even that faith is a gift from God. That's simple enough, but we have a tendency to think it's too simple. Surely there must be more to this grace and salvation thing, we reason. We model ourselves after this devout person or that one, and we set personal behavior goals. But we must be careful not to let any other person or code of behavior become more important than simple faith in the One who saved us.

Prayer: Lord, open my eyes and help me to discover the ruts that trap me. I claim Your promise to work in my life and change me.

92

Making God in Our Image

Woe to those who go to great depths to hide their plans from the Lord, who do their work in darkness and think, 'Who sees us? Who will know?' You turn things upside down, as if the potter were thought to be like the clay! Shall what is formed say to the one who formed it, 'You did not make me'? Can the pot say to the potter, 'You know nothing'? (29:15–16)

HERE IS THE THIRD woe: Woe to those who hide their plans from God and "do their work in darkness," who arrogantly think of themselves as equal to or even more important than God.

This image of the clay pot rebelling against the potter is hilarious! Can you imagine the scene? If you think about the many times you have questioned God, you can. "Been there, done that, read the book, and have the T–shirt!" What kind of potter would the clay create?

People create all sorts of images of God that are equally mistaken. They picture God as Santa Claus keeping a list of their naughty and nice actions or as a vending machine dispensing help when the right prayers are said. They perceive God as a "higher power" who will rescue them when they are in trouble or as a tyrant ready to squash them and make their lives miserable. They look at God as a Creator who abandoned humans long ago or as a meddler who is always trying to change them. Some people see God as white; others see God as black. Some imagine God as only male while others imagine Him as only female.

We humans seem to have a need to create God in our image. We ignore the fact that God created *us* in *His* image. We are God's creation, not the other way around. When the human race rebelled and fell away from grace, we forgot almost everything we knew about God our Creator. Still, if we are willing to be pliable clay in the Potter's hands, God will patiently work with us to reveal the truth about Himself.

How do you know what the true God is like? You have a Book that tells you all about Him.

Prayer: God, show Yourself to me. Open my eyes and let me see who You really are, not who I imagine You to be.

93

Chariots and Horses

Isaiah 30:1–17

THIS FOURTH WOE IS against God's own people. " 'Woe to the obstinate children,' declares the Lord, 'to those who carry out plans that are not mine, forming an alliance, but not by my Spirit, heaping sin upon sin; who go down to Egypt without consulting me; who look for help to Pharaoh's protection, to Egypt's shade for refuge.' ... This is what the Sovereign Lord, the Holy One of Israel, says: 'In repentance and rest is your salvation, in quietness and trust is your strength, but you would have none of it. You said, "No, we will flee on horses." Therefore you will flee! You said, "We will ride off on swift horses." Therefore your pursuers will be swift!' " (30:1–2, 15–16)

The people of Israel had learned very little from their own history, which was a record of God's delivering them in miraculous ways, time and again, despite their own waywardness.

Here in their time of need, to whom do the people turn for help? The Lord says they "go down to Egypt without consulting me; [they] look for help to Pharaoh's protection, to Egypt's shade for refuge." Really? Egypt? Had they truly forgotten a 400–year history of slavery and oppression there?

Their choice would bring consequences: shame and disgrace. But God still could not abandon His people. "Yet the Lord longs to be gracious to you; therefore he will rise up to show you compassion. For the Lord is a God of justice. Blessed are all who wait for Him!" (30:18)

Have we learned anything from our own personal history of bad decision–making? Who are the "allies" in whom we have placed false trust? Whom do we consult before making plans? Let this be our answer: "Some trust in chariots and some in horses, but we trust in the name of the Lord our God. They are brought to their knees and fall, but we rise up and stand firm. Lord, give victory to the king! Answer us when we call!" (Psalm 20:7–9)

Prayer: I have put my trust in You, God. You are my shield and my salvation.

More Scripture: Exodus 15, Psalm 20, Psalm 33:16–22, 2 Corinthians 6:14

94

Repeat the Lesson

Isaiah 31:1–9

WOE NUMBER FIVE SOUNDS like an echo of woe number four. Look back at the opening cry in Chapter 30:1, 2. "Woe to the obstinate children ... who go down to Egypt ... who look for help to Pharaoh's protection, to Egypt's shade for refuge." Chapter 31 begins in much the same way: "Woe to those who go down to Egypt for help ... "

The Genesis account of how Jacob's descendants ended up as slaves in Egypt and the Exodus account of their rescue and release by God through Moses are both historic and symbolic. The symbolism is simple and complex at the same time. The simple version: Egypt represents the bondage to sin that all humans experience. Moses is a type of Christ as he delivers his people from enslavement and sets them free.

The symbolism also has layers of complexity. Just as the Egyptians did not easily let go of their slaves, sin does not let go of its slaves without a fight. When God split the Red

Sea and made a safe pathway for the people, it represented a point of no return for them. We must recognize our own point of no return and celebrate it. Some Christians do this through the public ritual of baptism. Others celebrate it in some other public covenant service.

The trials of the wilderness represent many of the trials we face as we learn to live as God's people. Those trials included doubt, fear, longing for the old and comfortable, grumbling, and learning to trust. (Sound familiar?)

What practice of sin still enslaves you? What entices you to return to the bondage of sin? Work on breaking habits that tempt you to turn from God. He will help you. Trust in the Holy One of Israel.

Entering the Promised Land symbolizes the sanctification experience. Once again God marked that passage by miraculously making a way for the Israelites through the water, this time the Jordan River at flood stage. God enabled His people to claim their land, but they had to conquer the peoples who occupied it. God tells us that we must be holy like Jesus, and we can receive sanctification from Him if we ask for it. But if we are not careful, we can fall away. Daily we must claim the promises of God. Daily we must learn more from His Word. Day by day, we claim what belongs to us.

God does not want us to turn back to our Egypt. We must not go back to our old behaviors and alliances. When we need help, we must look to God.

Prayer: I will place my trust in God alone.

More Scripture: Romans 7, Numbers 14

95

Hope in God

Isaiah 33:1–9

ISAIAH DIRECTS THE SIXTH woe toward Assyria as he prophesies its eventual destruction. But in the meantime, God would allow Assyria to defeat and take into exile the people of the unfaithful northern kingdom, Israel. This would show the people of the southern kingdom, Judah, that God meant what He said about consequences for rebellion against Him. God was giving Judah a chance to repent because they had not totally turned their backs on Him the way Israel had.

Isaiah pleads: "Lord, be gracious to us; we long for you. Be our strength every morning, our salvation in time of distress. At the uproar of your army, the peoples flee; when you rise up, the nations scatter. ... Look, their brave men cry aloud in the streets; the envoys of peace weep bitterly. The highways are deserted, no travelers are on the roads. The treaty is broken, its witnesses are despised, no one is respected. The land dries up and wastes away, Lebanon is ashamed and withers; Sharon is like the Arabah, and Bashan and Carmel drop their leaves." (33:2–3, 7–9)

As an intercessor, Isaiah draws God's attention to the devastation of His people. He reminds God of what God already knows. When we intercede for our nation, for our cities, for our neighborhoods, and for our families, we know that God is perfectly aware of the details. Yet we must list them anyway. We list them for our benefit, not God's. It reminds us that God is in control of details and He cares about His people. It reminds us that God is the One who hears and answers our prayers.

Isaiah praises God: "The Lord is exalted, for he dwells on high; he will fill Zion with justice and righteousness." (33:5) Praise and thanksgiving are an important part of any kind of prayer. They remind us of the nature of God, and when we contemplate that, we are encouraged.

Isaiah recites a promise about God: "He will be the sure foundation for your times, a rich store of salvation and wisdom and knowledge; the fear of the Lord is the key to this treasure." (33:6)

This is a wonderful promise to claim for our day. God is our sure foundation. He is a rich storehouse of salvation, wisdom, and knowledge. What is the key to this treasure trove? The fear of the Lord. This is not a cowering fear that propels us away from God, but a respect and awe of power beyond our comprehension. Electricians respect electricity because they know what electricity can do. This very pale object lesson can help us understand what the Bible means when it instructs us to "fear" the Lord. The fear of the Lord is the starting point of a right relationship with God that develops into love.

Prayer: Help us to remember to turn to You, O Lord, for help.

More Scripture: Psalm 97, Proverbs 1:7

96

Childish Choices

'So then, the word of the Lord to them will become: Do this, do that, a rule for this, a rule for that; a little here, a little there ... '
(28:13)

NOW LET'S GO BACK to some other important verses interspersed within the "woes" chapters.

It is interesting to note that both Isaiah and Paul observed the same behavior in the people to whom they were responsible. Look at 1 Corinthians 3:1–2. Paul said that the believers in Corinth should be ready for the true meat of God's Truth, but they continued to exhibit childish behavior. That made them unable to "digest" the deeper truths of God's Word.

Isaiah told the people of Israel, both the northern and southern kingdoms, that God wanted them to understand and choose to live by the truths He had given them. However, the people continued to make childish choices.

You can imagine that Isaiah's message was not too well–

received. We don't like it when someone confronts us about our behavior any more than we like to confront others. This is a carryover from childhood, when we associated correction with negative feelings. But it's time to grow up and accept correction as something we need.

The people saw God's Word as "do this, do that," "a rule for this, a rule for that," "a little here, a little there." To them, God's Law had become a list of "do's" and "don'ts," and their obedience was half–hearted at best. God wanted His people to understand that He had given the Law for their benefit. God wanted them to mature, to love Him enough to desire to please Him through their obedience. Jesus said that the "first and greatest commandment" in the Law is "Love the Lord your God with all your heart and with all your soul and with all your mind." (Matthew 22:38, 37)

Are you obeying that commandment? If you are, your heart's desire will be to obey Him. You will come to an understanding that God's Law was created for your benefit. Your deep love for the Lord will cause you to want what He wants for you. We know that because of Jesus, we are living under Grace, not under Law. But when we love the Lord as Jesus said we should, God makes a covenant with us as His people: "I will put my law in their minds and write it on their hearts." (Jeremiah 31:33; see Hebrews 8:10.) We will find maturity in the Lord and desire the "meat" of God's Word.

Prayer: Lord, I want to love you with every fiber of my being so that I want nothing more than to walk in the way of obedience.

97

A Resting Place

*'This is the resting place, let the weary rest';
and, 'This is the place of repose'—but they
would not listen. ... The bed is too short to
stretch out on, the blanket too narrow to
wrap around you. (28:12,20)*

GOD GAVE THE PROMISED Land, the place of rest, to His people. They just had to follow His commands and trust Him to keep the nation strong. But they weren't doing that. So, to get the attention of His people, God made things uncomfortable for them, like a bed too short to stretch out on, and a blanket too narrow to wrap around the body. What a great image!

I always appreciate my own bed more when I sleep away from home on a bed that is less than comfortable. I love my sleep. I love my comfort. While I enjoy traveling, I just revel in coming home to my own bed. So this image that Isaiah painted for us really reaches me. Why would anyone choose substandard rest over the rest promised in God's Word?

Human nature hasn't changed much since the time of Moses. When he was leading the children of Israel to the Promised Land, they refused to trust and obey, so God sent them wandering in the desert until that stubborn generation passed away. They were not allowed to enter God's rest.

Jesus invites the weary and the burdened of this world to come to Him. (Matthew 11:28–30) The conditions of this rest are the same conditions that God gave the people of Israel. "Take my yoke upon you and learn from me ... my yoke is easy and my burden is light." They are the conditions of trust, surrender, and obedience.

Are you weary and burdened? Jesus invites you to come to Him. The conditions are simple. Don't be stubborn. Trust Him, surrender your will to Him, and obey Him.

Prayer: Lord, help all who are weary to come home.

More Scripture: Hebrews 4:1–11

98

Cornerstone

So this is what the Sovereign Lord says:
'See, I lay a stone in Zion, a tested stone, a
precious cornerstone for a sure foundation;
the one who relies on it will never be stricken
with panic. I will make justice the measuring
line and righteousness the plumb line ... '
(28:16–17)

MY GRANDFATHER WAS A carpenter. He taught my father important lessons: if you start the job with everything level, you end the job with everything level; measure everything at least twice before you cut; use a perfect measuring tool, because if you "eyeball" to save time, you end up wasting time; use the best materials, and your building will last.

God's message to Isaiah speaks of the same building principles for our lives. Start with a solid, level foundation. Matthew records the parable about the wise and foolish builders. Jesus told His listeners that anyone who hears and applies His teaching is like the wise builder, who started with a strong foundation, solid rock. Those who hear and ignore His teaching are like the foolish builder who started with a weak foundation, shifting sand. (Matthew 7:24–27)

After the foundation is ready, the cornerstone is laid. The cornerstone is the most important stone of the building. It determines the design and orientation of the building. In 1 Peter 2:4–12 we discover that Jesus is the cornerstone of God's design for the redemption of humanity.

God's measuring line is justice. It is a perfect measuring tool. His plumb line is righteousness. A plumb line is a string with a weight attached to the bottom. It serves as a way of making a wall straight. Righteousness is our plumb line and justice is our measuring stick. Together these tools ensure a level, sturdy, and right life when that life is built on the sure foundation of Jesus. Jesus is also the cornerstone. As the cornerstone, Jesus determines the orientation and design of our lives.

Prayer: Lord, keep us level and right as we build
our lives.

99

A Farmer Parable

Listen and hear my voice; pay attention and hear what I say. When a farmer plows for planting, does he plow continually? Does he keep on breaking up and working the soil? When he has leveled the surface, does he not sow caraway and scatter cumin? Does he not plant wheat in its place, barley in its plot, and spelt in its field? His God instructs him and teaches him the right way. Caraway is not threshed with a sledge, nor is the wheel of a cart rolled over cumin; caraway is beaten out with a rod, and cumin with a stick. Grain must be ground to make bread; so one does not go on threshing it forever. The wheels of a threshing cart may be rolled over it, but one does not use horses to grind grain. All this also comes from the Lord

*Almighty, whose plan is wonderful, whose
wisdom is magnificent. (28:23–29)*

"LISTEN AND HEAR MY voice; pay attention and hear what I
say. ... All this also comes from the Lord Almighty, whose plan
is wonderful, whose wisdom is magnificent." (28:23, 29)

To teach spiritual truths, Isaiah used a familiar picture of
the way a farmer treats the land and its produce during planting and harvest. Does a farmer continually plow the ground?
No. He prepares the soil only when it is time to plant. Then he
stops plowing and plants various types of seeds in conditions
just right for each one. After the harvest, the preparation for
use of each grain is different, depending on the crop. Certain
laws of nature dictate how the farmer is to plow, sow, harvest,
and prepare the grain. It's part of God's grand design.

In Galatians 6:7 we read: "Do not be deceived; God cannot
be mocked. A man reaps what he sows." Through their disobedience, the people of Israel continually broke the laws of God.
They sowed rebellion and would reap destruction. This is an
important truth for us to grasp. We do reap what we sow. May
God help us to be good "farmers"!

Isaiah warned the people that God would rise up and
"rouse himself" to do His work. (28:21) He described it as a
"strange work" and an "alien task" because it would involve
using the harvest of destruction to salvage the faithful remnant of His people. While it would appear that evil was about
to triumph, in the end, God and good would prevail.

God has a way of redeeming what we think of as the most
hopeless of situations. I like to believe that nothing is ever
truly wasted in the economy of God. If you are sowing rebel-

lion and reaping destruction, it is not too late to allow God
to redeem the situation. Turn to Him and learn what He is
teaching you. Sow better seeds, like love for God, obedience to
His Word, forgiveness, and love for others. Then see what God
will allow you to harvest.

Prayer: Lord, teach me to plant good seeds that will
yield a rich harvest.

More Scripture: Galatians 6:7–10, Philippians 4:4–9

100

Suddenly He Comes

Suddenly, in an instant, the Lord Almighty will come ... (29:5–6)

THE SECOND COMING OF the Messiah will occur in an instant: "It will happen in a moment, in the blink of an eye, when the last trumpet is blown. For when the trumpet sounds, those who have died will be raised to live forever. And we who are living will also be transformed." (1 Corinthians 15:52 *NLT*) What a promise!

Live your life as though each day may be your last. Do the most important things. Obey God. Live as the people of the early church lived, listening for the trumpet, the shofar, that would call them into the presence of God. We need to be ready when that call comes.

God instructed Moses to consecrate the people, to have them wash their clothes and be ready for the signal to come into His presence. (Exodus 19:10–11) Consecrated people are separated, set apart, for God. It means that wherever you are, you live for God. Whatever you do, you do for God. If you empty trash cans, you do it for God. If you wash pots, you do it for God. If you clean teeth for a living, you clean them for God. If you count money in a bank or enter data into a spreadsheet, you do those things for God. Your life is lived to bring honor and glory to the Kingdom of God.

The Israelites in the wilderness were instructed to wash their clothes. When we expect company or have a meeting with someone important, we put on our best. As we prepare to meet God, shouldn't we always be putting on our best—being devoted to Him in everything we say and do? He commands us to be holy because He is holy. That's what putting on our best truly means. We are dressed in robes of righteousness for Jesus' sake.

He will return in an instant. Be ready.

Prayer: God, help me to be consecrated and ready when You come.

More Scripture: Matthew 24:36–51, Matthew 25:1–13

101

Having Itching Ears

They say to the seers, 'See no more visions!'
and to the prophets, 'Give us no more visions
of what is right! Tell us pleasant things,
prophesy illusions. Leave this way, get off
this path, and stop confronting us with the
Holy One of Israel!' (30:10–11)

TURN TO 2 TIMOTHY 4:3–4 to see how these verses are echoed.
Do people really want to hear the truth? The other day I heard
some radio commentators ridiculing what they called conser-
vative, right–wing Christians for believing and teaching the
Bible. They were amazed that anyone in this "enlightened
age" could actually take the teachings of the Bible literally
or seriously. They thought it wasn't necessary to follow God's
Word in order to live a moral life with good values.

To those commentators, living a moral life would mean
things like not cheating or stealing and obeying the law. Their
good values included treating others as you want them to

treat you. Sound familiar? Where do these people think the blueprint for living such a life comes from? The fact is that most Americans appreciate many of the principles taught by the Bible without recognizing their source.

Beyond that, many like to hear what the Bible says, at long as it's the good stuff about God's love. The rub comes when God's Word deals with the not–so–nice things we humans do. People don't want to hear about sin and true repentance. When God's way seems too narrow, they abandon it. In effect, they are saying, "Tell us pleasant things ... stop confronting us with the Holy One of Israel!" (30:10–11)

Most of us don't enjoy confrontation, especially when God nudges us to stand in the path of people who are barreling down the wide road to destruction. Such people can be down-right mean. So our tendency is to love them to destruction instead of loving them enough to risk making them unhappy with us. We must be willing to risk rejection as we lovingly confront others with the Holy One of Israel and His Son, Jesus, the only one who can redeem them.

Prayer: God, help us to tell the truth in kindness so that we can help to rescue those who are destroying their lives through sin.

102

Principles of Blessing

Isaiah 30:15, 18–26

"YET THE LORD LONGS to be gracious to you; therefore he will rise up to show you compassion. For the Lord is a God of justice. Blessed are all who wait for Him! ... How gracious he will be when you cry for help! As soon as He hears, He will answer you." (30:18–19)

In Deuteronomy Chapter 11, God lays out a contract. "See, I am setting before you today a blessing and a curse—the blessing if you obey the commands of the Lord your God ... the curse if you disobey ... " (Deuteronomy 11:26–27, 28)

The choice between blessing and curse belonged to the individual and to the nation as a whole. In Deuteronomy 28, God's Word lays out the details of the blessing that would result from obedience to God and the curse that would result from disobedience. What comes through, however, is that God's desire is to give His people a blessing.

Here's a summary of the principles of blessing and curse:

- God wants to be gracious and show us compassion.

- God promises to bless those who acknowledge and obey His Word.

- We all have disobeyed God.

- Because of our disobedience, we deserve curse and not blessing.

- The ultimate curse is separation from God and death.

- Because of God's mercy, Jesus gave His life so that He could take away that curse.

- Still, we have a choice between blessing or curse.

- Blessing comes when we acknowledge, obey, and trust God.

- Curse comes when we deny, disobey, and doubt God.

- God is a just and holy God.

- God keeps His Word; He sticks to the contract.

- God expects His people to be holy and keep His commands (our part of the contract).

- We must claim and "own" God's promises.

The choice is yours today. Will you experience a blessed life or a cursed life? To experience a blessed life: Acknowledge God. Admit you have not kept God's commands. Ask for forgiveness and allow Jesus to take away the curse. Choose to live for God and obey His commands. Claim God's promises for yourself. Read the Bible and fellowship with other Christians so that you can learn about God's commands and promises. **You can live blessed. It's up to you!**

Prayer: Help me to choose blessing.

103

The Messianic Age

Isaiah 32

"SEE, A KING WILL reign in righteousness and rulers will rule with justice. Each one will be like a shelter from the wind and a refuge from the storm, like streams of water in the desert and the shadow of a great rock in a thirsty land." (32:1–2)

People who enjoy the privileges of authority often forget its responsibilities. When they forget or ignore those responsibilities, abuse abounds. The Righteous King, the Messiah, will not ignore or forget His responsibilities. His rule will be as refreshing streams of water in the desert and the shade of a great rock on a hot day. To really appreciate this metaphor, you would need to spend only about an hour in the desert. Obviously, water is a boon in such a dry place. But shade can also mean the difference between life and death. The great rocks of the desert cast their shadows and create shelter from the blistering sun. In the same way, the Righteous King—and the rulers assigned under Him—protects His subjects.

God longs to take care of you. Allow Him to touch and change your life in the way Isaiah says people will be transformed by the rule of the Righteous King. "Then the eyes of those who see will no longer be closed, and the ears of those who hear will listen. The fearful heart will know and understand, and the stammering tongue will be fluent and clear. ... the noble make noble plans, and by noble deeds they stand." (32:3–4, 8)

Recall the warning of Isaiah 6:9–10: "He said, 'Go and tell this people: "Be ever hearing, but never understanding; be ever seeing, but never perceiving." Make the heart of this people calloused; make their ears dull and close their eyes. Otherwise they might see with their eyes, hear with their ears, understand with their hearts, and turn and be healed.' "

In Matthew 13:11–17, Jesus cites that passage to describe people who can't understand His parables because their minds and hearts are closed to "the knowledge of the secrets of the kingdom of heaven." But, He says, those secrets are revealed to His disciples because they know Him: "Blessed are your eyes because they see, and your ears because they hear." Do you acknowledge Him as Messiah? If so, blessed is your heart because you understand. The Holy Spirit opens our eyes, our ears, and our hearts. This is the mystery of grace and salvation.

Pray for your unsaved family and friends and ask the Holy Spirit to work in their hearts. Pray for those who are blind and deaf to the truth because their hearts are hard. God's Spirit can make the difference.

Prayer: Open our eyes, Lord, and help us to see Jesus.

104

Complacent Women

Isaiah 32

THIS CHAPTER CLEARLY REFERS to the Messianic Age, yet it also applies to any age that requires a call to repentance. Incorporated within it is a message to women, calling them to intercession as it moves from a warning of trouble in the near future to a promise of glory and justice in the age to come.

In the first few chapters of Genesis, we learn that God decided that it was not good for the man He had created to be alone, so He formed a helper for him. That helper received the name woman. Throughout the ages and especially in this age, the concept of "helper" or "helpmate" has been viewed as a subordinate role. This was not God's intention. The same word *help* used here is used in Scripture for God as He comes alongside His people in battle. And the word we think of as "mate" is actually *meet,* meaning that this helper is the one who is appropriate for, and even equal to, Adam.

After Adam and Eve rebelled, God told Eve that her husband would rule over her. But that was not a curse that was to last forever. Because of Jesus, the curses of the Garden are canceled for those who accept Him as Savior.

Look at these "digger" questions. (Warning: They are somewhat provocative.)

- If God designed woman to be an equal partner, why do women who are saved often serve in subordinate roles? Is it because they are still choosing to live under the curse? Or is it because their church leaders have accepted the idea that women should be in subordinate roles?

- Did God create women to be more tuned into spiritual things as a way of ensuring that humans would always recognize their need for God? Is that why the serpent approached Eve first, and is Satan still setting his forces to attack women and distract them from obedience to the truth?

- Why does God specifically call the "complacent women" in this Isaiah passage to repentance, prayer, and intercession for their nation? Could He be calling them—and women today—to be warriors who will do spiritual battle for Him?

Prayer: Lord, help us to see the whole truth without prejudice.

More Scripture: Exodus 18:4, Deuteronomy 33:29, Psalm 40:13, 17, Psalm 46:1, Psalm 70:5, Psalm 118:7, Psalm 121. These are just a few of the passages in which same Hebrew word for "helper" that is used for Eve is used to describe God as a helper in battle.

105

Lift Him Up

*'Now will I arise,' says the Lord. 'Now will
I be exalted; now will I be lifted up.'* (33:10)

"JESUS SAID, '... I, when I am lifted up from the earth, will
draw all people to myself.' He said this to show the kind of
death he was going to die." (John 12:30–33)

"Just as Moses lifted up the snake in the wilderness, so
the Son of Man must be lifted up, that everyone who believes
in him may have eternal life in him." (John 3:14–15)

Jesus said that when He is lifted up, He will draw all people to Him. How do we lift Him up? The most obvious meaning is that we should exalt Him by the way we live. When the
Lord's people live out His justice and righteousness, we honor
Him. When our lives honor Jesus, He is lifted up.

But let's flesh out a deeper truth found in the passage in
John 3. Jesus was referring to a time in the history of Israel
when God's people were on their way to the Promised Land.
Their attitudes and complaints had gotten them in trouble

once again, so God sent venomous snakes among them. The people repented and looked to Moses to do something. Moses prayed, and God instructed him to make a bronze snake and put it on a pole, like a banner. Anyone who had been bitten needed only to look at the bronze snake to receive healing. (Numbers 21:4–9) Jesus told His listeners that just as Moses lifted up a snake in the wilderness to provide healing for the people, He would be lifted up as a banner for the people to bring them not just physical healing but eternal life. Isaiah 11:10 tells us that the nations, all peoples, will one day rally to the Root of Jesse, the promised Messiah.

All humans are victims of the Fall and suffer from the venom of the serpent of the Garden of Eden. The serpent's destroyer, Jesus Christ, the Son of Man, was lifted up so that we might live. He is the only antidote for the venom of sin.

Prayer: Help me to lift up Jesus so that others will be drawn to Him.

106

Forgiven and Indwelt

Look at Jerusalem, the city of our festivals. Look at Jerusalem, that beautiful place of rest. It is like a tent that will never be moved ... There the Lord will be our Mighty One. (33:20, 21 NCV)

"THEN THE CLOUD COVERED the tent of meeting, and the glory of the Lord filled the tabernacle." (Exodus 40:34)

God, the Creator of the entire universe, the Almighty and Holy One of Israel, chose to live among His people. His glory filled the Tabernacle. Once the people of Israel became established in the Promised Land, they built a Temple, and God's glory filled that place. (1 Kings 8:10–11) In Ezekiel 10, we read that God's glory departed from the Temple, which was then destroyed by the Babylonians. Seventy years later the Temple was rebuilt, but there is no record that God's glory returned. Then, hundreds of years later, Jesus came.

"The Word became flesh and made his dwelling among us.

We have seen his glory, the glory of the one and only Son, who came from the Father, full of grace and truth." (John 1:14) God's glory returns when Christ, the Word, is made flesh to "dwell" among His people.

When we first grasp that God loves us, we also recognize in the same instant that we can never make ourselves acceptable to a Holy God. But would God offer us a gift that is impossible to receive or enjoy? No! He made a way for us. That way is Jesus. "What can wash away my sin?" As the song says, "Nothing but the blood of Jesus." How can blood make us clean? In the system of sacrifice, only a life (blood) could atone for sin. The lives of cattle, sheep, and goats were traded as payment for the sin of the people. The sacrifices, the best the people had to offer, had to cost them something or they had no meaning.

Jesus, the Lamb of God, paid the ultimate price when He gave Himself as the once–for–all sacrifice that removes sin. Because of Him, you and I can be like a "tent that will never be moved," where the "Mighty One" dwells.

After Jesus left this Earth, He gave His Holy Spirit to us to live within us. God made it possible for *us* to become His dwelling place. "Don't you know that you are God's temple and that God's Spirit lives in you?" (1 Corinthians 3:16 *NCV*) Wow, what a gift!

Celebrate the sacrifice! Celebrate the Savior! Celebrate God's Spirit dwelling within us!

Prayer: Help me to live a forgiven and holy life, so
                that I might know You in all Your fullness!

107

Purified by the All–Consuming Fire

Isaiah 33:10–17

" 'WHO OF US can dwell with the consuming fire? Who of us can dwell with everlasting burning?' Those who walk right-eously ... " (33:14–15)

"John answered them all, 'I baptize you with water. But one who is more powerful than I will come, the straps of whose sandals I am not worthy to untie. He will baptize you with the Holy Spirit and fire. His winnowing fork is in his hand to clear his threshing floor and to gather the wheat into his barn, but he will burn up the chaff with unquenchable fire.' " (Luke 3:16–17)

God is the all–consuming fire that purifies and cleanses. His fire also destroys the "chaff," those people who are not worthy. Luke was describing Judgment Day, but in Leviticus, we see this promise coming true for rebellious people. "Aaron's sons Nadab and Abihu took their censers, put fire in them and added incense; and they offered unauthorized fire before the Lord, contrary to his command. So fire came out from the presence of the Lord and consumed them, and they died before the Lord. Moses then said to Aaron, 'This is what the Lord spoke of when he said: "Among those who approach me I will be proved holy; in the sight of all the people I will be honored." ' " (Leviticus 10:1–3) God will not tolerate sin. He is a holy God.

How then do we, as polluted as we are, escape being consumed by the fire of God's wrath? The blood of the Lamb, Jesus Christ, covers our sin and makes us clean. How do we keep clean? Through being willing to allow the fire of the Holy Spirit of God to purify us. The first thing we must do is yield to the "wonder–working power" of the Blood. Then we must allow God's Holy Spirit to refine us just as gold and silver are refined in a great furnace.

What impurities exist in your life? Yield them to the fire of God's furnace today.

Prayer: Send the fire!

More Scripture: Malachi 4:1, Lamentations 3:22

108

God of Details

Isaiah 34

THIS IS DEFINITELY ONE of those doom–and–gloom chapters. On first reading, we are immediately overcome with the
promise of judgment, destruction, and retribution. There are
very few people who would name this as their favorite passage of Scripture. Yet we still find encouragement and hope
in it. Two truths stand out: God is into details and He keeps
His word.

The chapter begins with God's anger against "all nations,"
then zeroes in on one, Edom, describing in detail the destruction that will come to that nation. *Edom* means "red," and it
is associated with the red–desert land of that name but also
with Esau, who sold his birthright to Jacob for a bowl of red
porridge. That began the enmity between Jacob's descendants
(Zion in this passage) and Esau's descendants (the Edomites).
The Lord here is describing His wrath against Edom, as representative of His wrath against all rebellious nations. He

promises it will happen, and He keeps His word.

Do you respect or trust people who do not keep their word? Most of us would rather deal with people who keep their word than those who break it. But it is sometimes very difficult to keep our promises. In fact, Jesus tells us that we should not "swear an oath" at all, but rather, simply say "yes" or "no," for anything beyond that "comes from the evil one." (Matthew 5:33–37)

Prayer: Help me to see God in the details of my life
and to rely on Him to keep His promises.
Help me so that my "yes" will truly be yes,
and my "no" will truly be no.

More Scripture: Numbers 30:2, Psalm 145:31

109

The Desert Blooms

Isaiah 35

FOLLOWING A DOOM—AND—GLOOM CHAPTER comes this chapter of encouragement. When the rains come to the desert, it springs to life. This object lesson stands to teach generation after generation about God's promises. When the Lord comes to bless His people with His presence, they also spring to life. These 10 verses promise that God will ransom and redeem His people and return them to their land. This was a promise that found literal fulfillment years later when the Jews returned from exile in Babylon.

But remember that prophecy has different layers of meaning. This same prophetic promise has a much richer fulfillment in God's ultimate plan of salvation. It looks forward to the day when " ... the eyes of the blind will be opened and the ears of the deaf unstopped. Then will the lame leap like a deer, and the mute tongue shout for joy." (35:5–6) In Jesus, all these miracles come to pass, and He redeems humankind from the clutches of Satan. The passage also says, " ... a highway will be there; it will be called the Way of Holiness; it will be for those who walk on that way." (35:8) This is the Way that Jesus opens for humankind to return to a right relationship with God. He sets our feet on the right path, the path of abundant life.

Have you heard the words to this old chorus? "Travel along in the sunshine/ on the king's highway;/Travel along, singing a song,/Follow Jesus day by day./Never mind what lies before you,/never mind what others do;/So travel along in the sunshine/On the king's highway." *(The Song Book of The Salvation Army,* #685) The King's Highway is the Way of Holiness. All who stay on this path not only enjoy safety but also gladness and joy.

Do you know of someone who needs a word of encouragement today? "Strengthen the feeble hands, steady the knees that give way; say to those with fearful hearts, 'Be strong, do not fear; your God will come, he will come with vengeance; with divine retribution he will come to save you.' " (35:3–4) God's word is full of encouragement. Every promise is true!

Prayer: Help me to take heart, as I face the dry times, that even the desert blooms in God's appointed time.

110

Time Out for History

Isaiah 36–39

THIS SECTION OF ISAIAH is drastically different from the rest of the book. It tells the story of a brief period in Judah's history. The Assyrians had conquered the northern kingdom of Israel and taken much of its population into exile. Not all the nations of the Middle East succumbed to Assyrian rule. King Hezekiah of Judah had chosen to rebel against Assyria by making an alliance with Egypt. Sennacherib, the Assyrian king, marched against Hezekiah. His armies took control of the major fortified cities of Judah and sent his commander to begin a siege of Jerusalem.

Chapter 36 deals with that siege and the challenge to Hezekiah from Sennacherib's field commander, who planted doubt, used intimidation and bribery, and called on the people of Judah to compromise. In his overconfidence, he mocked God's promise of deliverance. But the people remained silent because Hezekiah had commanded them not to answer.

Instead, the leaders tore their clothes as a sign of great distress and took the field commander's message to King Hezekiah.

Chapter 37 deals with deliverance. Hezekiah also tore his clothes, put on sackcloth, entered the Temple, and sent for Isaiah. The king called on priests, prophets, and the people to pray with him for the deliverance of Jerusalem, and God delivered them. As Sennacherib left to encounter the king of Cush, he sent a threatening letter to Hezekiah. Once again Hezekiah went before God in prayer: "Now, Lord our God, deliver us from [Sennacherib's] hand, so that all the kingdoms of the earth may know that you, Lord, are the only God." (v. 20) The Lord sent a message through Isaiah that He had heard Hezekiah's prayer and would deliver the city. Then the angel of the Lord killed 185,000 Assyrian soldiers. Sennacherib returned to Nineveh, the capital of Assyria, where he was killed by his own sons.

Chapter 38 tells of Hezekiah's illness. God sent Isaiah to tell him to get his house in order because he would not recover. Once again, the king turned to Lord in prayer, pleading for his life. Before Isaiah left the palace grounds, God sent him back to Hezekiah with the good news that he would recover and live for 15 more years.

In Chapter 39, we read of envoys coming from Babylon to celebrate Hezekiah's recovery. The king, delighted at the visit, showed them all the riches of his storehouses. Isaiah told Hezekiah that after his death, all these things would be carried off to Babylon. It is interesting that in this one case, the king did not turn to the Lord in prayer. Instead, he told

Isaiah that his prophecy was good because it would mean peace during his lifetime.

When do you turn to the Lord in prayer? In desperation when you are threatened or ill? Do you turn to Him as well when things are looking good for your immediate future?

Prayer: Remind me to humble myself and pray in
every circumstance.

More Scripture: Psalm 66 (perhaps written either for or by Hezekiah; note particularly verses 16–20); 2 Kings 18–20

111

Comfort My People

Isaiah 40:1–11

THE PROPHET ISAIAH DELIVERED a message of comfort that would have profound meaning in a future day. "Comfort, comfort my people, says your God. Speak tenderly to Jerusalem, and proclaim to her that her hard service has been completed, that her sin has been paid for, that she has received from the Lord's hand double for all her sins." (40:1–2) This prophecy was for the Jews who would one day be exiled to Babylon. The message was that exile would not last forever; there would be an end to their punishment.

This same message is echoed in the writings of the prophet Hosea, a contemporary of Isaiah. Both prophets served during the reigns of Uzziah, Jotham, Ahaz, and Hezekiah. God instructed Hosea to marry Gomer, an adulteress, who was quickly unfaithful to Hosea. Their marriage was meant to be a parable of Israel's unfaithfulness to God. Gomer's unfaithfulness caused her to be sold into slavery, but Hosea bought her back. God promised that Judah would be sold into exile because of its continual rebellion and unfaithfulness. God also promised that He would buy His people back.

Do you have sin habits that are taking you away from God? Most of the time, such a habit begins with an idea or temptation that tickles the imagination. You first entertain a sinful fantasy. The more you indulge in the fantasy, the easier it is for sinful behavior to be born. The more often you practice the behavior, the more deeply the sin habit becomes entrenched. Once the habit is entrenched, you find yourself far from God, in a kind of exile. Is there hope or comfort for you? Yes. God is waiting to restore you to the path of righteousness. Remember, He has bought you back with the blood of His son, Jesus Christ.

Prayer: I confess that my fantasies and habits have taken me to dark places and separation from You. Bring me back into your presence, O Lord.

112

Three Voices of Comfort

Isaiah 40:1–11

ISAIAH'S WORDS IN THIS chapter focus on the age of Messiah Jesus. Three voices reveal His characteristics.

The first is found in verse 3: "A voice of one calling: 'In the desert prepare the way for the Lord; make straight in the desert a highway for our God. Every valley shall be raised up, every mountain and hill made low; the rough ground shall become level, the rugged places a plain. And the glory of the Lord will be revealed, and all the people will see it together. For the mouth of the Lord has spoken.' " (40:3–5) This prophecy is about John the Baptizer, the herald of the Messiah. John's task would be to prepare the way of the Lord. In ancient days, when a sovereign ruler chose to visit his kingdoms, heralds would go in advance to alert the people of his coming. This obligated the ruler's subjects to prepare the road the ruler would use.

The first voice also describes how the Messiah will come.

"And the glory of the Lord will be revealed, and all people will see it together." (40:5) That glory would be revealed in Jesus: "For God, who said, 'Let light shine out of darkness,' made his light shine in our hearts to give us the light of the knowledge of God's glory displayed in the face of Christ." (2 Corinthians 4:6) The Messiah would come as a gift from God for all people. Once the glory of God was revealed in Jesus, He would become the Savior of the whole world. (John 3:16)

The second voice is found in verses 6–8: "A voice says, 'Cry out.' And I said, 'What shall I cry?' 'All people are like grass, and all their faithfulness is like the flowers of the field. The grass withers and the flowers fall, because the breath of the Lord blows on them. Surely the people are grass. The grass withers and the flowers fall, but the word of our God endures forever.' " This voice speaks of the fleeting nature of humankind and the eternal nature of God. John 1 tells us that Jesus is the eternal Word of God. Jesus said, "Heaven and earth will pass away, but my words will never pass away." (Matthew 24:35)

The third voice, Isaiah's own, pictures the Messiah first as a mighty Warrior King who comes in power. (40:10) In almost the same breath, the voice then describes the Lord as a gentle Shepherd King. (40:11) The image of the Son of God as the Mighty Warrior King would bring comfort to people who needed rescue. The image of the Messiah as the Gentle Shepherd King would bring comfort to those who needed to remember how much God loved them.

These three voices challenge us to explore the richness of God's Word that points to the promised glorious Savior.

Prayer: Help me to hear Your voice, the voice of Truth.

113

The Mighty Warrior King

*You who bring good news to Jerusalem, lift
up your voice with a shout, lift it up, do not
be afraid; say to the towns of Judah, 'Here
is your God!' See, the Sovereign Lord comes
with power, and he rules with a mighty
arm. See, his reward is with him, and his
recompense accompanies him.* (40:9–10)

ISAIAH'S WORDS IN THIS passage were addressed to a future
generation, one that would be born after the exile to Babylon.
That generation would need the comfort of Isaiah's words. They
would need to know that God is a Mighty Warrior King. The
Sovereign Lord comes with power. His arm rules for Him, His
reward is with Him, and His recompense accompanies Him.

Could the intended meaning for *recompense* be different from *reward* in this Scripture, or is Isaiah simply using
the literary device of repetition to emphasize his message?
Looking at the entire thought and image, we see that the

prophet uses these words: "The Sovereign Lord comes with power, and he rules with a mighty arm." *Rule* and *power* are two ideas that complete each other. The Mighty Warrior King comes in power, and that power establishes His rule. So *reward* and *recompense* can also be seen as two ideas that complete each other. The Mighty Warrior King will reward and repay; He will set things right. The power of the Mighty Warrior King will establish His Kingdom. Once His Kingdom is established, everything will be set right.

It should be a comfort and hope to us to know that these words were meant not just for the exiles in Babylon, but also for us. We must recognize God as our Sovereign Lord, know that He comes in power to establish His Kingdom, and that when He comes, He will bring reward and recompense. When His Kingdom is established in our lives, He begins to set things right. How is God working to set things right in your life?

Prayer: May Your Kingdom come and Your Will be done in my life today.

114

The Gentle Shepherd King

*He tends his flock like a shepherd: He
gathers the lambs in his arms and carries
them close to his heart; he gently leads those
that have young.* (40:11)

THE BIBLE USES THE imagery of a Gentle Shepherd King
to communicate how God cares for His people. "He tends his
flock like a shepherd ... "

King David, known as the Shepherd King, wrote that the
Lord was his Shepherd. (Psalm 23) David knew that God
would anticipate and take care of his needs. A shepherd provides shelter, nourishment, security, and physical well–being.
Because the shepherd carefully tends the flock, a level of trust
is built between sheep and shepherd.

However, the shepherd must be careful to watch for those
sheep that have a tendency to stray. David himself strayed
when he committed adultery with Bathsheba and tried to
cover up his sin by murdering her husband. For his sin, the

Lord punished David with the death of his and Bathsheba's child. Psalm 51:8, David's prayer of repentance, records these words: "Let me hear joy and gladness; let the bones you have crushed rejoice."

This verse may be connected with the common practice of a shepherd dealing with a stray sheep: breaking a bone in one of its legs. While the bone healed, the sheep would be carried on the shepherd's shoulders. After the bone healed, the sheep would no longer stray because it had grown so close to the shepherd. The shepherd knew that the brief amount of pain endured by the sheep because of the broken bone would ultimately save its life. After King David, the "straying sheep," was punished for his sin, he pleaded with the Lord to restore him, and the Lord did.

Jesus identifies Himself as the Good Shepherd who knows and cares for His sheep. He protects and leads them. He calls them by name, and they recognize His voice. Ultimately, the Good Shepherd lays down His very life for His sheep. (John 10:11–18)

Prayer: The Lord is my Shepherd. He takes care of my needs. Therefore, I can trust Him all the days of my life. Help me, Lord, to follow you closely.

115

Questions and Answers

Isaiah 40:12–28

"WHO HAS MEASURED THE waters in the hollow of his hand, or
with the breadth of his hand marked off the heavens? Who has
held the dust of the earth in a basket, or weighed the mountains
on the scales and the hills in a balance? ... Do you not know? Have
you not heard? Has it not been told you from the beginning? Have
you not understood since the earth was founded? ... Do you not
know? Have you not heard? The Lord is the everlasting God, the
Creator of the ends of the earth. He will not grow tired or weary,
and his understanding no one can fathom." (40:12, 21, 28)

When you were a child, did you ever ask when God was
born or who His parents were? It's difficult for humans to
grasp the idea that anyone could be eternal. Only when we
finally experience eternity will we truly begin to comprehend
its mysteries. For now, we have God's Word. For now, we have
faith. The questions "Who?" "How?" "Why?" are answered in
a simple declaration of faith: "The Lord is the everlasting
God, the Creator of the ends of the earth. He will not grow

tired or weary, and his understanding no one can fathom."

This passage from Isaiah is wonderful. It asks and answers questions about God's omnipresence, omnipotence, and omniscience. It is reminiscent of His reply to Job's cries and the counsel of his "miserable comforters": "Where were you when I laid the earth's foundation?" Through Chapters 38–41, the Lord's thundering challenge completely humbles Job, who ends up saying: "Surely I spoke of things I did not understand, things too wonderful to know ... My ears had heard of you but now my eyes have seen you. Therefore I despise myself and repent in dust and ashes."

Do you not know? Have you not heard? Within each of us, God implanted an ability to recognize the Truth. When we take off the trappings of pride in our own intelligence and accomplishments and look honestly into the Word of God, we recognize the Truth. "The Lord is the everlasting God, the Creator of the ends of the earth. He will not grow tired or weary, and his understanding no one can fathom." (40:28)

Read through this passage. Compare it with 1 Corinthians 1:20–31. Read Hebrews 11:1–3. Write on a piece of paper your questions about God or His Word that seem to have no answer. Add this to the bottom or back of the page: "What have I learned about this subject?" "Which of these questions are still important to me?" Place the paper in an envelope, put it aside, and open it in a year.

If you really open yourself up to learning Truth, God will help you find the answers to your questions.

Prayer: Father, there are mysteries that I cannot comprehend. Help me to trust You for the answers.

116

God Knows Where You Are

*Lift up your eyes and look to the heavens;
Who created all these? He who brings out
the starry host one by one and calls forth
each of them by name. Because of his great
power and mighty strength, not one of them
is missing. Why do you complain, Jacob?
Why do you say, Israel, 'My way is hidden
from the Lord; my cause is disregarded by
my God'? Do you not know? Have you not
heard? The Lord is the everlasting God, the
Creator of the ends of the earth. (40:26–28)*

WITH ALL OUR ADVANCED technology, we have found it more
and more impossible to count the stars. Every day astrono-
mers discover new ones. An astronomer who finds a "new"
star often has the privilege of giving it a name. This must
amuse God, since He has already named every one of them.
(40:26)

God may care about His vast universe, but does He really care about the details of our lives? In the passage best known as the Sermon on the Mount, Jesus tells His listeners to consider the flowers of the field: "They do not labor or spin. Yet I tell you that not even Solomon in all his splendor was dressed like one of these. If that is how God clothes the grass of the field ... will he not much more clothe you—you of little faith?" (Matthew 6:28–30)

If God cares for the flowers of the field so much, imagine how He cares for us. Yet there are times when we question whether God even knows us, much less cares about what troubles and concerns us. We turn to worry instead of to the Lord.

Think of the most beautiful and delicate flower you have ever seen. The God who took the time to design that fragile, exquisite flower is the same God who knows and cares about the details of your life. Trust Him.

Prayer: Lord, You are my God and I will trust in You.

More Scripture: Matthew 6:25–34

117

On Eagles' Wings

He gives strength to the weary and increases the power of the weak. Even youths grow tired and weary, and young men stumble and fall; but those who hope in the Lord will renew their strength. They will soar on wings like eagles; they will run and now grow weary, they will walk and not faint. (40:29–31)

"LET US NOT BECOME weary in doing good, for at the proper time we will reap a harvest if we do not give up." (Galatians 6:9)

We all grow weary. Some people seem to have more energy and endurance than others, yet eventually, we all come to the end of our own resources. That's when we learn to wait on God and tap into His abundance of power and strength. Jesus set the example. Jesus, the Word made flesh, spent hours in the presence of God. The psalmist wrote that in God's presence there is fullness of joy. (Psalm 16:11 *ESV)* Nehemiah said that the joy of the Lord is our strength. (Nehemiah 8:10) Psalm 46:1 states that God is our refuge and our strength.

We need to learn about true endurance. In this age of fast food and instant gratification, we quickly become bored with things that don't produce immediate results. We become impatient with God. We want to run ahead of Him and force the results. However, we must go back to the instruction and promise of Scripture: "Wait for the Lord ... " (Psalm 27:14) "Trust in the Lord ... " (Proverbs 3:5) "Be still, and know that I am God ... " (Psalm 46:10) "Let us not become weary in doing good, for at the proper time we will reap a harvest if we do not give up." (Galatians 6:9) We must tap into God's strength so we can endure.

This portion of Isaiah paints a picture for us: When we hope in the Lord, we will " ... soar on wings like eagles." (40:31) Eagles don't flap their wings; they spread them and allow the wind currents to carry them. Think of what we could accomplish for the Kingdom of Heaven if we spread our spiritual wings and trusted the wind of the Spirit to carry us. An eagle in flight looks perfectly still; believers who do not grow weary understand that they must "be still" and know that God is God. People who accomplish great things for God know this secret. (Can you see why this devotional book is titled *On Eagles' Wings?*)

Isaiah also says that those who hope in the Lord will " ... run and not grow weary, they will walk and not be faint." (40:31) They don't grow weak or stumble and fall because they are focused on the Lord. Paul puts it this way: "Let us run with perseverance the race marked out for us, fixing our eyes on Jesus ... " (Hebrews 12:1–2) If we keep our focus on

Him, not ourselves, we can be sure that our strength will be renewed for mission.

Prayer: Lord, help me to soar on wings like an eagle,
to run and not grow weary as I serve You.

118

No Contest

Isaiah 41:1–7, 21–29

" 'LET THEM COME forward and speak; let us meet together at the place of judgment.' ... The metalworker encourages the goldsmith, and the one who smooths with the hammer spurs on the one who strikes the anvil. One says of the welding, 'It is good.' The other nails down the idol so it will not topple. ... 'I look but there is no one—no one among the gods to give counsel, no one to give answer when I ask them. See, they are all false! Their deeds amount to nothing; their images are but wind and confusion.' " (41:1, 7, 28–29)

In this passage, God calls for a great showdown between Himself and the idols of the world. It is a challenge to the false gods of the surrounding nations and those of the Israelites themselves. He tells the people to bring their idols together for a contest. He asks the idols to "tell us what the future holds." The idol–makers tremble because they know the truth; that their idols can really do nothing. Yet they urge each other on because not showing up for this contest would be bad for business.

Do you sense the humor in Isaiah's account of the idol–makers as they egg each other on to win the contest? They do their best, yet the most perfectly crafted of their idols will topple if it's not nailed down. The idol–makers' very best work cannot even stand by itself, much less tell the future or explain the past.

Is your life idol–free? You may be tempted to say, "Of course!" but look deeper. What or whom do you rely on to get you through the day? Have any superstitions crept into your life? Do you trust in luck or good fortune? (Did you know that one theory of the origin of the word "luck" is that it comes from the name Lucifer and referred to the bad things he caused?) Is there something or someone you revere too much? Can any of these idols stand in a contest with God? There is no one like God. He is the winner of any contest in any court or arena. Keep an American coin with the motto "In God we trust" on it in a place where you will see it every day this week to remind you to trust in God alone.

" 'Do not be afraid ... for I myself will help you,' declares the Lord, your Redeemer, the Holy One of Israel." (41:14)

Prayer: Lord, reveal to me any idols I have allowed into my life. Help me to rid myself of them so that my trust is in You alone.

More Scripture: 1 Corinthians 10:1–14, Acts 19:23–41

119

Our Help

Isaiah 41:8–21

"DO NOT FEAR, FOR I am with you; do not be dismayed, for I am your God. I will strengthen you and help you; I will uphold you with my righteous right hand." (41:10)

God is speaking in this passage. Every time the personal pronoun "I" is used, the Lord is talking about what He has done for His chosen people or what He promises to do. You are also chosen of God. If you feel unsure of your future, or you are presently under attack by your enemies, read and commit this portion of Scripture to memory. Claim these promises as meant for you. Trust God for victory.

Hundreds of years before Isaiah's time, the Israelites left captivity in Egypt under the leadership of Moses. When the Egyptians pursued the people of God, God opened a way for them to pass through the sea on dry ground. This was a miracle that teachers and prophets constantly called attention to as a reminder that the God who had chosen them had not changed. Many years before the exile in Babylon, Isaiah speaks God's promise that He will deliver the people again. This time God will make a way for them to cross the desert in safety by turning the dry land into pools and springs of water. God will supply their needs and bring them out of exile and back to their own land.

The promise God made to deliver His people is one that transcends time. God can and will deliver you. How will He do that? We often want to tell Him how—and even when—we would like Him to rescue us, but His plans for us are beyond our imagining—and they are perfect. The important thing is that we trust God to do as He has promised. He is our Helper and our Deliverer. Let's claim the promises, then wait for God to act.

Prayer: God, my Helper, deliver me, in Your way and in Your time.

More Scripture: Psalms 57 and 59

120

Messianic Prophecy:
Servant Song 1

'Here is my servant, whom I uphold, my chosen one in whom I delight; I will put my Spirit on him and he will bring justice to the nations. He will not shout or cry out, or raise his voice in the streets. A bruised reed he will not break, and a smoldering wick he will not snuff out. In faithfulness he will bring forth justice; he will not falter or be discouraged till he establishes justice on earth. In his law the islands will put their hope.' This is what God the Lord says—the Creator of the heavens, who stretches them out, who spreads out the earth with all that springs from it, who gives breath to its people, and life to those who walk on it: 'I, the Lord, have called you in righteousness; I will take hold of your hand. I will keep you *and will make you to be a covenant for the people and a light for the Gentiles, to open eyes that are blind, to free captives from prison and to release from the dungeon those who sit in darkness. I am the Lord; that is my name! I will not yield my glory to another or my praise to idols. See, the former things have taken place, and new things I declare; before they spring into being I announce them to you.'* (42:1–9)

"HERE IS MY SERVANT, whom I uphold, my chosen one in whom I delight; I will put my Spirit on him and he will bring justice to the nations. ... See the former things have taken place, and new things I declare; before they spring into being I announce them to you." (42:1, 9)

Remember our analogy of prophecy being like a mountain range? The peaks of the tallest mountains are visible, but we can't see the hills and valleys between them. Now we know in part, but one day we will understand it all. (1 Corinthians 13:12) This portion of Scripture continues to speak about the person God will select and (in later chapters) will name as the king He will use to send the Jews home from the exile to Babylon. Matthew directly quotes from this passage, saying that Jesus is the One Isaiah prophesied would come. (Matthew 12:17–21)

So we understand that Cyrus, the king God would call to send the Jews back from exile in Babylon, was a type or foreshadowing of the deeper fulfillment of this prophecy about Jesus, the Messiah. Cyrus set the people free from physical exile and imprisonment. Jesus set people free from bondage to sin and death. Verse 6 speaks of the chosen people of God as a light of truth to the Gentiles; we also understand it to speak of Jesus as the true light to the Gentiles.

Are you concerned about your future? Rest assured, God has chosen you, so He has a plan for you. Are you feeling weary in walking God's way? Take heart. God promises that He will uphold His servants. Are you in need of direction? Listen to the voice of the Spirit to discern His will. Are you restless in your spiritual walk and bored with the same old things? Get ready! God has new things, deeper things to show you if you will look to Him.

Prayer: Help me to look for the new things You have promised to send.

121

The Real Thing

Isaiah 42:1–9

YOU READ SOMETHING ON a social media site and you're shocked. Could that really be true? Then, someone gently points out that the post is a hoax. In our world, it's sometimes hard to discriminate between fake and real.

God's Word promised that Messiah would come, and many would lay claim to that title. So how would people be able to recognize the real Messiah? They needed to look to the words of the Lord found in the prophecies of Isaiah.

In Jesus' day, many Jews were expecting a Messiah who would overthrow Roman rule, re–establish their nation, and reign on the throne of David. But the Lord says of the Messiah, "He will not shout or cry out, or raise his voice in the streets." (42:2)

Unlike the false messiahs, Jesus did not call the people to rebel against the established earthly government. He did not incite riots or encourage people to violence. Instead, he sought to establish the Kingdom of God through a radical message of love and grace. The true Messiah taught about spiritual power, not worldly power. His intent was to defeat the spiritual enemy, not an earthly one.

Through Isaiah, the Lord said that the true Messiah would encourage the weak and strengthen the fallen. "A bruised reed he will not break, and a smoldering wick he will not snuff out." (42:3) When the Pharisees criticized Jesus for spending time with the tax collectors and sinners, He told them that He was there to minister to the sick, not the healthy. The typical false messiahs didn't waste their time with such weak people.

The real Messiah would come for the benefit of the whole world, not just Israel. God says, "I, the Lord, have called you in righteousness; I will take hold of your hand. I will keep you and will make you to be a covenant for the people and a light for the Gentiles, to open eyes that are blind, to free captives from prison and to release from the dungeon those who sit in darkness." (42:6–7)

Jesus came to establish the healing and justice of the Kingdom of Heaven. He came as a light to the Gentiles as well as the Jews. He brought a message of love, grace, and truth, and He died on a Cross so that we might live. Jesus was a radical departure from many people's expectations. But He was the true Messiah Isaiah prophesied. Our Deliverer is the genuine article.

Prayer: God help us to recognize the real Messiah and follow Him.

More Scripture: Philippians 2:5–11, Luke 5:27–3

122

The Call

Isaiah 42:5–7; 49:1–6

ISAIAH WROTE THE WORDS in these passages about himself, about the Messiah, and about all who are called of the Lord.

God seems to delight in the impossible. He takes the most unlikely people and molds them into His servants. Isaiah was a young man when he felt God's call to be a prophet. He was from a noble family, but there were no priests or prophets in his background, so many of the adults in Isaiah's life must have questioned his call. His parents probably hoped it was just a young man's passing fancy.

Being a prophet wasn't easy for Isaiah. In Chapter 49, he expressed his discouragement. "I said, 'I have labored in vain; I have spent my strength for nothing at all.'" Then God encouraged him by revealing Isaiah's role in His master plan: "And now the Lord says—he who formed me in the womb to be his servant to bring Jacob back to him and gather Israel to himself, for I am honored in the eyes of the Lord and my God has been my strength—he says: 'It is too small a thing for you to be my servant to restore the tribes of Jacob and bring back those of Israel I have kept. I will also make you a light for the Gentiles, that my salvation may reach the ends of the earth.'" (49:4, 5–6) Wow!

God seems to delight in the impossible. He used an unlikely couple as parents for His Son. Mary was a teenage girl, and Joseph was a humble carpenter. Mary trusted God when He said she would conceive by the Holy Spirit and give birth to a Savior. Joseph obeyed God and took Mary as his wife, despite her condition and all the criticism that would be leveled against him.

God seems to delight in the impossible. Are you one of the unlikely people called to be His servant? Of course you are! All you have to do is trust and obey God, and He will fill your mouth with His words and guide your feet on the right path.

Prayer: Lord, it seems impossible that I could be one
who is called. But you have said so, and I
believe it. Use me.

123

Sing and Shout and Clap

Sing to the Lord a new song, his praise from the ends of the earth, you who go down to the sea, and all that is in it, you islands, and all who live in them. Let the wilderness and its towns raise their voices; let the settlements where Kedar lives rejoice. Let the people of Sela sing for joy; let them shout from the mountaintops. Let them give glory to the Lord and proclaim his praise in the islands. The Lord will march out like a champion, like a warrior he will stir up his zeal; with a shout he will raise the battle cry and will triumph over his enemies. (42:10–13)

HAVE YOU LOST YOUR zeal? Does it seem as if the fire of the Spirit has burned down to embers? Look at these words of Isaiah, and do exactly what he commands. Sing and shout to the Lord, even if you don't feel like it! Clap to the music. Just as a good game of pat–a–cake can calm a fussy baby, so can clapping in time to music raise our spirits.

I love attending The Salvation Army because when we sing our rousing praise songs, we clap along. As we do, we begin to feel joy in the Lord. Our actions are biblical: "Sing to the Lord a new song, his praise from the ends of the earth ... Let the people of Sela sing for joy; let them shout from the mountaintops. Let them give glory to the Lord and proclaim his praise ..." (42:10, 11–12) "Clap your hands, all you nations; shout to God with cries of joy." (Psalm 47:1) Even nature joins in praise to the Lord: "Let the rivers clap their hands, let the mountains sing together for joy ..." (Psalm 98:8) "You will go out in joy and be led forth in peace; the mountains and hills will burst into song before you, and all the trees of the field will clap their hands." (Isaiah 55:12)

Do you want the Lord to "march out like a champion" and triumph over your enemies? Do you want to renew your zeal and fan the flame of the Spirit within you? Shout His praise from the mountaintops. Give Him glory for the things He has done and for who He is. Burst into song! Be like the mountains and trees and clap your hands in total praise. Lift Him up and feel the joy of the Lord wash over you.

Prayer: Praise the Lord, O my soul. Let all that is within me praise His Holy Name.

More Scripture: Psalm 47

124

'I Will'

Isaiah 42:10–17

LOOK AT THE "I will" promises of God in this portion of
Scripture. "*I will* lay waste the mountains and hills and dry
up all their vegetation; *I will* turn rivers into islands and
dry up the pools. *I will* lead the blind by ways they have not
known, along unfamiliar paths *I will* guide them; *I will* turn
the darkness into light before them and make the rough
places smooth. These are the things *I will* do; *I will* not forsake them."

If God's people do not turn to idols, He promises, "I will
not forsake them." God promises to do what is necessary for
His people, including altering the landscape. Some people
would look at what God did and say, "Those things were going
to happen anyway because of a drought." People are always
looking to explain away God's miracles.

Scientists have offered theories about how the parting of
the Red Sea could have occurred. Some say a volcanic explo-

sion caused a tidal wave effect that pulled the water back. Others say that a strong, hurricane–force wind could have blown the water apart. But one thing no one can explain is the timing. Why did the water part just as millions of Israelites came to its edge? And why did the water come back together just as the Egyptians began to cross? With faith, I believe that God performed a miracle. He did that because He had to be true to Himself and His promises to bring His people out of Egypt and into the Promised Land. His main promise is the same one found in this passage from Isaiah: "I will not forsake them."

God will never forsake us—unless we forsake Him. God's people had to learn that lesson the hard way. But if we follow Him and do not harden our hearts through sin, this is His promise: "Never will I leave you; never will I forsake you." (Hebrews 13:5)

Prayer: God, help me to trust in Your promise.

125

Intercede for Your Nation

'Hear you deaf; look you blind, and see! ...
You have seen many things, but have paid
no attention; your ears are open, but you do
not listen.' It pleased the Lord for the sake
of His righteousness to make his law great
and glorious. But this is a people plundered
and looted, all of them are trapped in pits or
hidden away in prisons. They have become
plunder, with no one to rescue them; they
have been made loot, with no one to say,
'Send them back.' Which of you will listen to
this or pay close attention in time to come?
Who handed Jacob over to become loot,
and Israel to the plunderers? Was it not the
Lord, against whom we have sinned? For
they would not follow his ways; they did
not obey his law. So he poured out on them
His burning anger, the violence of war. It

enveloped them in flames, yet they did not understand; it consumed them, but they did not take it to heart. (42:18, 20–25)

IF YOU HAVE A call to be an intercessor for your nation or your community, your heart will burn with understanding as you read this Scripture.

God handed over His chosen and beloved people to the Assyrians and the Babylonians because His righteousness demanded it. God's chosen people had broken His law and flaunted their rebellion, both as a nation and as individuals. The leaders of the people, the priests, and the kings became corrupt. Both church and state leaders led the people to rebellion. God's righteousness demanded punishment.

We are on shaky ground in our day. Church and state leaders have failed, and corruption is rampant. How can we intercede for our nation? One of the best examples of a prayer on behalf of a people is found in Daniel 9. Daniel acknowledges the character and position of God. He then identifies and confesses the sins, both attitudes and actions, of his nation. He prays, " ... we have sinned and done wrong. We have been wicked and have rebelled; we have turned away from your commands and laws. We have not listened ... refusing to obey you." (Daniel 9:5–6, 11) Daniel was a righteous man who was known for his obedience to the Law and to God. Yet he realized that he had to count himself among the wicked people, just as Isaiah called himself a man of unclean lips who lived among unclean people. The most effective intercessors love and trust God and care for others enough to set aside their own claims to righteousness. In this true state of humility, they are able to pray for others.

Are you more righteous than Daniel or Isaiah? If these great men of God could humble themselves and pray, you surely should be able to follow their example.

Prayer: Lord God, I want to pray for my nation. Help me to first humbly confess my own sin.

126

Kinsman Redeemer

Isaiah 43:1–3

IN GENESIS 14 WE read of Abram acting as a kinsman redeemer for his nephew Lot. In Jewish tradition, a kinsman redeemer was a male relative who had the privilege and responsibility of coming to the aid of a family member who was in trouble or in need. We see this concept developed throughout Scripture, and it becomes a "type" or object lesson of the ultimate Kinsman Redeemer, Jesus.

To understand the idea of the kinsman redeemer a little better, look to the book of Ruth. When Naomi returned from Moab to Israel, she went back to claim her house and property in Bethlehem. Naomi's daughter–in–law, Ruth, a Moabite and the widow of Naomi's son, went to work gleaning in the fields, one of the few honorable jobs open to single women. Naomi asked Ruth whose field she had gleaned in that first day. Ruth told her it belonged to Boaz. Naomi recognized that

Boaz was a kinsman and a good man. She knew that God had provided a solution for them; he would act as a kinsman redeemer and marry Ruth.

The Lord Himself promised to act as a Kinsman Redeemer for His people in exile. To the people "plundered and looted," "trapped in pits or hidden way in prisons ... "with no one to rescue them," the Lord says, "Do not fear, for I have redeemed you; I have summoned you by name; you are mine." (42:22; 43:1)

Why would God care for these people He had rejected for their sin? He answers: "For I am the Lord Your God, the Holy One of Israel, your Savior." (43:3) In His time, God Himself would redeem His people, and His act of deliverance would show the world not only His love for His chosen people but also His own character and faithfulness.

This act of redemption was only a foretaste of the ultimate act of redemption for the "whosoever." All of us have been a people looted and plundered, in pits and in prison. God gave His Son, Jesus Christ, as a Kinsman Redeemer to ransom us from the sin that imprisons us. 1 Peter 1:18–19 reminds us that our redemption price was not silver and gold; it was the precious blood of Jesus.

Prayer: Thank You, Lord, for paying the ultimate price to redeem me.

127

Deliverer

Isaiah 43:1–13

"Do not fear, for I have redeemed you; I have summoned you by name; you are mine. When you pass through the waters, I will be with you; and when you pass through the rivers, they will not sweep over you. When you walk through the fire, you will not be burned; the flames will not set you ablaze. For I am the Lord your God, the Holy One of Israel, your Savior ... Do not be afraid, for I am with you ... I have revealed and saved and proclaimed ... No one can deliver out of my hand. When I act, who can reverse it?" (43:1–3, 5, 12, 13)

At the same time God is making a promise for His people's future, His words remind them of other times they had passed through the waters: when Noah and his family were rescued from the flood; when God opened the Red Sea for His people to escape from Egypt; when He opened the waters of the Jordan for the Israelites to pass into the Promised Land. They might also have been reminded of other occasions when

God allowed his prophets Elijah (2 Kings 2:8) and Elisha (2 Kings 2:14) to part the Jordan. Isaiah helps us to connect with the truth that the God of the past is also God of the present. If God did this before, He can do it again. God is faithful and we can trust Him to deliver us.

God claims the future with this promise: "When you walk through the fire, you will not be burned; the flames will not set you ablaze." (43:2) When we read this, we can't help but be reminded of an incident that took place years after God made this promise through Isaiah. In the time of the exile, three Jews—Shadrach, Meshach, and Abednego—refused to bow to an idol that King Nebuchadnezzar had set up. The king threw the men into a blazing furnace for their disobedience, but God protected them from the heat and flames. Their clothes did not smell like smoke and not a hair on their bodies was singed. (Daniel 3) Isaiah's promise was for these men, and for us as well. We can be assured that when we go through fiery trials, the Lord will protect us, and we will not be burned.

" 'Do not be afraid, for I am with you. ... I have revealed and saved and proclaimed ... You are my witnesses,' declares the Lord, 'that I am God. Yes, and from ancient days I am he. No one can deliver out of my hand. When I act, who can reverse it?' " (43:5, 12–13)

Prayer: I trust You, Lord, to be with me and deliver me.

128

Sovereignty

Isaiah 43:1–13

OUR CLEAR UNDERSTANDING FROM the New Testament is
that God sent Jesus to die for "whosoever" will come. Yet here
we read in black and white that God gave preference to His
chosen people. A quick glance at the Old Testament reveals
that God seemed to play favorites. He honored Abel's sacrifice over Cain's. He chose Noah and his family to survive the
flood. He chose Abram and Sarai to be the father and mother
of nations. He chose Jacob over Esau. Out of all the baby boys
marked for death by the Egyptians, God chose Moses to survive. Jesus seemed to play favorites too. He chose 12 men to
serve as His closest disciples and three out of the 12 as His
closest friends.

God's ways don't always seem fair, and that causes many
people to stumble in their faith. But we must accept that
He knows what He's doing, and that His perspective is very
different from our own. Consider this as a simple example.

A toddler sees her brother eating a peanut butter cookie. It looks better than the oatmeal cookie she has, so she asks for one. But her dad knows that she is allergic to peanuts and refuses her request. She cries that it's unfair for her sibling to have something she can't have. Finally, she stops sobbing and accepts her dad's decision. She doesn't understand, but she knows her dad loves her.

Do you have questions about God that seem to have no answers? Have you taken an earnest request before Him, but He seems to be answering no? Or providing no answer at all? When we're confused about what the Lord is up to or even angry at Him, *we must trust what we know about God,* that He is sovereign and knows what is best. Even when life seems unfair, we must stand back in awe and recognize Him for who He is. " 'Before me no god was formed, nor will there be one after me. I, even I, am the Lord, and apart from me there is no savior. I have revealed and saved and proclaimed—I, and not some foreign god among you. You are my witnesses,' declares the Lord, 'that I am God. Yes, and from ancient days I am he. No one can deliver out of my hand. When I act, who can reverse it?' " (43:10–13)

Prayer: God, there are some things in life that don't seem fair. Give me wisdom to know when to keep pleading for answers and when to simply surrender in faith.

129

Names for God

Isaiah 43:1–13

LOOK AT ALL OF the names for God and the descriptions of
God's nature used in this passage. Here are a few things we
can learn about God from this list:

- "The Lord" signifies majesty.

- "He who created you" connotes preeminence and
  loving care.

- "I have redeemed" implies that there is a pur-
  chase price.

- "I am the Lord your God" declares sovereignty
  and relationship.

- "The Holy One of Israel" confirms a covenant and
  reveals God's purity.

- "Your Savior" proclaims His desire and power to

rescue.

- "I am with you" establishes hope.

- "Everyone who is called by my name" implies ownership and kinship.

- "I am he" discloses His transcendent glory. This was the answer given to Moses when he asked God for His name.

- "Before me no god was formed, nor will there be one after me" states His exclusive claim as God and His eternal nature.

- "I, even I, am the Lord" announces His unique supremacy beyond question.

- "I have revealed and saved and proclaimed" describes God's actions on behalf of humanity.

- "From ancient days I am he" affirms God's constancy.

- "No one can deliver out of my hand" establishes God's invincible might and trustworthiness.

- "When I act, who can reverse it?" certifies God's omnipotence and control.

What other lessons have you learned about God from this passage? Make your own list.

Prayer: Help me to know more about You each day, Lord.

130

Symmetry

Isaiah 43:14–21

LOOK AT THE SYMMETRY of Isaiah 43. In verse 1, God promises deliverance from exile to His chosen people; then in verse 14, He promises exile to their enemies. In both sections, God reminds His people of the past. He is the One who made a way for them through the Red Sea in their exodus from Egypt. Now He promises to make a way for them through the desert in their exodus from Babylon.

This is a good time to look at the book of Ezra. Isaiah, as a prophet, was a receptor of visions of the future sent to him by God. Ezra, Nehemiah, Zerubbabel, Joshua, and those who returned to Jerusalem from Babylon were people who believed in and envisioned the fulfillment of God's promises. "Ezra had devoted himself to the study and observance of the Law of the Lord, and to teaching its decrees and laws in Israel." (Ezra 7:10) He was the one chosen by God to lead His people out of Babylonian exile and back to Jerusalem. Ezra wrote:

"I proclaimed a fast, so that we might humble ourselves before our God and ask him for a safe journey for us and our children, with all our possessions. I was ashamed to ask the king for soldiers and horsemen to protect us from enemies on the road, because we had told the king, 'The gracious hand of our God is on everyone who looks to him, but his great anger is against all who forsake him.' So we fasted and petitioned our God about this, and he answered our prayer." (Ezra 8:21–23)

Ezra believed that God would make a way for His people through the desert and deliver them, so he didn't ask King Artaxerxes for soldiers and horsemen to protect them. Could it be that he was claiming the very promises of God for deliverance found in Isaiah 43?

Look at what Ezra did to prepare himself and the people to act on God's promises. First, he dedicated himself to the study of Scripture. Second, he lived a holy life modeled after the commands of God. Third, he boldly proclaimed the Word of God, teaching others and calling the people to fast and pray. In doing so, he got them to rely on God instead of a pagan army for their protection. The exiles faced dangers from nature and from bandits on the desert journey home. Yet God was faithful to deliver them.

Do you feel as if you are in a wasteland, a wilderness of trials? God promises to make a way. He says, "See, I am doing a new thing. Now it springs up; do you not perceive it?" (43:19)

Prayer: Lord, make a way for me as You did for Your chosen people.

131

Give God His Due

Isaiah 43:14–28

THE IRONY OF THE comparisons made in this portion of Scripture still rings true today. God promised He would deliver His people from exile. He reminded them of their deliverance from Egypt by " ... a path through the mighty waters." (43:16) It is good to call to mind what God has done for us in the past. But we shouldn't dwell there. God told His people to forget those "former things" because He was about to do "a new thing ... making a way in the wilderness and streams in the wasteland." (43:19)

Yet, unlike the wild animals of the desert that recognized God and gave Him praise for His provision, His people were not calling on Him or honoring Him. Worse, they were burdening God with their sins and wearying Him with their offenses.

Is the Lord talking about the people of Isaiah's day or the people who would live for 70 years in exile in Babylon? Perhaps it's both.

In the ancient days of the Tabernacle and the Temple, people acknowledged God by bringing sacrifices and offerings. A constant offering of incense symbolized their prayers. The priests tended the incense as the faithful prayed and interceded on behalf of their nation. The people brought their grain and animal offerings and gathered as a community to acknowledge God as their Sovereign, to praise Him for His provision, and to confess their sins and repent.

When the Temple was destroyed and the people were taken into exile, the sacrifices and offerings ceased. However, there were faithful people who still prayed and fasted as they called on the Lord for deliverance. But even the faithful remnant shrank in size as people became busy with things other than worshiping God. The Lord needed the faithful to intercede for and prepare the others to receive His promises. Who would have ears to hear and eyes to see? Who would have hearts to understand and begin to pray?

God created the world and everyone in it. He loves all people and has provided deliverance for all. However, many are still living in exile in the kingdom of Satan. God calls us who know Him to intercede and pray for those people so that they will be ready to recognize God and receive His good promises. Will you have eyes that see the need? Will you have ears to hear God calling you to pray? Have an obedient heart. Ask God to show you for whom He wants you to pray and how He wants you to do it. God may call you to pray for criminals in and out of prison. He may call you to intercede on behalf of children and teenagers tempted to join gangs or to try drugs. God may call you to pray for a specific people group such as

Hindus or Muslims. Is God calling you to walk in your neighborhood and pray for the people who live there?

Prayer: Lord, give me a heart for those who do not
yet know You and for those who have known
You but have turned away.

132

Chosen of God

Isaiah 44:1–5

WHEN I WAS IN junior high school, the physical education teacher would often appoint two captains to "choose up" teams. I was not the best player in any sport and would often end up one of the last to be chosen. The most painful experience was being the absolute last person put on a team because that meant I was really not chosen at all. When you are chosen, you feel worthy. When you are not, you feel like a leftover. You feel worthless.

When humans choose people to be on their team, they choose their friends and they choose the most skilled at the game. They choose because they want to win. God chooses differently. "God chose the foolish things of the world to shame the wise; God chose the weak things of the world to shame the strong. God chose the lowly things of this world and the despised things—and the things that are not—to nullify the things that are, so that no one may boast before him." (1

Corinthians 1:27–29) God chose Moses, an 80–year–old shepherd and murderer, to deliver His people from bondage. God chose David, the youngest brother, over all his older, stronger, and better–looking brothers. God chose Paul, a persecutor of Christians, to be His emissary to the Gentiles.

In this day of grace, because of Jesus' sacrifice, God still chooses and uses ordinary people. As we respond in faith to God's call, Jesus becomes "the captain of our salvation." (Hebrews 2:10 *NKJV)* When we join God's team, we are winners. But we don't boast about that. Instead, all we can do is "boast in the Lord." (1 Corinthians 1:31)

When a man and a woman fall in love, they choose to belong to each other in the bonds of marriage. One may take the other's surname or the couple might combine their surnames to signify their commitment to one another. In Western culture, we wear wedding rings as an outward sign of that commitment. "Some will say, 'I belong to the Lord'; others will call themselves by the name of Jacob; still others will write on their hand, 'The Lord's,' and will take the name Israel." (44:5) As the Lord's chosen, we take His name. By the way we live our lives, we show that we belong to Him. And we know that our names are written on the palm of His hand.

Are you living as the chosen of God or as one of the world's leftovers? Beloved of God, wear His name like the winner you are.

Prayer: Oh, God help me to choose to live for You
each day of my life.

133

I AM

'This is what the Lord says—Israel's King and Redeemer, the Lord Almighty: I am the first and I am the last; apart from me there is no God. ... This is what the Lord says—your Redeemer, who formed you in the womb: I am the Lord, the Maker of all things, who stretches out the heavens, who spreads out the earth by myself ... ' (44:6, 24)

THE NAME OF GOD, "I Am," has rich meaning. The word *I* is the *first* person pronoun. God is the First, the Creator, the Original. The word *am* denotes being or existence. God is the origin of existence. He is the First and the Last. This is a lesson humankind has great difficulty comprehending. From the 3–year–old who has a million and one questions about life to the scientist who devotes herself to discovering the origins of the universe, we all need to come to a point where faith supersedes all doubt. It must be enough to accept that God is the Great I Am.

"Now faith is confidence in what we hope for and assurance about what we do not see. ... By faith we understand that the universe was formed at God's command, so that what is seen was not made out of what was visible. ... And without faith it is impossible to please God, because anyone who comes to him must believe that he exists and that he rewards those who earnestly seek Him." (Hebrews 11:1, 3, 6)

Jesus claims the "I Am" title numerous times in the book of John: as the Bread of Life; the Light of the World; the Gate for the Sheep; the Good Shepherd; the Resurrection and the Life; the Way, the Truth, and the Life; and the True Vine. When the woman at the Samaritan well speaks of the coming Messiah, Jesus says, "I, the one speaking to you, I am he." He even says, echoing His Father, " ... before Abraham was born, I am!" (John 8:58) The Jewish hearers of Jesus' day would have clearly understood the claim He was making. Some considered it blasphemy and thought He should be stoned to death. Others recognized Jesus as the Messiah.

In Colossians, Paul says of Jesus, "He is before all things, and in him all things hold together." (1:17) In Revelation, Jesus Himself says, "I am the Alpha and the Omega, the First and the Last, the Beginning and the End." (22:13)

Jesus, as a manifestation of the Three in One, shows us God, the great I Am. God reminded His people in the day of Isaiah and reminds us today that He alone is worthy of our worship and our praise. In Him, we can find all we need.

Prayer: Lord God, You are the First and Last in my life.

More Scripture: Exodus 3:13–15; Colossians 1:15–20; Revelation 1:8, 17

134

Wooden Gods

Isaiah 44:9–20

"THOUGH THEY KNEW GOD, they did not honor him as God or give thanks to him, but they became futile in their thinking, and their senseless minds were darkened. Claiming to be wise, they became fools; and they exchanged the glory of the immortal God for images resembling a mortal human being or birds or four–footed animals or reptiles." (Romans 1:21–23 *NRSV)*

As you read these verses of Isaiah 44, try to catch the irony and humor in his words. The carpenter cuts down trees to use as fuel, to warm himself, to bake bread and roast meat. But out of that same wood that can be burned to cinders, he " ... fashions a god and worships it; he makes an idol and bows down to it." He prays to this wood, " 'Save me! You are my god!' ... No one stops to think, no one has knowledge or understanding to say, 'Half of it I used for fuel; I even baked bread over its coals, I roasted meat and ate. Shall I make a detestable thing from what is left? Shall I bow down to a block of wood?' Such a person feeds on ashes; a deluded heart misleads him … " (44:15, 17, 19–20)

When Moses went up to the mountain for 40 days to meet with God, Aaron took it upon himself to have a golden calf made for the people to worship. The people couldn't even wait 40 days for God without turning to something else to worship. Throughout Scripture, we see the people of God mixing with pagan culture and creating gods for themselves.

Such idol worship brought the judgment of God. We don't like to think about that. But God is just and holy. He holds us accountable for our sin, which separates us from His love. Ultimately, Jesus will judge all humanity and separate the sheep from the goats, the wheat from the chaff.

God is grieved when we worship anything but Him. He loves us, but He can't stand sin. Because He is holy, He simply can't abide it.

I'm sure you are not carving out wooden idols to worship. But is there anything or anyone in your life—including your-self—that you have bowed down to, that has become the lord of your life? If you have, your "deluded heart" is misleading you. Look to the Lord Jesus. He alone can save.

Prayer: Lord, open my eyes to see if I have placed anyone or anything above You.

135

I Have Redeemed You

'Remember these things, Jacob, for you, Israel, are my servant. I have made you, you are my servant; Israel, I will not forget you. I have swept away your offenses like a cloud, your sins like the morning mist. Return to me, for I have redeemed you.' Sing for joy, you heavens, for the Lord has done this; shout aloud, you earth beneath. Burst into song, you mountains, you forests and all your trees, for the Lord has redeemed Jacob, he displays his glory in Israel. (44:21–23)

THESE VERSES, FOLLOWING GOD'S condemnation of idol worship, paint a wonderful word picture of the enduring, redeeming love that God has for His people. He says, "I have made you ... I will not forget you." (44:21) Then He makes this amazing statement: "I have swept your offenses away like a cloud, like the morning mist." (44:22) Isn't it wonderful to know that when God forgives, He forgets? Our sins evaporate before Him like clouds, like the morning mist, and we can live in the sunlight of blamelessness, of righteousness. "For he chose us in him before the creation of the world to be holy and blameless in his sight." (Ephesians 1:4)

The Lord implores His people, "Return to me, for I have redeemed you." (44:22) Why do the people need to be invited in this way? Isn't it sometimes true that even though our sins are forgiven, we don't always immediately turn back to God? I think that sometimes we are reluctant to believe that our shame could really be completely gone. We still have an instinct to hide our faces from Him. But we need not do that! The Lord invites us, like the father of the Prodigal Son, "Return to me, for I have redeemed you."

We should rejoice that God loves us this much. "Sing for joy, you heavens, for the Lord has done this; shout aloud, you earth beneath. Burst into song, you mountains, you forests and all your trees, for the Lord has redeemed Jacob, he displays His glory in Israel." (44:23) And in us.

Prayer: I sing for joy that you have forgiven my
sins and made me blameless once more.
Hallelujah!

136

There Is No Other

'I am the Lord, and there is no other ... '
(45:5)

THE FIRST 14 VERSES of Chapter 45 are an address to King Cyrus, who, at the time of this writing, had not even been born. In verses 5, 6, 14, 18, and 22 of this chapter, the Lord introduces Himself to Cyrus and adds these words: " ... and there is no other ... " God offers further important assurances as well.

Verse 5 declares, "I will strengthen you ... " God is all–powerful.

Verse 6 teaches that when God strengthens someone, it is for a purpose " ... so that from the rising of the sun to the place of its setting people may know that there is none beside me." God is the one true God.

Verse 14 promises that Cyrus's enemies will be subdued. "They will bow down before you and plead with you, saying, 'Surely God is with you, and there is no other ...'" Whoever has God as champion cannot be defeated.

Verse 18 teaches Cyrus that the Lord formed the Earth and everything in it. God is Creator.

Verse 22 implores Cyrus—and all people—"Turn to me and be saved, all you ends of the earth." God is Savior. This passage foreshadows the One who provides salvation for the whole world. "For God so loved the world that he gave his one and only Son, that whoever believes in him shall not perish but have eternal life." (John 3:16)

God made these proclamations to a pagan king whom He would use to accomplish His purposes. Imagine what He will do for those who have turned to Him for salvation. The Lord is on your side, so you can trust that victory is assured.

Prayer: You are the Lord of my life, and there is no other. Thank you that I can depend on You for victory.

137

Authority Figures

Isaiah 45:1–6

EVEN THOUGH KING CYRUS would not acknowledge God, God would give him power, treasures, and strength. God would do these things "For the sake of Jacob my servant, of Israel my chosen ... " (45:4) and to show that He is the one true God.

Scripture teaches repeatedly that even evil rulers who do not acknowledge God can still serve His purposes. Think about Pharaoh in the book of Exodus and Nebuchadnezzar in the book of Daniel. In the New Testament, the Caesars and even the leaders of the Sanhedrin were against Jesus and the Apostle Paul, but God worked through their opposition to accomplish His plan.

Scripture also teaches that we should submit to those governing us and lift them up in prayer. Paul writes to Timothy, urging " ... that petitions, prayers, intercession and thanksgiving be made for all people—for kings and all those in authority, that we may live peaceful and quiet lives in all godliness and holiness." (1 Timothy 2:1–2)

Paul commands the Christians living in Rome, "Let everyone be subject to the governing authorities, for there is no authority except that which God has established." If we rebel against authority, then, we are rebelling against God. He says that rulers "hold no terror" for those who do right, but for those who do wrong. Christians, he says, should pay taxes, respect, and honor to those who rule over them. (Romans 13:1–7)

No matter who has earthly control, the Lord asserts that He has ultimate control. When Pontius Pilate said to Jesus, " 'Don't you realize I have power either to free you or crucify you?' Jesus answered, 'You would have no power over me if it were not given to you from above.' " (John 19:10–11)

So God is in control. We know that. But are there times when rebellion against authority is called for? During the Civil War, Quakers set up stations along the Underground Railroad for people escaping slavery. During World War 2, Christian leader Dietrich Bonhoeffer engaged in a plot to kill Adolf Hitler because he believed evil would triumph if he stood by and did nothing. He took action after much prayer and was hanged when the plot was discovered.

The rule is that we should submit to authority—unless that authority asks us to break the laws of God. Presidents, prime ministers, governors, mayors, bosses, and pastors—all people in positions of leadership—are there by either God's direct will or His permissive will. We are bound to respect their authority and pray for them. Are you in conflict with a person in a position of authority? Pray for that person and submit, out of reverence for the Lord. If the person's orders or actions go against the law of God, seek His will and ask Him to direct you as to what you should do.

Prayer: Lord, touch parents, teachers, people in government, law enforcement officers, employers, property owners, and pastors and cause them to be just, fair, and wise.

138

Holy Witness

Isaiah 45:22–25

"BY MYSELF I HAVE sworn, my mouth has uttered in all integrity a word that will not be revoked: Before me every knee will bow; by me every tongue will swear. They will say of me, 'In the Lord alone are deliverance and strength.' " (45:23–24)

God swears by Himself. He does not need any other witness. Yet He does provide them. God called upon the heavens and the Earth to be witnesses in His case against His children. (Isaiah 1:2) He provided the Law to stand as a witness against rebellion. He would send two very important witnesses, Jesus and the Holy Spirit, to testify to His sovereignty and saving power. And Jesus said to the Pharisees who argued that He couldn't appear as His own witness: "In your own Law it is written that the testimony of two witnesses is true. I am one who testifies for myself; my other witness is the Father, who sent me." (John 8:13, 18)

God says through Isaiah: "Before me every knee will

bow; by me every tongue will swear." (45:23) Once again, the prophet's words foreshadow the coming of Jesus. Listen to the echo in this passage about Him: " ... he made himself nothing by taking the very nature of a servant ... he humbled himself by becoming obedient to death—even death on a cross! Therefore God exalted him to the highest place and gave him the name that is above every name, that at the name of Jesus every knee should bow, in heaven and on earth and under the earth, and every tongue acknowledge that Jesus Christ is Lord, to the glory of God the Father." (Philippians 2:7, 8–11)

After we are saved, we wait for the final witness, the Holy Spirit, to fill us with the same power that Jesus had when He was on Earth. When we are anointed with that power, Jesus said, " ... you will be my witnesses ... to the ends of the earth." We are called to be the means by which God's invitation, given through Isaiah, is extended: "Turn to me and be saved, all you ends of the earth ... " (45:22)

Prayer: Lord, empower me by your Spirit to be a
witness for You.

More Scripture: John 8:12–18, 1 John 5:7–10

139

Carry Me

Isaiah 46

I REMEMBER WHEN I finally realized that I was too big for Daddy to carry me. I lifted my arms to indicate that I wanted him to lift me up. He said: "Sweetness, you are just too big for me to carry anymore. You need to walk." My older sister smiled knowingly, but I was upset. This was a crisis time for me. I couldn't accept the fact that Daddy had limitations. Surely my daddy the hero could do anything. So the questions came: Was I too fat? Didn't Daddy love me anymore? Then I reasoned that there were just too many of us kids, that my daddy could not carry all of us, so to be fair, he had to stop carrying me. It was a sobering realization for a 3–year–old.

I felt security in being carried by someone bigger and stronger. I felt safe, cared for, and most of all, I felt loved. Even though I am an adult, I still need to be carried. God knows this. Chapter 46 of Isaiah speaks of a God who has no limitations. He is our Maker, our Parent, our Sustainer, and the One who carries us.

Do you catch the irony of this chapter? Bel and Nebo are Babylonian gods, and the people and their beasts of burden become weary carrying the images, the idols, of those gods. The gods "stoop low," but they can't relieve the people of their burdens. (46:1) Even God's own people—"you rebels"—make an idol of gold or silver to worship, and they have to lift it to a place of honor, a place from which it cannot move on its own. But as much as they cry out to their idol, it " ... cannot answer; it cannot save them from their troubles." (46:6–8) The idols and false gods we make to give us the security and love we crave cannot carry us or answer us. The one true God who can carry us is also the One who will respond to us when we cry out to Him.

" 'Listen to me, you descendants of Jacob, all the remnant of the people of Israel, you whom I have upheld since your birth, and have carried since you were born. Even to your old age and gray hairs I am he, I am he who will sustain you. I have made you and I will carry you; I will sustain you and I will rescue you.' " (46:3–4)

Do you hunger for security and love? Turn to God. He will hear your cries and He will carry you.

Prayer: Lord, help me to remember the assurance
of 1 Peter 5:7: "Cast all your care upon Him,
because He cares for you." *(MEV)*

140

The Bigger They Are

Isaiah 47

THE BIGGER THEY ARE, the harder they fall. So the proverb goes. It came true for Babylon. Long before it rose to the
height of its power, God spoke through Isaiah and told of
its fall. God would use the kings of Babylon to accomplish
His purposes in the lives of His people. He would allow the
Babylonians to destroy Jerusalem and carry the Jews off into
captivity. Yet even as God allowed this to happen, He would
still weep for His beloved people when He saw how their captors treated them.

God says through Isaiah, "I was angry with my people and
desecrated my inheritance; I gave them into your hand, and
you showed no mercy." (47:6)

This oppression would not last forever. The city of Babylon
is likened to a haughty virgin queen who, because of God's
wrath, would no longer be called "tender and delicate." "Lift
up your skirts, bare your legs, and wade through the streams.

Your nakedness will be exposed and your shame uncovered. I will take vengeance; I will spare no one." (47:1, 2)

Ironically, the Lord says that Babylon had considered herself the "eternal" queen who had said to herself, "I am, and there is none beside me." (47:7, 10) There is a sardonic echo here of God's own words, repeated over and over in Isaiah 45: "I am the Lord, and there is no other." Only the one true God can make such claims!

This passage speaks to us of arrogance, of thinking that we are so in control of our own lives that nothing can touch us, no matter what we do. This queen city went so far as to indulge in sorceries and spells. God says, "You have trusted in your wickedness and have said, 'No one sees me.' " That kind of pridefulness and waywardness brings disaster. The Lord says, "A calamity will fall upon you that you cannot ward off with a ransom; a catastrophe you cannot foresee will suddenly come upon you." God taunts this queen, telling her to go on with her sorceries and call out her astrologers and stargazers to save her. But He knows they can't do that. "Surely they are like stubble; the fire will burn them up. They cannot even save themselves from the power of the flame." Ultimately, God says to Babylon, " ... there is not one that can save you." (46:10, 11, 13–14)

Babylon's leaders arrogantly thought they were untouchable, that they were, as we often say of large businesses, "too big to fail." They trusted in their false gods, in magic, and in their own power. We must never turn to anything or anyone else but God for answers. We must not be tempted to think that we are in control. Remember the old proverb, as it is stated in Scripture: "Pride goes before destruction, a haughty spirit before a fall." (Proverbs 16:18)

Prayer: Lord, keep me from prideful thinking.

141

Refining Fire of Affliction

Isaiah 48

WHAT DO YOU DO with people who give lip–service to obedience? God says that His people had sworn by Him and invoked His name, "but not in truth or righteousness." God had given His people fair warning, telling them what would happen if they continued in their own way, but then He was forced to act. "For I knew how stubborn you were; your neck muscles were iron, your forehead was bronze." (48:1–4) Have you ever been that stiff–necked, refusing to go the way God wants you to go because you thought you knew best?

The Lord's people would be sent into exile. Even then, He would show restraint: "For my own name's sake I delay my wrath; for the sake of my praise I hold it back from you, so as not to destroy you completely." God refined His people in "the furnace of affliction" just as silver is refined in fire. God reminds His people who He is, the One who is the First and the Last, who laid the foundations of the earth. Yet His people continued to worship idols. "Come together, all of you and listen: Which of the idols has foretold these things?" (48:9–10, 14)

The Lord laments that His people have not listened to Him: "I am the Lord your God, who teaches you what is best for you, who directs you in the way you should go. If only you had paid attention to my commands, your peace would have been like a river, your well–being like the waves of the sea." (48:17–18)

Would you rather experience the refining fire of affliction or peace like a river? God has amazing patience with us, even when our neck muscles are like iron with stubbornness, even when we willfully stray from Him. But how much better it would be for us if we would truly hear His voice, completely surrender to His will, and say, "I'm in his hands, I'm in his hands,/Whate'er the future holds/I'm in his hands./The days I cannot see/Have all been planned for me;/His way is best, you see;/I'm in his hands." *(The Song Book of The Salvation Army,* #848)

Prayer: Lord, help me to yield to Your will in all
             things.

142

Faithful When No One Listens: Servant Song 2

Isaiah 49:1–13

PASTORS GIVE SERMON AFTER sermon and the words seem to fall on deaf ears. Teachers give lesson after lesson and no one seems to learn. The cry comes: "Why, God? Why am I wasting my time and Your words on these people? They are no different now than they were when I started." Then God gives the assurance: "You be obedient to the task I have given you. I will take care of the results. I will reward your faithfulness in My time."

When Isaiah started his prophetic ministry, God warned him that his words would fall on deaf ears, and that his message would not change the fate of the nation. However, God expected Isaiah to obey. Isaiah's words were important to the people of his day, and they were even more important to the people of the future. "It is too small a thing for you to be my servant to restore the tribes of Jacob and bring back those of Israel I have kept. I will also make you a light for the Gentiles, that my salvation may reach to the ends of the earth." (49:6) This word from the Lord applies not only to the prophet Isaiah but also to Jesus, the servant Lord.

Isaiah's prophecies would one day be honored and taken to heart: "In the time of my favor I will answer you, and in the day of salvation I will help you ... " (49:8) Isaiah's words—through Jesus—would bring salvation, restoration, and freedom for those dwelling in darkness. Jesus sent His disciples to be His witnesses to the ends of the Earth (Acts 1:8), and the Gospel has indeed been carried around the world. "Shout for joy, you heavens; rejoice, you earth; burst into song, you mountains! For the Lord comforts his people and will have compassion on his afflicted ones." (49:13)

Be faithful and obedient to the call God has given you. What you are doing may seem sometimes like a waste of your time and God's resources, but God will take care of the results. Even the Lord Jesus wept over Jerusalem and pleaded with His Father in Gethsemane to take the cup from Him. But He submitted Himself to His Father's will, and the way was opened, through His death and resurrection, for all of us to live in freedom.

God called His servants Isaiah and Jesus to proclaim His Word. God also called you, even before you were born, to do His will. Trust Him to bring about the results. Like the heroes of faith in Hebrews 11, you may not see them right away, or even in your lifetime. But your job is to remain obedient and to trust in God.

Prayer: God, help me be faithful to preach and teach Your Word even when it seems to fall on deaf ears.

143

I Love You More Than ...

Isaiah 49:14–26

WHEN I WAS LITTLE, our family had a love language. My mom would say something like, "I love you more than 'taters.'" Then she would give me a hug. I was raised with the need to know not just *that* I was loved but also how *much* I was loved. After I was married, I found myself using the same kind of love language with my husband, only in reverse. I would ask him how much he loved me. This confused him at first, but soon he caught on. He would say, "I love you more than all the raindrops in Seattle."

How much does God love His people? The Bible is full of God's love language to us. Look at what the Lord says in this passage: "Can a mother forget the baby at her breast and have no compassion on the child she has borne? Though she may forget, I will not forget you! See I have engraved you on the palms of my hands ... " (49:15–16)

God compares His love for His people to that of a mother

for a baby. It is said that there are few bonds stronger than those between a mother and her child. Human mothers are often compared to a protective mother bear that ferociously defends her cub. It is not a wise thing to get between a mother bear and her cub or between a human mother and her child. Yet even a mother's love is not as great as God's love for us!

The other word picture in this passage is of an engraving of God's people on the palms of His hands. An engraving is not simply a tattoo; it is a cut that becomes a scar. How could God ever forget how much He loves us when all He has to do is look at the scars on His hands?

God goes even further with His love language. He says He will bless His people with children born in their bereavement over their exile. Those sons and daughters will have kings for "foster fathers" and queens for "nursing mothers." God loves His people so fiercely that He will " ... contend with those who contend with you ... " until all people know " ... that I, the Lord, am your Savior, your Redeemer, the Mighty One of Jacob." (49:20, 23, 25, 26)

How much does God love you? It's far more than "taters," or raindrops in Seattle, or the love of a mother for her baby. He loves you so much that He has engraved your name on the palm of His hand. He loves you so much that He will bless you beyond measure. He loves you so much that He will fight for you against anyone and anything.

Thought: I asked the Lord how much He loved me, and He opened His hands to show me the nail prints.

144

The Long Arm of God

Isaiah 50:1–3, 10–11

THE PEOPLE OF JUDAH felt abandoned, and that they had been "sold" by God because of their sins. They wondered if God could help them and if He even still cared enough to help. Their land was in a battle zone between the great powers. Daily they lost ground as the borders of their beloved nation shrank. Where was the God of Abraham, Isaac, and Jacob? Where was the God of Moses, Joshua, David, and Solomon? Where was the great I Am who had worked wonders in the past to deliver His people?

God had not abandoned them; they had abandoned Him. When the people began worshiping other gods and trusting in their own might, the nation as a whole turned their back on God and broke their covenant relationship with Him.

God continued to uphold His part of the covenant long after the people dissolved their part of it. He continued to try to help, but He got no response. "When I came, why was there no one? When I called, why was there no one to answer? Was my arm too short to deliver you? Do I lack the strength to rescue you?" (50:2) God was asking His people, "Why do you doubt my power? Why do you put your trust in other gods, and even in human beings?"

We often walk through dark times. Sometimes we bring them on ourselves by wrong decisions or "in–your–face" rebellion. Sometimes the darkness descends because of the actions of others. Always, God gives us the choice to trust in Him to redeem the situation. "Who among you fears the Lord and obeys the word of his servant? Let the one who walks in the dark, who has no light, trust in the name of the Lord and rely on their God." (50:10)

God also allows us the freedom to "light our own fires," to trust our own "flaming torches" to guide us. But He warns us that this choice leads to destruction. "But now, all you who light fires and provide yourselves with flaming torches, go, walk in the light of your fires and of the torches you have set ablaze. This is what you shall receive from my hand: You will lie down in torment." (50:11) Extinguish those torches and let God be the Light to guide you!

Prayer: God help me to realize that You have not abandoned me. Help me trust in You to lead me through the dark places. Please deliver me!

More Scripture: Genesis 3, Psalm 23, John 1:1–9

145

Unashamed and Unafraid:
Servant Song 3

Isaiah 50:4–11

"BECAUSE THE SOVEREIGN LORD helps me, I will not be disgraced. Therefore I have set my face like flint, and I know I will not be put to shame." (50:7)

This Scripture reveals that God's servant would suffer. Because we live in this time of Grace, we understand that this passage refers to Isaiah; to the Messiah, Jesus; and to all God's faithful servants.

First, it applies to Isaiah, a servant and prophet of God. When a prophet has to obey God and deliver bad news, rejection and persecution inevitably follow. Isaiah was not an exception to the rule: he suffered scorn and physical abuse. Tradition records that Isaiah was even martyred for delivering God's message.

Second, it applies to the Messiah. These words from Isaiah (50:6) are mirrored in the Gospels: "I offered my back to those who beat me, my cheeks to those who pulled out my beard; I did not hide my face from mocking and spitting." Jesus obeyed God to the point of giving His life for others. From the Cross, Jesus prayed for those who persecuted and mocked Him. "Father, forgive them, for they do not know what they are doing." (Luke 23:34) The people who had cried out, "Crucify him! Crucify him!" were the very people He came to save. (Luke 23:21)

Third, it applies to every servant of God who brings a message from God that people don't want to hear. Stand firm in the Truth, even when the people who need to hear your message turn on you. God may choose to deliver you from your enemies. However, God may choose to deliver you *to* your enemies so that a greater good may come. Ultimately, God will deliver us from all evil. "Who among you fears the Lord and obeys the word of his servant? Let him who walks in the dark, who has no light, trust in the name of the Lord and rely on his God." (50:10) Say with Isaiah, "It is the Sovereign Lord who helps me. Who will condemn me? They will all wear out like a garment; the moths will eat them up." (50:9)

Prayer: Lord, help me to remain faithful to proclaim
Your Word even when it could mean rejection—
and so much more.

More Scripture: Psalm 56

146

Look for the Names of the Lord

Isaiah 51

LOOK AT SOME OF the names and descriptions of God found in this passage. Did I miss any?

- Multiplier: " ... I blessed [Abraham] and made him many." (v. 2)

- Loving One: " ... [The Lord] will look with compassion ... " (v. 3)

- Teacher: "Instruction will go out from me ... " (v. 4)

- Righteous One: "My righteousness draws near speedily ... " (v. 5)

- Savior: " ... my salvation is on the way ... " (v. 5)

- Judge: " ... my arm will bring justice to the nations." (v. 5)

- Source of Hope: "The islands will look to me and wait in hope for my arm." (v. 5)

- Eternal One: " ... my righteousness will last forever, my salvation through all generations." (v. 8)

- Mighty God: " ... arm of the Lord, clothe yourself with strength!" (v. 9)

- Way–Maker: "Was it not you who dried up the sea ... so that the redeemed might cross over?" (v. 10)

- Redeemer and Joy Bringer: "Those the Lord has rescued will return. They will enter Zion with singing; everlasting joy will crown their heads." (v. 11)

- Comforter: "I, even I, am he who comforts you." (v. 12)

- Deliverer: "The cowering prisoners will soon be set free ... " (v. 14)

- Lord Almighty: "For I am the Lord your God, who stirs up the sea so that its waves roar—the Lord Almighty is his name." (v. 15)

- Creator: " ... I who set the heavens in place, who laid the foundations of the earth ... " (v. 16)

- Defender: " ... your God, who defends his people ..." (v. 22)

What did you learn about God? Which name means most to you right now?

Prayer: Creator, Deliverer, Judge, Loving One, help me to learn more about You.

147

Listen, Look, Hear

Isaiah 51:1–8

READ THROUGH THESE VERSES and notice the commands from God to listen, to look, and to hear. They are placed for us to learn specific lessons from God.

> "Listen to me, you who pursue righteousness and who seek the Lord … " (v. 1)

> "Look to the rock from which you were cut and to the quarry from which you were hewn … " (v. 1)

> " … look to Abraham, your father, and to Sarah, who gave you birth." (v. 2)

As you pursue righteousness, have you ever felt as though you were walking in a storm, uphill, against the wind? Do you worry that your life is making no difference for the Kingdom? God's Word has a lesson for you that is full of encouragement: Be faithful in your pursuit of righteousness. Keep on seeking the Lord, who has chosen you. Remember how God did the impossible with Abraham and Sarah as He gave them a son in their old age and multiplied their descendants. He is true to His promises, and he can multiply your efforts.

> "<u>Listen</u> to me, my people; <u>hear me</u>, my nation:
> Instruction will go out from me; my justice will
> become a light to the nations. My righteousness
> draws near speedily, my salvation is on the way, and
> my arm will bring justice to the nations." (vv. 4–5)

> "<u>Lift up your eyes</u> to the heavens; <u>look</u> at the
> earth beneath; the heavens will vanish like
> smoke, the earth will wear out like a garment and
> its inhabitants die like flies. But my salvation will
> last forever, my righteousness will never fail. (v. 6)

> "<u>Hear me</u>, you who know what is right, you people
> who have taken my instruction to heart:
> Do not fear the reproach of mere mortals or be
> terrified by their insults. For the moth will eat
> them up like a garment; the worm will devour them
> like wool. But my righteousness will last forever,
> my salvation through all generations." (vv. 7–8)

The lesson: We can believe God when He says He has a plan. We can trust Him to do just what He promises. He has already won the ultimate victory. In the meantime, we need to trust God to help us win the daily battles. Jesus said, "Heaven and earth will pass away, but my words will never pass away." (Matthew 24:35)

Prayer: Help me to look, listen, and hear.

148

Awake, O Lord; Awake My People

Isaiah 51:9–23

WHEN ISAIAH PLEADS WITH God to awake and deliver His people, it is the prayer of an intercessor. Isaiah reminds the Lord of his past deeds: "Was it not you who cut Rahab to pieces, who pierced that monster through? Was it not you who dried up the sea, the waters of the great deep, who made a road in the depths of the sea so that the redeemed might cross over?" (51:9–10) The Rahab mentioned here is not the prostitute who helped to save the day in Jericho (and who became an ancestor of Jesus!) but a female god of chaos often associated with Egypt and Pharaoh. Isaiah was reminding God that He had defeated that monster and brought His people safely out of captivity.

Throughout Scripture, we read about people who stepped forward to pray for the deliverance of God's chosen. When the Lord said he would destroy His wayward people in the wilderness, Moses interceded with Him to turn from His fierce anger, and "the Lord relented." (Exodus 32:9–14) When the promised 70 years of exile in Babylon were about to end, Daniel reminded the Lord and called on Him to keep His promise. (Daniel 9) Rarely was there a time when God could find no one to stand in the gap for His people. (Ezekiel 22:30)

Intercessors also often plead with the people for whom they are praying. Isaiah cried, "Awake, awake! Rise up, Jerusalem ... " He knew that God's people were in the midst of suffering the wrath of God, but He also called their attention to God's promise: "See, I have taken out of your hand the cup that made you stagger; from that cup, the goblet of my wrath, you will never drink again." (51:17, 22) Sometimes, a prophet brings Good News!

Standing in the gap as an intercessor—and pleading with people to change—is spiritually dangerous work. Do not enter into it lightly. Pray first that God will protect your loved ones and livelihood because the enemy will attack whatever will bring the most distraction to you. Put on the full armor of God (Ephesians 6:10–18). Claim His promise: "Ask and it will be given to you; seek and you will find; knock and the door will be opened to you." (Matthew 7:7) Obey those nudges you receive from the Holy Spirit, and pray in faith. If God is telling you to speak words of prophecy directly to the people, take courage and do that too.

Prayer: Let God arise, let people obey Him, and let His enemies be scattered.

More Scripture: Psalm 68:1–3

149

Wake Up and Get Ready

Isaiah 52

ISAIAH TELLS THE PEOPLE, "Awake, awake, Zion, clothe your-self with strength." (52:1) He is prophesying about the return from Babylonian exile. "Free yourself from the chains on your neck, Daughter Zion, now a captive." (52:2) Why would the Lord release His people? Because the rulers He allowed to take them into captivity would mock and blaspheme His name. "Therefore my people will know my name; therefore in that day they will know that it is I who foretold it. Yes, it is I." (52:6) The Lord instructs His people to prepare for their exo-dus from Babylon: "Touch no unclean thing! Come out from it and be pure, you who carry the articles of the Lord's house. But you will not leave in haste or go in flight; for the Lord will go before you, the God of Israel will be your rear guard." (52:11–12)

God would enable the people to rebuild Jerusalem, and He would restore the nation of Judah. This would be a partial and temporary fulfillment of the Scripture: "For this is what the Lord says: 'You were sold for nothing, and without money you will be redeemed.' " (52:3)

True redemption would come through a different kind of ransom: the blood of Jesus. Those who witnessed Jesus' arrival in Jerusalem on Palm Sunday must have heard the echo of Isaiah's words: "How beautiful on the mountains are the feet of those who bring good news, who proclaim peace, who bring good tidings, who proclaim salvation, who say to Zion, 'Your God reigns!' " (52:7)

Jesus came as the Messiah, the Suffering Servant, to give His life as an atoning sacrifice. "See, my servant will act wisely; he will be raised and lifted up and highly exalted. Just as there were many who were appalled at him—his appearance was so disfigured beyond that of any human being and his form marred beyond human likeness—so will he sprinkle many nations, and kings will shut their mouths because of him." (52:13–15) Before Jesus was "raised and lifted up" on the Cross, He suffered a beating that made Him almost unrecognizable. For His sacrifice, He was "highly exalted." The same blood that would "sprinkle many nations" also sanctifies us.

In this time of Grace, the Holy Spirit enables us to understand the past and encourages us to hope in the future. Eagerly we wait for Jesus to come and for all God's promises to find fulfillment. Get ready! "For now we see only a reflection in as in a mirror; then we shall see face to face. Now I know in part; then I shall know fully, even as I am fully known." (1 Corinthians 13:12)

Prayer: Lord, help us to be ready for Your return.
Help us to be ready for the grace of new revelation each day.

More Scripture: Ezra 8:21–36, 1 Peter 1:18–19, Revelation 19

150

His Suffering and Glory:
Servant Song 4

Isaiah 52:13–53:12

THIS PORTION OF ISAIAH about the Suffering Servant is precious to those who love Jesus. Our Savior did not come as the son of a king or even as a rich man. There was nothing royal about His earthly disguise. "He had no beauty or majesty to attract us to him, nothing in his appearance that we should desire him." (53:2) He really was the prince who became a pauper so that we paupers could become princes.

When Jesus walked the Earth, He was fully human. Many people reject the idea that He could ever have had a headache or growing pains. But if He did not experience these things, what was the point of God bringing Him into the world as a baby? "He grew up before [the Lord] like a tender shoot, and like a root out of dry ground." (53:2) What was the point of a sinless life if it was not a human life? Paul writes that though Jesus is God, when He came to Earth, He " ... emptied himself, taking the form of a slave, being born in human likeness." (Philippians 2:7 *NRSV*)

When Jesus began to teach, many people did not accept His message. "He was despised and rejected by mankind, a man of suffering, and familiar with pain." He was scorned by His own people. "By oppression and judgment he was taken away. Yet who of his generation protested?" (53:1, 3, 8)

When Jesus was beaten and crucified, some people thought it was His just reward for claiming to be the Son of God. "Surely he took up our pain and bore our suffering, yet we considered him punished by God, stricken by him, and afflicted." In obedience to His Father, He stood before His accusers in silence: "He was oppressed and afflicted, yet he did not open his mouth; he was led like a lamb to the slaughter, and as a sheep before its shearers is silent, so he did not open his mouth." In His death, " ... he was pierced for our transgressions, he was crushed for our iniquities ... " That should make us feel great sorrow and shame. "We all, like sheep, have gone astray, each of us has turned to our own way; and the Lord has laid on him the iniquity of us all." But thanks be to God, " ... the punishment that brought us peace was on him, and by his wounds we are healed." (53:4, 5–7)

Because of Jesus' obedience, " ... God exalted him to the highest place and gave him the name that is above every name, that at the name of Jesus every knee should bow, in heaven and on earth and under the earth, and every tongue acknowledge that Jesus Christ is Lord, to the glory of God the Father." (Philippians 2:9–11)

Prayer: Let every knee bow and every tongue confess that Jesus is Lord.

151

Who'd a thunk it?

Isaiah 53:1–3

WHEN YOU LOOK AT the plan of God, that's what you have to say: "Who'd a thunk it?" Or, in Isaiah's language, "Who would have believed what we heard?" (53:1 *NCV)* The Savior of the world born to an unwed teenager? Birthed in a stable, not a palace? Raised as a carpenter? In Nazareth, a town on the edge of nowhere?

What was so special about Him? At the time of His "bar mitzvah" Temple visit, Jesus did impress the scribes with His knowledge of Scripture and His astute questions. So would this be the fairytale start of the Messiah's ministry? No, His family collected Him and took Him home, and He lived in obscurity for another 18 years. Even His own parents, who knew what had been prophesied for their son, probably began to have their doubts. Who but God would set out such a plan?

No one thought of Jesus as anything but an ordinary man. Even John seemed surprised that when God revealed the promised Messiah to him, it was Jesus. Instead of a cousin, a commoner, a carpenter, he saw "the Lamb of God, who takes away the sin of the world." (John 1:29) As Jesus entered the water, symbolizing not repentance (for He had never sinned) but a new beginning, He laid aside 30 years of normalcy and took up a new life of public ministry. He started His three-year journey to the Cross, the tomb, and ultimately, the throne. God's plan was finally unfolding.

Even then, it continued to confound. Jesus was not the Messiah anyone was expecting. He was not a Pharisee, Sadducee, scribe, priest, or zealot. He didn't lead a rebellion against Roman oppressors, storm the palaces of the false rulers, and establish an earthly kingdom. Jesus was a storyteller, a healer, and a teacher who turned things upside down. Still hunted by those who opposed Him, still haunted by the dubious details of His conception, and still misunderstood by those closest to Him, Jesus was not the image of the expected Savior. When He was arrested and nailed to a cross, Jesus looked even less like the Savior. He was "despised and rejected," and in His beaten state, looked like someone any sane person would avoid.

Yet in all His ugliness, He was bearing our sin. Three days in the grave and one resurrection later, people finally began to understand. The secret was revealed: " 'What no eye has seen, what no ear has heard, and what no human mind has conceived,'—the things God has prepared for those who love him … " If the powers of darkness and rulers of this world had known who Jesus was and the plan God had laid out for Him, "they would not have crucified the Lord of glory." (1 Corinthians 2: 9, 8, quoting Isaiah 64:4) Who'd a thunk it? God! And He wins!

Prayer: Thank you, God, for revealing Your plan,
Your Son, our Savior, in Your time.

152

Like Shepherdless Sheep

Isaiah 53:6–7

"KNOW THAT THE LORD IS GOD. He made us, and we belong to him; we are his people, the sheep he tends." (Psalm 100:3 *NCV)* Scripture often uses sheep to symbolize humans. There are a lot of similarities. None is as descriptive as: "We all have wandered off, like shepherdless sheep, scattered by our aimless striving and endless pursuits." (Isaiah 53:6 *VOICE)* Just like sheep, we easily wander off and pursue our own ends rather than God's plan for us. We all need the Lord as our Shepherd, but we often don't want Him around. Like independent 2–year–olds or moody teenagers, we exert our independence, refuse to follow, and say petulantly, "I don't want to ..." We become lost lambs, covered in mud, dung, brambles, with our skin torn and bleeding. We are afraid, starved, and claimed by a new master who does not have our best interests in mind. What a disaster!

Who can rescue us? Ironically, it's another Lamb! "The

Eternal One laid on him, this silent sufferer, the sins of us all. And in the face of such oppression and suffering—silence. Not a word of protest, not a finger raised to stop it. Like a sheep to a shearing, like a lamb to be slaughtered, he went— oh so quietly, oh so willingly." (Isaiah 53:6–7 *VOICE)* We have a Savior. The Lamb of God came, in all humility and in sin- less obedience, to pay the ransom. "You were bought, not with something that ruins like gold or silver, but with the pre- cious blood of Christ, who was like a pure and perfect lamb." (1 Peter 1:18–19 *NCV)* What a triumph!

Jesus is not just Lamb but also Shepherd. As His sheep, yes, I sometimes wander off. But then I realize how much I need and want Him. He desires only the best for me. He restores my soul, and my cup of blessing overflows. (Psalm 23) I will follow where He leads me.

Prayer: Lord, You are my Shepherd. I want to follow, trust, and obey You. Help me.

153

Revelation

Isaiah 54

IN THIS CHAPTER WE see the revelation of Israel's future glory. The allegory describes Zion as being like a barren, husbandless, desolate woman who can sing because she has at last borne children. In our modern day, we may find it difficult to understand the anguish of such a woman. But in that day, the measure of a woman's worth was her success at marrying and giving children to her husband. If she didn't have children, her husband could divorce her, no questions asked. The restoration of God's nation would be as wonderful as when a barren woman gives birth and is restored to a place of security. God tells the woman, "Enlarge the place of your tent, stretch your curtains wide ... For you will spread out to the right and to the left; your descendants will dispossess nations and settle in their desolate cities." (54:2, 3)

Before restoration could occur, a ransom payment would be required. God says He Himself will redeem the woman (the people in exile). " 'For a brief moment I abandoned you, but with deep compassion I will bring you back. In a surge of anger I hid my face from you for a moment, but with everlasting kindness I will have compassion on you,' says the Lord your Redeemer." (54:7–8)

Once the people returned to their holy city, the Lord would rebuild it with precious jewels like turquoise, lapis lazuli, and rubies. (Sounds like the heavenly city, doesn't it?) God says that He will be the children's teacher, " ... and great will be their peace." (54:11, 13) This allegory tells us that God will redeem, restore, and rebuild His people. They will know the security, love, peace, and prosperity that a beloved wife enjoys. This promise has yet to be fulfilled in its entirety. We, the Church of which Jesus is the head, are the bride of Christ. We, the ransomed ones, will one day be part of " ... the Holy City, the new Jerusalem, coming down out of heaven from God, prepared as a bride beautifully dressed for her husband." (Revelation 21:2) Until that day, the Lord blesses us with hints of heaven. Open your eyes and discover those glimpses God is revealing to you today.

Prayer: Open my eyes to see the beauty of the full redemption of the Lamb.

154

The Battle Belongs to the Lord

'See, it is I who created the blacksmith who fans the coals into flame and forges a weapon fit for its work. And it is I who have created the destroyer to work havoc; no weapon forged against you will prevail, and you will refute every tongue that accuses you. This is the heritage of the servants of the Lord, and this is their vindication from me,' declares the Lord. (54:16–17)

GOD SAYS HE IS behind the forging of weapons, and He is the one who " ... created the destroyer to work havoc" in this world. That sounds like very bad news. But what is the heritage of the servants of the Lord? We have God on our side. God says, in verse 17, " ... no weapon forged against you will prevail." Here are a couple of other versions of that sentence. " ... no weapon that is used against you will defeat you." *(NCV)* "No weapon that is formed against you shall prosper ... " *(MEV)* " ... no weapon that can hurt you has ever been forged." *(The Message)*

Likewise, with God on your side, " ... you will refute every tongue that accuses you." "You will show that those who speak against you are wrong." *(NCV)* " ... every tongue that shall rise against you in judgment, you shall condemn." *(MEV)* "Any accuser who takes you to court will be dismissed as a liar." *(The Message)*

This is God's promise to us: He will vindicate us, give us victory, see to it that everything works out for the best. God has won the ultimate victory, and He desires to help us win the battles. Ephesians 6:10–18 reminds us that our battle is not really with flesh and blood, (even though it can take that form); it is against spiritual forces. We are instructed to put on the whole armor of God so that we can stand. If we claim the promise put before us in Isaiah 54:16–17, we will stand and we will win. But before we can claim any promises from God, we have to discover them. Ask God to help you hunger and thirst for His Word. Ask God to help you comprehend and apply His promises. Take your stand and know that God is on your side. Remember, the battle really belongs to God, and He wants to deliver you.

Prayer: Lord God Almighty, the battle belongs to You.

155

Come, Drink and Eat

'Come, all you who are thirsty, come to the
waters; and you who have no money, come,
buy and eat! Come, buy wine and milk
without money and without cost. Why spend
money on what is not bread, and your labor
on what does not satisfy? Listen, listen to me,
and eat what is good, and you will delight
in the richest of fare. Give ear and come to
me; listen, that you may live. I will make an
everlasting covenant with you, my faithful
love promised to David. (55:1–3)

LOOK AT THIS GENEROUS invitation to those who are in need.
Come if you are thirsty. Come if you are hungry. Blessed are
the ones who recognize their hunger and thirst for God. Their
souls will live. Cursed are those who try to fill their hunger
and thirst for God with other things. They will starve and die.
The prophet Haggai challenged the people of God who had

returned from exile to rebuild Jerusalem: Quit seeking your own way. Look to God and obey Him and He will grant you success. Jesus also said it. His words are recorded in Matthew 6:33: "Seek first his kingdom and his righteousness, and all these things will be given to you as well."

What are you hungry and thirsty for in your life? Can that hunger and thirst be satisfied by material possessions and physical indulgence? Obviously, the answer is no. We have a God hunger and thirst that only God can satisfy. He is willing. We only have to respond to His gracious invitation.

Jesus said, "I am the bread of life. Whoever comes to me will never go hungry, and whoever believes in me will never be thirsty." (John 6:35) Remember Jesus' invitation to the woman at the well? She came seeking water, but Jesus offered her "living water." He said, "Everyone who drinks this [well] water will be thirsty again, but whoever drinks the water I give them will never thirst. Indeed, the water I give them will become in them a spring of water welling up to eternal life." (John 4:13) The very last chapter of the New Testament echoes this invitation: "Let the one who is thirsty come; and let the one who wishes take the free gift of the water of life." (Revelation 22:17)

God says, "Listen, listen to me, and eat what is good and you will delight in the richest of fare." (55:2) That promise is an everlasting covenant God makes with us.

Prayer: Fill me with the Bread of Life, Lord, and satisfy my thirst with the Living Water.

156

The Word of God Produces

'For my thoughts are not your thoughts, neither are your ways my ways,' declares the Lord. 'As the heavens are higher than the earth, so are my ways higher than your ways and my thoughts than your thoughts. As the rain and the snow come down from heaven, and do not return to it without watering the earth and making it bud and flourish, so that it yields seed for the sower and bread for the eater, so is my word that goes out from my mouth: It will not return to me empty, but will accomplish what I desire and achieve the purpose for which I sent it. You will go out in joy and be led forth in peace; the mountains and hills will burst into song before you, and all the trees of the field will clap their hands. Instead of the thornbush will grow the juniper, and instead of briers

the myrtle will grow. This will be for the Lord's renown, for an everlasting sign, that will endure forever.' (55:8–13)

CAN ANYONE UNDERSTAND THE mind of God? Paul raises this question in 1 Corinthians 2:6–16. He concludes that only the Spirit of God Himself can know God's thoughts. That same Holy Spirit who inspired the written Word of God lives within each Christian and will teach us to understand that Word. What a wonderful gift!

God promises that His Word will accomplish its purpose: "It will not return to me empty, but will accomplish what I desire and achieve the purpose for which I sent it." (55:11) God uses precipitation as an object lesson to emphasize this truth. Rain and snow water the earth. When the earth receives that water, the plants bud and flourish, yielding "seed for the sower and bread for the eater." (55:10)

When God's purposes are accomplished, we respond, and all nature rejoices. "You will go out in joy and be led forth in peace; the mountains and hills will burst into song before you, and all the trees of the forest will clap their hands." (55:12)

The passage ends with a promise of blessing. Where once thorn bushes and briers cursed the dry land, pine trees and myrtle trees would spring up in soil now soaked with rain. Likewise, God restores our dry, barren, cursed souls by providing the water of life.

Prayer: Plant the Word of Life in my heart, Lord, and water it so that it may yield rich fruit.

More Scripture: John 12:23–25, Galatians 5:22

157

God Says

Isaiah 56:1–8

"HE HAS SHOWN YOU, O mortal, what is good. And what does the Lord require of you? To act justly and to love mercy and to walk humbly with your God." (Micah 6:8) In Isaiah 56, the Lord adds a promise to His command: "Maintain justice and do what is right, for my salvation is close at hand and my righteousness will soon be revealed." (56:1) God is addressing His people. But then, He goes a step further, saying that neither eunuchs nor foreigners would be excluded from salvation. In ancient kingdoms, eunuchs were (typically) castrated men who served as harem attendants or court officials. Mosaic Law excluded eunuchs from worship in the Temple. Likewise, foreigners (those who were not Jews) were also left out of the congregation.

But this passage from Isaiah shows that God sees beyond the letter of the Law. Eunuchs who keep the Sabbath, " … who choose what pleases me and hold fast to my covenant—to them

I will give within my temple and its walls a memorial and a name better than sons and daughters; I will give them an everlasting name that will endure forever." (56:4–5) What grace!

God promises that the same grace will be lavished on foreigners " ... who bind themselves to the Lord ... these I will bring to my holy mountain and give them joy in my house of prayer." Their sacrifices will be acceptable, the Lord says, " ... for my house will be called a house of prayer for all nations." (56:6, 7)

The same Lord who would deliver His people from exile would " ... gather still others to them besides those already gathered." That's the "whosoever." That's us!

God does not exclude anyone from His grace. Jesus said: "I have other sheep that are not of this sheep pen. I must bring them also. They too will listen to my voice, and there shall be one flock and one shepherd." (John 10:16)

We are sheep who have followed the Good Shepherd. We are recipients of His grace. We respond to that grace in our desire to please Him. What pleases God? He wants us to maintain justice and do what is right.

Prayer: Lord, thank you for your grace to me. Help me to act justly, love mercy, and walk humbly with You.

158

Sabbath Rest

Isaiah 56:4–8

ONE OF THE IMPORTANT criteria God gave for acceptance of eunuchs and foreigners into His Kingdom was the keeping of the Sabbath. God's people had been commanded to keep the Sabbath for two reasons. First, it was to remind them that God is their Creator. When He was forming the universe, God worked for six days and saw fit to rest on the seventh day. God commanded His people to do as He did, to labor for six days but rest on the seventh, which would be called the Sabbath. (Exodus 20:8–11) Second, they were to keep the Sabbath to remember God as Deliverer. He had brought them out Egypt, releasing them from their bondage. So they were also to give their servants, foreigners residing in their towns, and even their animals rest on the Sabbath, one day of release from their work. In remembering God as Creator and Deliverer, the people would be reminded of their covenant relationship with the Lord. (Deuteronomy 5:12–15)

By the time of Jesus, rabbis had added so many commands and laws concerning the Sabbath that the people had
forgotten the true reasons for it. Observing the Sabbath was
no longer worshipful but a rigid and legalistic exercise. When
Jesus allowed His disciples to glean grain from a field on the
Sabbath, the Pharisees rebuked Him because what they were
doing was not "legal." Jesus reminded them that David, their
national hero, had allowed his hungry warriors to eat consecrated bread that was intended only for the priests. (Matthew
12:1–3) When Jesus healed on the Sabbath, the Pharisees
called Him out. Jesus pointed out that they would certainly
rescue a trapped sheep on the Sabbath. "How much more
valuable is a person than a sheep! Therefore it is lawful to do
good on the Sabbath." (Matthew 12:9–13) Jesus observed the
spirit, not the letter, of the Law. He said, "The Sabbath was
made for man, not man for the Sabbath. So the Son of Man is
Lord even of the Sabbath." (Mark 2:27–28)

How do we keep the Sabbath in this New Testament age?
Most Christians meet together on Sunday as the Body of
Christ to celebrate the new covenant of Grace God made with
us through the blood of Jesus. When we meet, let us keep the
Sabbath by remembering God as Creator, Deliverer, Savior,
and Risen Lord. If we do that, we are pleasing God and will
receive the promised blessings of Isaiah 56.

Prayer: Lord, help me to remember the Sabbath and
worship You every day of my life.

159

Sleepy Shepherds

Come, all you beasts of the field, come and devour, all you beasts of the forest! Israel's watchmen are blind, they all lack knowledge; they are all mute dogs, they cannot bark; they lie around and dream, they love to sleep. They are dogs with mighty appetites; they never have enough. They are shepherds who lack understanding; they all turn to their own way, they seek their own gain. 'Come,' each one cries, 'let me get wine! Let us drink our fill of beer! And tomorrow will be like today, or even far better.' (56:9–12)

CAN THERE BE ANYTHING more pathetic than leaders who care more about their own comfort and needs than the needs of their people? We see it happen all the time. Some bosses are more interested in climbing the ladder than in everyone who is stranded below them. Some parents indulge in their own pursuits to the neglect of their children. Some government leaders seek to line their own pockets yet fail to address the problems of their constituents. Some church leaders become more concerned about the politics of the church than about meeting the spiritual needs of their congregations. Some church members become so totally focused on feeding their own souls that they fail to reach out to others.

Why do these things occur? Most of us start out with the best of motives. We understand our mission and responsibilities and gladly shoulder them. Then somewhere along the way, we grow frustrated or tired and begin to focus on our own needs. Self becomes our master. The self is a very tricky thing to keep in balance. If it gets overindulged (or underfed), we are in big trouble.

Sheepdogs help the shepherd care for the sheep. They are trained to gently but firmly keep the sheep together. The best sheepdogs are alert, full of energy, and passionate about their job. They do their work for the sheer love of it and to please the shepherd. But what happens to sheepdogs that neglect or even feed on the sheep they are supposed to protect? I imagine the shepherd would be forced to destroy them for the sake of the sheep.

We are all "sheepdogs" for someone. Whom has God assigned to you? Do not neglect or cause harm to one of these "sheep." Be alert and allow God to awaken or reawaken your passion for others.

Prayer: Lord, give me a heart for those You have
called me to care for.

More Scripture: Jeremiah 23:1–4 and Ezekiel 34:1–16

160

Who Is the Author?

Isaiah 57

THIS PASSAGE IS FULL of lust, violence, and betrayal. As you read it, ask yourself if anything has really changed in the years since Isaiah wrote these words. People still sacrifice their children through neglect, abuse, and abortion. People are still driven by their sexual appetites: Young people sleep with their partners before marriage; husbands and wives cheat on one another; and people accept all kinds of alternative lifestyles as the norm. People trust not in God but in a lottery ticket. Pagan practices like worship of Satan and goddesses are making a strong comeback. People are still entangled in the consequences of wrong choices, yet they don't recognize the hopelessness of continuing to make such choices.

Long before the foundation of the world was formed and people fell from grace, Lucifer began to write evil on the pages of history. Using the same old formula, he continues to author book after book. We've seen the evil spilling out of their pages, yet we continue to be tempted to pick up the latest volume.

Before the laying of the foundation of the world, another Author was already at work writing the story of salvation. Hebrews 12:2 describes Him as the Author and Finisher of our faith. Give Him full rein to write the pages of your life story. God promises to provide healing and restoration for all who will humbly turn to Him.

" ' ...whoever takes refuge in me will inherit the land and possess my holy mountain.' And it will be said: 'Build up, build up, prepare the road! Remove the obstacles out of the way of my people.' For this is what the high and exalted One says—he who lives forever, whose name is holy: 'I live in a high and holy place, but also with the one who is contrite and lowly in spirit, to revive the spirit of the lowly and to revive the heart of the contrite. I will not accuse them forever, nor will I always be angry, for then they would faint away because of me—the very people I have created. I was enraged by their sinful greed; I punished them, and hid my face in anger, yet they kept on in their willful ways. I have seen their ways, but I will heal them; I will guide them and restore comfort to Israel's mourners, creating praise on their lips. Peace, peace, to those far and near,' says the Lord. 'And I will heal them.' " (57:13–19)

Prayer: Lord, write Your story on my heart that I
may be healed and live in Your peace.

161

Appearances Can Be Deceiving

Isaiah 58

WE HAVE ALL BEEN taken in by people who know the right words to say to make them appear to be genuine in their faith, only to find out later that they do not really know God. Some people attend church and model great church behavior. They have even fooled themselves into believing they are alive in Christ because they do good things. Many faithful church attendees, and yes, even some church leaders, have a form of godliness but deny the power of God. (2 Timothy 3:5)

The people Isaiah was prophesying against kept their scheduled fasts. They denied themselves food, wore sackcloth, and sat in ashes. God saw that though they seemed to be asking for His counsel, what they really wanted was for God to notice them bowing their heads. On the day of their fasting, they exploited their workers and quarreled with one another. The Lord let the people know that this kind of fasting is not acceptable to Him; true fasting would yield action on behalf of others.

"Is that what you call a fast, a day acceptable to the Lord? Is not this the kind of fasting I have chosen: to loose the chains of injustice and untie the cords of the yoke, to set the oppressed free and break every yoke? Is it not to share your food with the hungry and to provide the poor wanderer with shelter—when you see the naked, to clothe them, and not to turn away from your own flesh and blood?" (58:5–7)

We can go through the motions of worship but miss the point of it entirely. We can have a form of godliness yet deny God's power to change us—and the world. But Isaiah has an encouraging word—and a challenge—for us. " 'If you do away with the yoke of oppression, with the pointing finger and malicious talk, and if you spend yourselves in behalf of the hungry, and satisfy the needs of the oppressed, then your light will rise in the darkness, and your night will become like the noonday. The Lord will guide you always; he will satisfy your needs in a sun–scorched land and will strengthen your frame.' " (58:9–11)

Prayer: Help me, Lord, to act on Your behalf in this world.

More Scripture: Isaiah 29:13, Matthew 7:21–23

162

The Long Arm of the Lord

Isaiah 59

GOD IS HOLY AND will not tolerate evil. Look at the gap that had grown between God and His chosen people. Here's a partial list of the sins, the iniquities, God saw among them: false speaking, wicked talk, injustice, lack of integrity, lies, acts of violence, and evil scheming. Do any of those things separate you from God? When we are in that state, "We look for light, but all is darkness; for brightness, but we walk in deep shadows. Like the blind we grope along the wall, feeling our way like people without eyes. ... We look for justice, but find none, for deliverance, but it is far away." (59:9–10, 11)

The problem for God's people of that time—and for us—is that " ... our sins testify against us." (59:12) God had always sought a man or a woman who would stand up and intercede for the people—at times, to no avail. (See Ezekiel 22:29–31) In the day Isaiah talks about in this chapter, "The Lord looked and was displeased that there was no justice. He saw that there was no one, he was appalled that there was no one to intervene." So God was compelled to act Himself: " ... his own arm achieved salvation for him, and his own righteousness sustained him. He put on righteousness as his breastplate, and the helmet of salvation on his head; he put on the garments of vengeance and wrapped himself in zeal as in a cloak." (59:15–17)

Throughout history, people have persisted in their sinful ways. Our sins, great and small, separate us from God. However, He has acted on our behalf. Jesus stands in the gap for us. "The Redeemer will come to Zion ... " (59:20) He Himself is the Way for those stumbling in darkness to walk in the light of salvation. No matter how far you are from God and how hopeless you think your situation is, if you reach out to God for help, He will reach you. How long is God's arm? It is long enough.

This is God's promise to the redeemed: "My Spirit, who is on you, will not depart from you, and my words that I have put in your mouth will always be on your lips, on the lips of your children and on the lips of their descendants—from this time on and forever." (59:21) Isn't that wonderful news?

Prayer: Lord, I acknowledge that my sin has separated me from You. Restore me once more, and let Your Spirit rest upon me.

More Scripture: 1 Corinthians 10:1–14, 1 Timothy 2:5–6

163

Rise and Shine

Isaiah 60

ISAIAH SOUNDS THE CALL to the people of God to rise and be restored. The Word of God always has balance. Things come full circle to constantly reinforce God's message. Even the sub–topics, the "by–the–ways," come back around for fulfillment. Look at this chapter and pick out the familiar themes.

Your list should include the main themes of light, glory, and darkness. These themes are introduced in the first words of the Bible. The world was in darkness until God turned on the light. (Genesis 1:1–3) We see the same themes addressed in the first chapter of the Gospel of John. Jesus is described as "the light of all mankind. The light shines in the darkness, and the darkness has not overcome it." (John 1:4–5) The promised light is the Lord Himself. "The sun will no more be your light by day, nor will the brightness of the moon shine on you, for the Lord will be your everlasting light and your God will be your glory." (60:19) Jesus said, "I am the light of the world. Whoever follows me will never walk in darkness, but will have the light of life." (John 8:12)

When we are redeemed, we have the Lord's light within us. Jesus told His followers that we are the light of the world, and we should not hide that light. "A town built on a hill cannot be hidden. Neither do people light a lamp and put it under a bowl. Instead they put it on its stand, and it gives light to everyone in the house. In the same way, let your light shine before others, that they may see your good deeds and glorify your Father in heaven." (Matthew 5:14–16) In Revelation, the seven lampstands, representing the Church, remind us that God's people are to shine their light upon this dark world. (Revelation 1:20) "Nations will come to your light, and kings to the brightness of your dawn." (Isaiah 60:3)

Imagine our world covered by a thick cloud of evil that blocks out the light of God. The cloud is growing thicker every day. Darkness becomes familiar, and people are blinded; they can no longer see the light of truth. Instead of becoming alarmed by the dark cloud of evil, they almost begin to find a familiar comfort in it. But God calls His people, those with the light within them, to pray and punch holes in the dark cloud so that the light of Truth can shine through. Some will run to that light while others will flee from it, preferring the darkness. But our mission, no matter how discouraging it sometimes seems, is to be God's lights in this dark world, to pray and proclaim the Gospel. Arise and shine, for the glory of the Lord has come to dwell in you.

Prayer: Help me to shine for Jesus' sake.

164

Rise and Be Restored

Isaiah 60:4–22

CONSIDER THE "FULL–CIRCLE" TOPICS of the Bible. Looking at this chapter of Isaiah, after listing the main topics of light, glory, and darkness, we can add unity and restoration. At first glance you may not recognize every detail of the promised restoration that would lead to unity. Why did Isaiah mention Midian, Ephah, Sheba, Kedar, Nebaioth, and Lebanon? Midian was one of the sons of Abraham by Keturah, the woman he married after Sarah died; Ephah was one of the sons of Midian. The Midianites were chronic enemies of Israel. The Queen of Sheba once visited King Solomon to make an alliance. Kedar and Nebaioth were sons of Ishmael, tradition-ally thought to be the progenitor of the Arabs. Lebanon had a long history of alliance with Israel. Looking at the present–day situation in the Middle East, we could easily doubt the validity of this promise of unity. Yet God's Word declares that it will occur. I believe we are called to pray for unity in the Middle East and restoration for Israel.

This chapter of Isaiah also alludes indirectly to two other occasions when God's people enjoyed His blessing or provision. The first occasion was when the baby Moses was spared certain death by the daughter of Pharaoh. He experienced the care and nurture of the royal household, the same royal household that had sentenced him and all the other Israelite babies to death. Moses represents the remnant of God's people who are spared and nurtured by the very hands that seek to destroy them. History repeats. The second occasion occurred in the days of Solomon when the territory of Israel reached its greatest extent and enjoyed a long period of peace and prosperity. It was the best of times for the nation. God's Word through Isaiah let the people of his day know that if they would only repent, He would restore them to that state. The remnant of the people coming out of exile would receive the blessing of God.

This is more than history. Romans 9–11 helps us to understand that these promises are for both the chosen children of Abraham—the original branches of God's chosen vine—and for the adopted children, the engrafted branches—the Gentiles—whom God has redeemed. We are all a part of the same vine. (John 15:1–8) Every promise of the Bible belongs to us all.

How do we apply these truths of Isaiah 60 to our everyday experience? The lesson of topics or themes that come full circle is repeated in every aspect of our lives. A full circle is completed when the results of an action or choice, whether good or bad, come back to you or your descendants. What unfinished business confronts you today? If you have made a bad choice, ask God to help you face it and deal with it so that it will not come full circle to work harm. If you are making good choices, remember that they too will come back full circle in the form of blessings upon you and yours.

Prayer: Lord, I pray for peace and blessing upon me and upon my family.

165

The Spirit of the Lord

Isaiah 61

ISAIAH WROTE THESE WORDS about himself, yet they are also about the Messiah. At the beginning of His ministry, Jesus went to the synagogue and was handed the scroll of Isaiah. He looked up this passage and read: "The Spirit of the Lord is on me, because he has anointed me to proclaim good news to the poor. He has sent me to proclaim freedom for the prisoners and recovery of sight for the blind, to set the oppressed free, to proclaim the year of the Lord's favor." After he rolled up the scroll, he said, "Today this scripture is fulfilled in your hearing." (Luke 4:16–21) This might be called Jesus' mission statement.

What is the mission of your life? How does your life make a difference for God? Could it be that Jesus' mission statement is also your own? How can you proclaim good news to the poor? Throughout His ministry, Jesus showed a preference for the poor and downtrodden. Perhaps we should too by doing such things as providing community meals and offering assistance to those in crisis. Do we give the poor who walk through our doors the best seats in our sanctuaries? How can you bind up the broken–hearted? You might have a ministry to those who are grieving or suffering distress from fractured relationships. How can you proclaim freedom for the captives and release prisoners from darkness? You might become involved in the fight against human trafficking or in helping people recover from addiction. Perhaps you have a ministry visiting in prisons or helping those who have been imprisoned to become productive citizens. This part of the mission statement doesn't have to be taken literally. Any time you reach people with the Good News of the Gospel, you are setting captives free and releasing prisoners from darkness.

How can you proclaim the year of the Lord's favor? Perhaps you do that when you treat others as if they are the Lord Himself: "For I was hungry and you gave me something to eat, I was thirsty and you gave me something to drink, I was a stranger and you invited me in, I needed clothes and you clothed me, I was sick and you looked after me, I was in prison and you came to visit me." (Matthew 25:35–36) Jesus said that when we do these things for the "least of these," we are ministering to Him.

Notice that in the synagogue that day, Jesus didn't read the whole passage from Isaiah. He stopped with the phrase, "to proclaim the year of the Lord's favor." For the time to fulfill the whole passage had not yet arrived. God's timing is always perfect. He will keep His whole promise in His time.

Prayer: God, help me to understand the purpose for my life. Help me to trust You for the details. Let Your Spirit rest upon me.

More Scripture: Ecclesiastes 3:1–11

166

The Garments of Salvation

Isaiah 61:1–11

VERSES 2–3 SAY THAT the Lord will comfort all who mourn and
" ... bestow on them a crown of beauty instead of ashes, the oil
of joy instead of mourning, and a garment of praise instead of
a spirit of despair." In verse 10, Isaiah says he delights in the
Lord, who has " ... clothed me with garments of salvation and
arrayed me in a robe of his righteousness." These verses foreshadow the personal transformation brought about by Jesus:
"Therefore, if anyone is in Christ, the new creation has come:
The old has gone, the new is here!" (2 Corinthians 5:17) Paul
uses Isaiah language when he says that believers in the Lord
Jesus should not sin any longer because " ... you have taken
off your old self with its practices and have put on the new
self." (Colossians 3:9–10) When Jesus comes into our lives, He
makes changes. We are to take off our old clothes—the filthy
rags of self–righteousness—and put on our new clothes—the
robes of righteousness that come with salvation.

Revelation 7:9–17 describes a scene in heaven. A multitude of people from every nation, tribe, and language stand before the throne of the Lamb. Dressed in white robes, they are holding palm branches and praising God. One of the 24 elders seated around the throne asks John who these people are. John answers, "Sir, you know." The elder replies, "These are they who have come out of the great tribulation; they have washed their robes and made them white in the blood of the Lamb." Can blood make anything white? The literal, laundry answer is no, but the spiritual, salvation answer is yes. Jesus, the once–for–all sacrificial Lamb, shed His blood so that we might be clean.

Because of Him, we no longer have to live in sin or mourn over it. Instead, the Lord gives us " ... a crown of beauty instead of ashes, the oil of gladness instead of mourning, and a garment of praise instead of a spirit of despair." (61:3) Because of Him, we can wear "garments of salvation," "a robe of righteousness." (61:10) Receive your royal robes!

Prayer: Thank you, Lord, for washing my sins away with Your blood and clothing me in "a robe of white." That's possible only because of You.

167

The Seed Cycle

They will be called oaks of righteousness,
a planting of the Lord for the display of
his splendor ... For as the soil makes the
sprout come up and a garden causes seeds
to grow, so the Sovereign Lord will make
righteousness and praise spring up before
all nations. (61:3, 11)

ISAIAH USES YET ANOTHER metaphor to help us understand how God's people will be transformed. Look at a seed you buy at the nursery. It's hard and dry. While there is potential for life, it remains dormant. But when a seed is planted in good soil, it germinates. Its dried–up husk of a seed casing falls away as a new sprout springs up.

As long as we are hardened to the Gospel message, our potential remains dormant. But when we put off the dry husk of self–righteousness and accept the righteousness of Christ for our own, we sprout to life. We push down through the soil, forming deep roots and growing into a flourishing plant. With nurture and cultivation, we become an "oak of righteousness, a planting of the Lord for the display of his splendor." We take our place among the people of God, a well–watered garden that produces righteousness and praise.

Prayer: Lord, I want to be " ... like a tree planted by streams of water, which yields its fruit in season and whose leaf does not wither ... " I want whatever I do to prosper for You. (Psalm 1:3)

168

A New Name

Isaiah 62:1–5, 11–12

IN BIBLE TIMES, GENTILES converting to Judaism would be immersed in water to represent death and burial. When the proselytes emerged from the water, they were considered reborn. As new creatures, part of the Jewish nation, they were given a new name.

In this passage of Isaiah, the prophet says " ... you will be called by a new name that the mouth of the Lord will bestow. You will be a crown of splendor in the Lord's hand ..." Zion would no longer be called "Deserted" or "Desolate" but "Hephzibah" ("my delight is in her") and "Beulah" ("your land will be married"). The new names show a change in covenant relationship, which would now be one of reunion and delight instead of abandonment and despair. "As a young man marries a young woman, so will your Builder marry you; as a bridegroom rejoices over his bride, so will your God rejoice over you." (62:1–5)

Once again, Isaiah's words resonate with our New Testament understanding. Jesus is the bridegroom and we, the Church, are His bride. When people asked Jesus why His disciples weren't fasting while John's disciples and the Pharisees were, He answered, "How can the guests of the bridegroom fast while he is with them? They cannot, so long as they have him with them. But the time will come when the bridegroom will be taken from them, and on that day they will fast." (Mark 2:18–20)

That day came when our Bridegroom bade farewell to His wondering disciples and ascended into Heaven. But in one of the great promises of His return, He said, "Look, I am coming soon! My reward is with me." (Revelation 22:12)

The Lord had proclaimed this long before when He said to "Daughter Zion": "See, your Savior comes! See, his reward is with him, and his recompense accompanies him." Because of Jesus, like Zion, we are called "the Holy People, the Redeemed of the Lord." Zion was given beautiful, hopeful names, like "Sought After" and the "City No Longer Deserted." (62:11–12) We too are blessed of the Lord. "Once you were not a people, but now you are the people of God; once you had not received mercy, but now you have received mercy." (1 Peter 2:10)

The Lord chose to be merciful to us by sending us His Son. When we are born again, we take on His family name: Christian. That name speaks to us of belonging to the Lord, our Bridegroom. Aren't you looking forward to the wedding feast of the Lamb?

Prayer: Thank You, Lord, for Your mercy to us.

More Scripture: Revelation 2:17

169

Persistent Prayer

Isaiah 62

GOD EXPECTS PERSISTENCE IN our praying. It is not that God wants or expects us to beg. It is not that God doesn't hear us the first time we ask. So why does God seem to require persistence in prayer before the outcome manifests itself? Isaiah's prayer was for the eventual restoration of Israel. God had already promised this. It was already on its way. So why did Isaiah say he would continue to speak out and continue to pray until this promise came about? Why did Isaiah point out that God had placed watchmen on Jerusalem's walls specifically to pray for the city? (62:6–7)

Jesus told His followers to ask, seek, and knock if they wanted something from God. (Matthew 7:7) God knows what we want and need, but He chooses to involve us in the process. Prayer is one of the greatest gifts God gives to us. It allows us to participate in God's plan.

Reading Luke 18:1–8 will help shed light on this portion

of Isaiah. If the unrighteous judge would finally give in to the persistence of the widow, how much more will our righteous God choose to hear us when we pray? Persistent praying develops us and challenges us. If God were to answer all your prayers immediately and exactly as you want Him to answer, you would have a very shallow and messy life. It would also mean that God serves you, not the other way around. It would make God into a giant wish–granting genie in the sky. But God is not an overindulgent parent who spoils His children, making them unfit for life. Instead, He is a loving and firm parent who teaches His children how to live abundantly and eternally.

God posted watchmen on the walls of Jerusalem who would "never be silent night or day." They had the job of calling on the Lord in prayer for the city. He has also posted us as watchmen on the walls of our cities. We all have the responsibility of praying for them. Isaiah says we should pray relentlessly, without ceasing, so that our cries to God give Him no rest until He answers.

Prayer: Lord, we lift Your name on high. We ask that You move in the hearts and minds of our city government leaders. We ask that You move in the hearts and lives of those who live in our city neighborhoods. Help them to hunger and thirst after Your righteousness.

170

Making a Name

Isaiah 62

WE SAY THAT PEOPLE set out to "make a name" for themselves, to build their reputations. Mention the name of a person who has a reputation for following through with their promises, and that name inspires confidence that a project will succeed. Mention the name of a person known for kindness or generosity, and that name brings a smile to people's lips.

But mention the name of a person who never completes a project, and that name will cause people to lose faith when they learn that person is in charge. Mention the name of a person known for outbursts of anger, and that name will cause people to shudder. It's hard to live down a bad name.

God's people had made a bad name for themselves through their rebellion. When people mentioned the name of Zion, the words "Deserted" and "Desolate" came to mind. I can imagine that people said these words with a sneer.

Let's do an experiment. What reaction do you have to these names?

Benedict Arnold
Abraham Lincoln
Adolf Hitler
Mother Teresa

For better or worse, these people made a name for themselves in history. We make a name for ourselves too—perhaps not in history, but among our family, our friends, our co-workers. We who are believers especially want to have a good name. In a Christian community, we should be quick to help each other build up and maintain that good name. But we can do damage to it by an unwise decision, a word said with malice, a bad attitude. Repairing the damage may be difficult, but it is possible, especially among brothers and sisters in Christ, because we can repent and ask and receive forgiveness. Just like Israel, we can be known by a new name that reflects the Lord's delight in us.

How do you think people react when your name is mentioned? Do you have a habit of tearing down others? If you do, you are damaging your own name in the process.

Do you need to repair a bad name you have made for yourself? Do you need a "new" name?

There is one name, of course, that we can trust without question. Blessed be the name of the Lord!

Prayer: Help me to build a reputation that others can trust because they know I trust in You.

171

The Grapes of Wrath

Isaiah 63

ISAIAH 63:1–6 SPEAKS OF the day of the Lord's wrath. We see a picture of a furious God dressed in garments spattered with the blood of the people he has trampled down. In Revelation, we read of rider on a white–horse, the Word of God, dressed in a robe dipped in blood. "He treads the winepress of the fury of the wrath of God Almighty." (19:11–16) Both passages reveal that God will wreak vengeance against those who reject Him.

But there is still time. Isaiah 63:7–19 is the prophet's plea, his prayer for remembrance, repentance, and redemption. Isaiah uses the history of God's choosing Israel and His faithfulness to them as a springboard to ask God, their Savior, for mercy. The prophet reminds the Lord of His compassion and kindness toward His people and of the times " ... he lifted them up and carried them all the days of old." The prophet brings up the days when the people didn't stumble, when the Lord " ... sent his glorious arm of power to be at Moses' right hand. ... you, Lord, are our Father, our Redeemer from of old is your name." (63:9, 12, 16)

In the midst of this plea comes this verse: "Why, Lord, do you make us wander from your ways and harden our hearts so we do not revere you?" (63:17) It reminds me of this part of the Lord's Prayer: "And lead us not into temptation, but deliver us from evil." Is God, in His sovereign power, in complete control of what we do, or do we have free will? Does God harden people's hearts, make us wander from His ways, lead us into temptation? We think of the Scripture saying that " ... the Lord hardened Pharaoh's heart." (Exodus 9:12) Even then, Pharaoh still had freedom to choose, and his choice was not to listen to Moses and Aaron and, therefore, to defy God. Likewise, the people of Israel had always had freedom to choose, and so many times, they rebelled against God.

In the New International Version of the Bible, this passage is titled, "God's Day of Vengeance and Redemption." How can both be happening at the same time? Look at this verse: "It was for me the day of vengeance; the year for me to redeem had come. I looked, but there was no one to help, I was appalled that no one gave support; so my own arm achieved salvation for me, and my own wrath sustained me." (63:5) The Day of Judgment is coming when God will visit vengeance on those who have rejected Him. That's inevitable. But the Day of Redemption is also coming when the Lord will save those who call upon Him. In the meantime, it's up to us to soften as many hard hearts as we can.

Prayer: Lord, I call upon You to deliver me from evil.
Set my feet on the path of life and do not let
me depart from it.

172

Give Us a Sign

Isaiah 64

WHEN SKEPTICS HAVE CONFRONTED you or heaped scorn upon you because of your faith, have you ever wished that God would silence them by revealing Himself in all His might? Do you long to see the look on their faces when that happens? If so, then you can identify with both Isaiah and Habakkuk. Quickly scan the three chapters of Habakkuk and compare his writings with this chapter of Isaiah. Both prophets plead with God for a renewal of the miracles He had performed on behalf of His people in the days of the exodus from Egypt. When God finished with Pharaoh, there was no doubting God's existence. The Egyptians, as well as the Hebrews, could not mistake the power of God. Even other nations, when they heard what God had done, stood in awe and fear of the God of Israel.

Now, hundreds of years later, Isaiah asks God to display His power again. "Oh, that you would rend the heavens and come down, that the mountains would tremble before you!"

(64:1) "Lord, I have heard of your fame; I stand in awe of your deeds, Lord. Repeat them in our day, in our time make them known ... " (Habakkuk 3:2)

Yet even as the prophets pray, they know that the sin and unbelief of the people will incite God's wrath. "All of us have become like one who is unclean, and all our righteous acts are like filthy rags ... " (64:6) Both Isaiah and Habakkuk turn their prayers from asking for a sign of God's power to asking for His mercy, for Him to remember His love for His people. "We are the clay, you are the potter; we are all the work of your hand. Do not be angry beyond measure, Lord; do not remember our sins forever. Oh, look upon us, we pray, for we are all your people." (64:8–9) The last line of Habakkuk 3:2 says, " ... in wrath remember mercy."

Because Jesus came to Earth and died for our sins, we are the recipients of God's grace and mercy. That grace and mercy is available to anyone who repents. But this present age will end—perhaps soon. When Jesus comes again, He will rend the skies and appear in His full splendor, and many will suffer the wrath of His judgment. But because God has had mercy upon us, we will be ready for His appearance. We can say, with Habakkuk, " ... I will rejoice in the Lord, I will be joyful in God my Savior. The Sovereign Lord is my strength; he makes my feet like the feet of a deer, he enables me to tread on the heights." (3:18–19)

Prayer: Lord, I am grateful for Your mercy, for I am a sinner saved by grace.

More Scripture: Psalm 144:5–8; Daniel 7:13, 14; Acts 1:9–11, Revelation 1:7–8

173

A Request for Salvation

Isaiah 64

PAUL AND SILAS WERE in jail for casting out a demon from a fortune–teller. They were shackled, but they sang hymns and praised God. When an earthquake came in the night, their chains were broken and the prison doors opened. Their jailer, who had been asleep, thought all the prisoners had escaped, and he was ready to kill himself. But Paul shouted, "Don't harm yourself! We are all here!" The jailer was so amazed that he asked Paul and Silas, "Sirs, what must I do to be saved?" (Acts 16:16–34) Isaiah, aware of the people's sinfulness and God's absolute right to destroy them, asks: "How then can we be saved?" (64:5) It is the question of the ages. When we come face to face with a holy, powerful God, we are confronted with our sin. We recognize our need for salvation.

People who consider themselves "good" often have dif-ficulty understanding that they need cleansing from sin. They may say that they have basically abided by the Ten

Commandments; they haven't murdered anyone or cheated on their spouse. But remember what Jesus said about hateful thoughts being the same as murder and lustful thoughts being the same as adultery? (Matthew 5:21–22, 27–28) These "good" people may love their families, give money to charity, and volunteer on a regular basis. Surely, they think, the good will outweigh the bad. But we know, "There is no one righteous, not even one ..." (Romans 3:10)

How then can we be saved? Romans 3:23–26 and Ephesians 2:4–10 hold our answer. No one, not even a "good" person, can earn salvation. We are not saved by our deeds but by the sacrifice of Jesus. Salvation is a gift that can only come through faith in Him. Help the "good" people in your life see the Truth, so that they, like you, can be set free.

Prayer: Lord, I pray for all the people in my life who consider themselves good, that they would recognize their need for a Savior.

174

The Righteous Response of God

Isaiah 65:1–16

GOD RESPONDS TO ISAIAH'S request for His appearance. When you first scan this part of chapter 65, you may notice that God is reminding Isaiah of His grace. Or you may be overwhelmed by God's condemnation. But look more closely: God's response is a complicated mix of both grace and condemnation.

As recorded in the previous chapter, Isaiah has asked God to show Himself and His power to both the people of Israel and their enemies. God replies that He is there for all who have eyes to see, but they are choosing to ignore Him. In fact, they are turning away from Him and taunting Him with their rebellion. So His righteous answer to Isaiah is yes, I will reveal Myself in a mighty way. However, the result will not be exactly what you had in mind. "See, it stands written before me: I will not keep silent but will pay back in full; I will pay it back into their laps—both your sins and the sins of your fathers." (65:6–7)

However, God says He will continue to show grace to His people. Just as grapes are not destroyed as long as juice can be found in them, so the Lord will not destroy all the people but will save a remnant who have served Him.

God is Holy, so He cannot tolerate sin. Those who continue to rebel, the Lord says, will go hungry and thirsty and be put to shame while His servants eat and drink and rejoice. "My servants will sing out of the joy of their hearts, but you will cry from anguish of heart and wail in brokenness of spirit." (65:13–14) Note the balance of judgment and grace.

The Apostle Peter reminds us that the " ... day of the Lord will come like a thief"; in other words, very quickly and unexpectedly. In the meantime, Peter says, we " ... ought to live holy and godly lives ... ," "to be found spotless, blameless and at peace with him." (2 Peter 3:10, 11, 14)

Prayer: Lord, help us to live in such a way that we do not take Your mercy and grace for granted.

175

In That Day

Isaiah 65:17–25

THE APOSTLE PETER WROTE " ... in the last days scoffers
will come ... They will say, 'Where is this "coming" he promised?' " (2 Peter 3:3, 4) There have been countless skeptics
since Peter's time who didn't believe the Lord would keep
His promise to return. Today, even some people who know
Jesus as Savior and Lord doubt that He will come again
soon. They say: "It's been over 2,000 years and Jesus hasn't
returned. Why should we be looking for Him in our lifetime?"
Some skeptics point out that people throughout history have
been sure that Jesus would come at a certain date and time.
Because He didn't arrive then, they argue, He isn't coming
today. Such arguments may seem to have a ring of truth. Yet
our perspective is so finite, so limited. Peter challenges us to
remember that time doesn't mean the same thing to God as
it does to us; His perspective is infinite and eternal. "Do not
forget this one thing, dear friends: With the Lord a day is like

a thousand years and a thousand years are like a day." (2 Peter 3:8)

As in other places in Isaiah, in Chapter 65, the prophet tells of a time of restoration for the people of Judah, but he also points toward the day of the Lord's coming. We see a glimpse of a glorious future for those who love Him: "See, I will create new heavens and a new earth." In that day, the Lord says, "The wolf and the lamb will feed together, and the lion will eat straw like the ox, and dust will be the serpent's food. They will neither harm nor destroy on all my holy mountain." (65:17, 25)

We should all be pleading, "Oh, Lord, come quickly, so this will come to pass." But then we remember that so many people are still lost. We need to pray that they will partake in this season of Grace before their opportunity passes. Some Christians pray: "O Lord, don't return until my loved ones accept You as Savior." We should really be praying: "O Lord, help my loved ones accept You as Savior before You return." We don't know when that day will be. It could be today or 100 or 1,000 years from now. God has one reason for waiting. "The Lord is not slow in keeping His promise, as some understand slowness," Peter says. "Instead he is patient with you, not wanting anyone to perish, but everyone to come to repentance." (2 Peter 3:9) That's grace.

Prayer: Give us hearts to rescue the perishing.

176

God Answers Prayer

*'Before they call I will answer; while they
are still speaking I will hear.' (65:24)*

" ... YOUR FATHER knows what you need before you ask him."
(Matthew 6:8)

If God knows what we need before we ask, then why do we
need to ask at all? Prayer is a gift from God. Prayer causes
us to exercise faith, and it allows us to participate in God's
miraculous work. It is important to understand the laws and
limits God has put in place regarding prayer. Understand
that He is a God of order. Just as God's physical creation has
basic laws that define order, so does His spiritual creation. We
must ask before God will answer. If this were not so, we would
be puppets operated by a divine hand rather than humans
with free will. We choose to exercise our faith through the
process of prayer.

Perhaps the development of a child's ability to walk will
help illustrate this idea. An infant exercises her legs while

her diaper is being changed or while her parents hold her up. The infant next learns to use her legs to flip herself over. Then she learns to push up on hands and knees and begin to crawl. Soon, she pulls herself up and stands, holding onto a table or the crib. All of those first steps are important in helping the child learn to balance and coordinate movement. Parents (especially first–time parents) may want to hold on to their child, doing everything for her. However, that is not the best thing for the child. The parents' role is to keep a child safe but allow her to develop.

God also does what He must do to keep us safe while He allows us to exercise our spiritual "legs" and develop spiritually, at just the right pace. We develop as we are in communication with God. And remember: God is the One "who is able to do immeasurably more than all we ask or imagine." (Ephesians 3:20) Solomon asked God for wisdom. God said yes—and added wealth, honor, and a long life to His answer.

Prayer: Help me to trust You enough to ask.

177

Judgment and Hope

Isaiah 66

THERE ARE SEVERAL FAMILIAR themes in this last chapter of Isaiah; we'll explore them more fully in the devotions to follow.

Theme 1: God is Creator and no building can contain Him. We can't box God in. Yet, thanks to Jesus' sacrifice, God grants that His Spirit can dwell within us.

Theme 2: Obedience is better than sacrifice. Those who offer God displeasing sacrifices will be treated harshly. But the Lord looks with favor on " ... those who are humble and contrite in spirit, and who tremble at my word." (66:2–4) We don't make literal animal sacrifices today, but is our worship and the way we live our lives pleasing to Him?

Theme 3: The righteous will be vindicated. "Rejoice with Jerusalem and be glad for her ... I will extend peace to her like a river, and the wealth of nations like a flooding stream." The Lord says He will comfort His people like a mother comforts her child. (66:10, 12, 13) Like the Israelites, we may be waiting for some of God's wonderful promises to be fulfilled. But this prophecy encourages us to hang in there and trust that those promises are sure. Hebrews 11:1 tells us that "faith is the assurance of things hoped for, the conviction of things not seen." *(ESV)* If God said it, He will do it.

Theme 4: Live pure lives. The Lord speaks against "Those who consecrate and purify themselves to go into the gardens, following one who is among those who eat the flesh of pigs, rats and other unclean things—they will meet their end together with the one they follow." (66:17) Are you living your life for the Lord or following someone or something that is less than pure?

Theme 5: Proclaim God's glory. God will place a sign on the surviving remnant and send them out to proclaim His glory among the nations. (66:19–21) Jesus told His disciples that when the Spirit came upon them, they would be His " … witnesses in Jerusalem, and in all Judea and Samaria, and to the ends of the earth." (Acts 1:8) Are you taking the Gospel to the ends of the Earth—or even to your own neighborhood?

Theme 6: The Lord will create "the new heavens and the new earth" that will endure forever for those who are faithful. (66:22) Romans 8:18–25 tells us that all Creation waits for this day. The fall of humankind in the Garden of Eden set the events in motion, and God will bring it to its conclusion.

Prayer: Lord, I want to worship you in Spirit and in truth. Help me to trust that all Your promises, even to the end of days, are sure.

178

Theme 1: God's Dwelling Place

This is what the Lord says: 'Heaven is my throne, and the earth is my footstool. Where is the house you will build for me? Where will my resting place be? Has not my hand made all these things, and so they came into being?' declares the Lord. (66:1–2)

TO BUILD A DWELLING place for God is an impossible challenge. Yet consider the ways He accommodated the human need for something physical to stand for Him.

After their parents fell from grace, Cain and Abel brought gifts to God. The Bible doesn't specify where they brought their gifts. It must have been some sort of altar or meeting place. From that time on, people constructed physical places to meet with God.

There are significant meeting places identified in the Bible. The ark became a place of physical salvation for Noah and his family, those who obeyed the Lord. For the Israelites in the wilderness, the Tabernacle became the dwelling place of God's glory.

In 2 Chronicles 2–7 we read about the construction and dedication of the Temple under the direction of King Solomon. Once again, God sanctioned the building of a meeting place. When the Temple was dedicated, God's glory filled it, and it became a physical point of reference for the people's worship of God. Ezekiel 10 records the departure from the Temple of God's glory because of the attitudes and actions of His people.

Then the glory returned in Jesus. "The Word became flesh and made his dwelling among us. We have seen his glory, the glory of the one and only Son … " The expression "made his dwelling" that is used here means "tabernacled" or "pitched a tent." *The Message* puts it this way: "The Word became flesh and blood, and moved into the neighborhood."

After the death and resurrection of Jesus, we believers became the "place of meeting" for God. The Apostle Paul writes, "I pray that out of his glorious riches he may strengthen you with power through his Spirit in your inner being, so that Christ may dwell in your hearts through faith." (Ephesians 3:16–17) We meet together on Sundays in what we call the "house of God," but God is there because we are there. Jesus said: "Where two or three gather in my name, there am I with them." (Matthew 18:20)

God has been gracious in giving us physical ways to understand His presence. We should be grateful that because of His grace, we have access to His presence wherever we are.

Prayer: Lord, help me to be a dwelling place fit for Your presence.

179

Theme 2: Obedience, Not Sacrifice

'These are the ones I look on with favor: those who are humble and contrite in spirit, and who tremble at my word. But whoever sacrifices a bull is like one who kills a person, and whoever offers a lamb is like one who breaks a dog's neck; whoever makes a grain offering is like one who presents pig's blood, and whoever burns memorial incense is like one who worships an idol. They have chosen their own ways, and their souls delight in their abominations; so I also will choose harsh treatment for them and will bring on them what they dread. For when I called, no one answered, when I spoke, no one listened. They did evil in my sight and chose what displeases me.' (66:2–4)

"DOES THE LORD DELIGHT in burnt offerings and sacrifices as much as in obeying the Lord? To obey is better than sacrifice, and to heed is better than the fat of rams." (1 Samuel 15:22) The prophet Samuel was delivering the bad news to Saul that the Lord had rejected him as king. Saul had been told to destroy the Amalekites along with their cattle, sheep, camels, and donkeys. But Saul disobeyed God and spared their king, along with the best of their livestock, which Saul told God his men would offer as sacrifices.

"Stop bringing meaningless offerings!" said the Lord to His people, as He likened them to the wanton citizens of Sodom and Gomorrah. (Isaiah 1:13)

It may be easy for us to read these passages and condemn those who practice meaningless rituals. But we have to think about whether we do the same thing. God wants a real relationship with us, not rote religion and empty ritual. There are many people who sit in church every week, dutifully read the Bible every day, pray several times a day, and live law–abiding, moral lives, yet miss out on the essence of Christian living. Their hearts are far from God.

Jesus said: "I have come that they may have life and have it to the full." (John 10:10) Jesus came to give spiritual life that would flow into every area of our being. What does it mean to truly live for Him? It means that the love of God and love for others should affect every choice and decision you make. For example, does your love for God and others have an influence on the way you drive? Next time you are in heavy traffic, use it as an opportunity to pray for the people on the road with you. Pray for that person who cut you off. Pray for the bad drivers. Pray for the spiritually lost people. If you are living abundantly for God, it will affect everything you do.

Prayer: Help me to give my best and obey.

180

Theme 3: Vindication

Isaiah 66:5–14

IN THIS PASSAGE, THE Lord says He will repay His enemies as they deserve. (66:6) We don't like to think of God as a God of vengeance. That's possibly because we think of retribution as an Old Testament concept. Under the Old Covenant, God's people were allowed to exact retribution. But before the Law came, that practice had escalated out of control. The Law put limits on retribution. Allowing people to take "an eye for an eye and a tooth for a tooth" was a way to ensure that justice was fair. But Jesus turned that idea on its head. Instead of seeking retribution (even fair retribution like an eye for an eye), He said, we should turn the other cheek and love our enemies. (See Matthew 5:38–48.)

The Apostle Paul says, "Do not repay anyone evil for evil." Instead of taking revenge ourselves, we should " ... leave room for God's wrath, for it is written: 'It is mine to avenge; I will repay,' says the Lord." Our job is not just to refrain from revenge but also to love our enemies: "If your enemy is hungry, feed him; if he is thirsty, give him something to drink. In doing this, you will heap burning coals on his head." (Romans 12:17, 19, 20) Love just might change our enemies; our kind actions might cause them to recognize their sin and repent. After all, we were God's enemies until we accepted the gift of salvation from Jesus. Jesus suffered our sentence of death, which was the just expression of God's wrath, so that we could experience God's love.

In the last days, God's wrath will be unleashed on the unrighteous, and the righteous will be rewarded: " ... the hand of the Lord will be made known to his servants, but his fury will be shown to his foes." (66:14) But in the meantime, it's not for us to self–righteously act on His behalf against those who wrong us. An eye for an eye and a tooth for a tooth cannot be our standard for action. Instead, we must obey our Lord, who said " ... love your enemies and pray for those who persecute you, that you may be children of your Father in heaven." (Matthew 5:44–45)

Prayer: Lord, I have been forgiven. Help me to
forgive.

181

Theme 4: Live Pure Lives

Isaiah 66:17

GOD HAS NO PATIENCE with sin. The people the Lord condemned in this passage practiced pagan rituals and ran after others who lived filthy, unclean lives. Our lips can say: "He is God, and there is no other." But our actions may not back up that claim.

We can be sucked in by gossip or snarky comments on social media. We can give in to temptation to find excitement outside our marriage. We can be dragged down by pornographic images in magazines or on the internet. Or we can entertain hateful thoughts about our own brothers and sisters in Christ. No matter how beautifully we are dressed on Sunday or how energetically we participate in worship, we cannot cover our sins.

We may have accepted the Lord Jesus as Savior, but if we keep returning to sin habits, we separate ourselves from God.

Our human tendency is to slink away in shame, as Adam and Eve attempted to do, but we can't hide from God. We must confess our sin (and remember, there is no such thing as a small sin) with a contrite spirit and ask forgiveness.

If we want to live pure lives, we must have a desire to surrender ourselves completely to Him. We must give the Lord "All my days and all my hours,/All my will and all my powers,/All the passion of my soul,/Not a fragment but the whole." *(The Song Book of The Salvation Army, #566)* We may sing that song but balk at spending 15 minutes in prayer, let alone a "sweet hour." We may say that we want to surrender our will to Him, but at the first temptation, we go our own way.

If purity before the Lord is our desire, we must " ... not conform to the pattern of this world, but be transformed by the renewing of [our] mind[s]." (Romans 12:2) The Apostle Paul also writes, " ... whatever is true, whatever is noble, whatever is right, whatever is pure, whatever is lovely, whatever is admirable—if anything is excellent or praiseworthy— think about such things." (Philippians 4:8)

Prayer: "Create in me a pure heart, O God, and renew a steadfast spirit within me." (Psalm 51:10)

182

Theme 5: Go into All the World

'I will set a sign among them, and I will send some of those who survive to the nations— to Tarshish, to the Libyans and Lydians (famous as archers), to Tubal and Greece, and to the distant islands that have not heard of my fame or seen my glory. They will proclaim my glory among the nations. And they will bring all your people, from all the nations, to my holy mountain in Jerusalem as an offering to the Lord—on horses, in chariots and wagons, and on mules and camels. They will come in chariots and wagons,' says the Lord. (66:19–20)

NOTE THE SIMILARITIES BETWEEN this portion of Isaiah and Matthew 28:18–20. Both passages are concerned with the nations who have not heard about God. God's people are called to proclaim His glory among the nations.

Read Revelation 19 and 20 and broaden your perspective on this last chapter of Isaiah. There is a definite period of grace when the Gospel can be preached so that people will be able to respond and be saved. There is a definite time when Christ will come as Warrior and Judge. We do not know how long this age of Grace we enjoy will last. There should be some urgency for those of us who know about God's glory and grace to go and tell. God has placed you where He can best use you. You are unique and only you can reach your "end of the earth." Live to proclaim God's glory. Jesus said that when He is lifted up, He will draw all people to Himself. (John 12:32) Your job is to be faithful in lifting up Jesus as you proclaim God's glory. You don't have to worry about the results—those are up to God!

The Day of Judgment is coming, but the Day of Grace is here. Go forth and proclaim His name in all the Earth!

Prayer: Inspire in me a new sense of urgency, Lord.

183

Theme 6: New Heavens, New Earth, New Us

'As the new heavens and the new earth that I make will endure before me,' declares the Lord, 'so will your name and your descendants endure.' (66:22)

THE DAY OF THE Lord is coming. "For with fire and with his sword the Lord will execute judgment on all people ... " (66:16) That's the bad news, but we who know the Lord don't have to fear it, for He will also create "the new heavens and the new earth" that will endure forever for those who are faithful. (66:22)

It's not just that we need not be afraid but also that we look forward to this new day with great joy. The Apostle Paul tells us, "I consider that our present sufferings are not worth comparing with the glory that will be revealed in us. For the creation waits in eager expectation for the children of God to be revealed." (Romans 8:18–19)

In the Garden, the man and woman God made in His image were one with Him. They walked and talked with God in the cool of the evening, and they were naked but unashamed. When they fell, the greatest curse they experienced was separation from God. Jesus came to effect reconciliation, and we find it in His blood. But even we, " ... who have the first fruits of the Spirit, groan inwardly while we wait for adoption, the redemption of our bodies." (Romans 8:23, *NRSV)*

We won't be raised and restored in isolation. Paul says that restoration is also about "creation itself," which " ... will be liberated from its bondage to decay and brought into the freedom and glory of the children of God. We know that the whole creation has been groaning as in pains of childbirth right up to the present time." All creation has been waiting to be made new again. (Romans 8:21, 22)

Isaiah had a glimpse of the "new heavens and the new earth." John described them in Revelation. "I saw the Holy City, the new Jerusalem, coming down out of heaven from God, prepared as a bride beautifully dressed for her husband. And I heard a loud voice form the throne saying, 'Look! God's dwelling place is now among the people, and he will dwell with them. They will be his people, and God himself will be with them and be their God.' " (21:2–3)

As Paul says, we "hope for what we do not yet have" and we " ... wait for it patiently." (Romans 8:25) For now, it has to be enough for us that because of Jesus and the Holy Spirit, we have that promise.

Prayer: Lord, I know I am supposed to be patient. But my heart can't help but cry, "Haste the day!"

9 780865 440678